JIM AND ANA

JIM AND ANA

*The Lives of James Hector Munn (1864-1926)
and Ana Mae Edwards Munn (1871-1955)
of Leland, Jefferson County, Washington*

By
Hector John Munn (1930-   )
Grandson

iUniverse, Inc.
Bloomington

Jim and Ana
The Lives of James Hector Munn (1864-1926) and Ana Mae Edwards
Munn (1871-1955) of Leland, Jefferson County, Washington.

iUniverse books may be ordered through booksellers or by contacting:

iUniverse
1663 Liberty Drive
Bloomington, IN 47403
www.iuniverse.com
1-800-Authors (1-800-288-4677)

Because of the dynamic nature of the Internet, any web addresses or links contained in
this book may have changed since publication and may no longer be valid. The views
expressed in this work are solely those of the author and do not necessarily reflect the
views of the publisher, and the publisher hereby disclaims any responsibility for them.

ISBN: 978-1-4502-7566-8 (sc)
ISBN: 978-1-4502-7567-5 (ebk)

Printed in the United States of America

iUniverse rev. date: 01/13/2011

Contents

PREFACE

The purpose of this project is to provide a record of the lives of Jim and Ana Munn for their descendents that live today or may one day wonder about the origins of this side of their family. Facts get lost or more difficult to recover and memories fade into confusion. The hope is to preserve in one place the essential facts of the origins of Jim and Ana and the life they had together at Leland. The primary audience then is the Munn Family.

The main context of these two lives is the community that formed on the edges of Lake Leland and for a time was the community of Leland. There have been gaps in the information about the Leland community that may be filled as a result of detailing the lives of Jim and Ana Munn. There may be an additional audience among the friends and neighbors that lived in Leland, that now live at the lake edge or that one day may wonder a bit about who once lived here and what the area once looked like. It was a most vibrant place for a time.

If you are one of the interested readers, we hereby invite you to share in the story of one Jefferson County, Washington family's origins and experiences. The account is presented without censure. Your family story may have had many similar joys, sorrows, successes and failures. We all are a product of our past and if we don't look back now and then we might be more proud than we should. But then, we realize that growing up in Leland was actually quite interesting and worth sharing.

This is what the Homesteads of Jim and Ana Munn and Captain Edwin and Adelia Nichols looks like today.

Jim and Ana "homesteaded" the 40 acres shown as "Orchard 40". In 1900 they purchased nearly 160 acres from the Nichols couple after Ed Nichols died. The Nichols "homestead" consisted of "Lots" that bordered the western shore of what was then Lake Hooker. Lots 1, 2, and 4 were odd shaped portions of 40s. Lot 3 was more than 40 acres. The "Hill 40" was a true 40 acre piece. As the years have gone by, the streams the flow through Lot 2 and 4 have added soil to the lake edge. Lot 4 now appears as a full 40 acres with even more "land" beyond its measured northern edge. Note also the "40" that was first cleared by Thad Smith and G.W. Edwards. (See Map 3)

I: INTRODUCTION

James Hector Munn and Ana Mae Edwards arrived in Port Townsend, Jefferson County, Washington Territory about the same year, 1889. For Ana Mae, the date is known exactly from the diary of her mother Matilda, 3 May 1889 at 1:15 PM, Union Dock, Port Townsend. The Edwards family had travelled from Minneapolis, Kansas by train to Tacoma and by side-wheeler across Puget Sound. Ana Mae would take her elementary school teachers' examination in September.

Mr. and Mrs. James H. Munn, on the "main street" of Leland, Arcadia Road, circa 1917. (George Munn Collection).

For James Hector, the arrival date is approximate. He purchased an unproven homestead in Jefferson County from the original homesteader on 6 June 1891. Before he could officially purchase a homestead, he had to declare an intent to become a citizen. This he did before the Superior Court of Jefferson County on 14 September 1890, which is his earliest documented presence in Port Townsend. He may have spent the better part of the year before in search for an available property and settling the purchase. He had come from Prince Edward Island, Canada by way of Boston. He came to Vancouver, British Columbia, then to Everett, Washington. He was then on his way to Discovery Bay by way of Port Townsend. Ana Mae records a chance encounter with Jim sometime in the fall of 1889 when she was in an orchestra that played at the Seaman's Bethel in Port Townsend.

Jim and Ana were married 2 December 1892 in Everett, Washington. Jim was 28 and Ana was 21. Earlier in 1982 they were together in Port Townsend where Jim had paid $150 to take over an additional 40 acre unproven homestead. The "40" had been offered to Ana the summer of 1892, but she was too young to purchase the property. Instead, Jim paid for it and had it recorded in his name.

This "40" was situated on the hillside west of Lake Hooker, a name that was changed to Lake Leland. The original owner of the homestead had built a one-room shack where Jim and Ana lived in order to earn the homestead patent. Jim then built a new house on a flat place on a hill between the two creeks on that property. This house was the birth place of 5 children, Viola, Hector, Alice, Sarah, and Evangeline. The youngest child, George, was born in the lakeside log house on the land purchased from the original homesteaders, Edwin and Adelia Nichols.

Jim and Ana lived on the Nichols homestead the remainder of their lives. Jim died in Seattle at St. Luke's Hospital (which became Virginia Mason Hospital) on April of 1926 at the age of 61. Ana died in her own bed in the house that was a converted cookhouse where she moved after Jim died. She died in August 1955 at the age of 84. They had two sons and four daughters, seven grandsons and eight granddaughters. Of the fifteen grand children, 9 are still living in 2010. It is important for those who are alive to remember Jim and Ana while we still remember details.

Fortunately, there has been significant recorded information. Great grandmother Matilda Edwards kept a terse but vital diary. She usually wrote one line a day for most of her adult life. Ana's brother Grant Edwards wrote a family genealogy in 1930. This was followed by a more detailed genealogy written by their niece, Elva Salome Edwards Cole, Joel Edwards' daughter. Ana wrote a weekly article for the Port Townsend Leader in which she documented Leland community life. She then wrote her memoirs in 1951. Finally, granddaughter Mary Beth (Munn) Yntema wrote about her lively childhood in Leland with her siblings and cousins and included what she knew about her grandfather Jim and a few choice paragraphs about her grandmother Ana.

These written records will be drawn on heavily for this story. Each writer wrote what was important to them in the space and time they set out. So it is with this "book". The writer has previously written a summary of the origins of James Hector Munn starting with somewhat speculative account of the 1645 massacre of many members of the Lamont Clan in Dunoon, Argylleshire (Cowal Peninsula), Scotland by the Campbell Clan. In that account it is argued that the "Munns" are members of the Lamont Scottish clan, though some family members hold that the Munns are connected to the Stewart of Bute clan.

After about two or three generations of Munns at Kilfinan, on the Cowal mainland of Argyllshire, Duncan Munn and wife Flora Brown took up residency in a cotter's stone house at the edge of Port Mor, a bay on Colonsay. Colonsay is an island at the Atlantic edge of Scotland where Duncan was probably a fisherman. Here they gathered their family and become part of a 115 person exodus on the ship *Spencer* that took them to Prince Edward Island (PEI), Canada in 1806. Duncan and Flora brought with them 4 sons and 2 daughters, while a fifth son, we think, remained on Colonsay to come later with his twin sons Neil and Alexander Munn.

5

The family of Malcolm McMillan was also on the *Spencer*. One of his daughters, Elizabeth (Betsy) McMillan and James Munn, a son of Duncan Munn, had wed in December 1805 before emigrating on the *Spencer*. James McMillan and Ann Munn, brother and sister of James Munn and Betsy McMillan, come to Prince Edward Island (PEI) with the Malcolm McMillan family on the *Spencer*. The two families, the McMillans and the Munns were thus very close and settled in the same Belle River/Wood Islands region of eastern PEI. It is speculated that Malcolm McMillan was an heir to some of the wealth of his father, Hector McMillan. It was from this resource it is speculated that most of the *Spencer* passengers were able to pay for the passage and to buy property in Canada.

For Ana, we will pick up her story as she tells it in her 1951 memoirs. She writes with great detail about her childhood on the Edwards homestead, her high school days in Minneapolis, Kansas, and the Edwards family journey to Port Townsend from Minneapolis, Kansas and her life with Jim at Leland. She writes less and less detail as their children grew up, leave home, and get married. Jim contracted throat cancer and died. Ana continued living alone as the family matriarch for an additional twenty-nine years.

I (the author) had a unique relationship with grandma Ana that was different from that of any other of her grandchildren. Following my entry into the world 7 February 1930 in Index, Washington, west of Everett where the family lived near dad's work at Sunset Mine, my mother became very sick and was hospitalized. Aunt Sarah Albright came over from Leland to bring my brother Bob (Robert) and me to Leland in July 1930. Helen and Mary Beth remained in Index under the care of some high school girls. Helen and Mary were brought to Leland in September so they could begin at Leland School that year. The older children lived with Sarah and Roy Albright and their daughter Lorraine in grandma's house. Grandma Ana became my principle care giver. My bed was in her bedroom in the "office". She was the one who fed and changed me. By Thanksgiving of 1930, mother was well enough to leave the hospital and go to her parents' home in Great Falls, Montana. Then she came to Leland after New Years and took over my normal care.

During the 7 months I was in grandma Ana's care, there was time for us to bond. Bonding goes two ways, perhaps. I always knew that grandma treated me specially and I always felt relaxed with her and she was always interested in everything that I did. Even as a grade school student, grandma thought nothing of putting me in charge of the Leland Post Office after school while she was out doing evening chores. I gave out mail, sold stamps, and locked up at 5 PM before going home.

Meanwhile, brother Bob was helping our grandmother Ana with the evening dairy chores, milking, turning the separator, feeding the calves, getting hay down from the hay mow and cleaning up after the cows. The time came when Bob wanted to stay after school for high school sports. Grandma was able to retire from the Post Office and gave the postmaster job to her daughter Viola Alden. I was then in line to assist Ana with milking chores. We didn't help with the morning chores, but just the evening milking after school. We'd do the work for grandma and then go home and milk our own cows.

Grandma and I would have long conversations while we were doing the milking. While the hands were busy, the mind and mouth could carry on. Grandma had a high pitched voice and sometime she was hard to hear if we were at separate ends of the row of milk cows. Yet grandma talked about most anything in her mind, her life as a child, current politics, religious beliefs, community events. The topics were endless. At this time she was Leland correspondent for the Port Townsend *Leader*. I had to be somewhat circumspect about relating current gossip as she might just put my words in her weekly column. For a year, I was correspondent for Quilcene High School "Ranger", a column for the Port Townsend *Leader* as well. What's more, we used the same typewriter for our news writing. The typewriter was a permanent fixture on grandma's dining table. She had a pile of her notes and I had mine. We were often trying to hit the same deadlines with the articles.

When the book "The Egg and I" by Betty McDonald was published about life on a Chimacum chicken farm, grandma announced that she could write a story that would be better as it would be all true and wouldn't have any dirty words. That is how she came to write her memoirs, "Pioneering in Four States and I'll Tell You All about It", by Ana Mae Munn, Leland, Washington. She finished it in 1951 when she was 80 years old. I bought her a ream of legal paper with properly sized carbon paper. She religiously made a carbon copy. She never copied over and never needed to make corrections. Sometimes she would forget to make a carriage return and letters would pile up on the right margin. By that time, brother Bob had finished with the merchant marines and had taken over the farm. So grandma had unencumbered time to sit and write. As said, she wrote historically straight through once without recopying.

Now in 2010, I'm doing just what my grandmother did, but not my memoires. I am finishing her story. I'm the fourth youngest of the grandchildren. Perhaps I will have the freedom to write some things that my older cousins would leave out. I intend to write just the facts as I can sort them out. If I recall something others would not like to hear or know, please grant me the license of age. Grandma Ana was much more cautious with her story. She was careful to leave out awkward information. She would write some accounts in obscure phraseology and not mention names, if there was a hint of possible harm.

II: JAMES HECTOR MUNN, 1864 TO 1891

James Hector Munn, circa 1893. (Munn family collection).

BELLE RIVER, PRINCE EDWARD ISLAND, CANADA

James Hector Munn was born 26 July 1864 in the house his grandfather James had built. It was on the "Old Farm" which James had given to son Hector. The original 100 acre "French long lot" was one of four 100 acre lots that the four Munn brothers settled on in Lot 62, Queens County, from the Selkirk lands. These were at Bell River in eastern Prince Edward Island.

Hector Munn, James Hector's father, was born in 1825. He was the 7th child and 3rd son of James and Betsy. His older brothers were Duncan Howard and John. He was named for Betsy's grandfather Hector McMillan. His birth was 19 years after the four Munn brothers and their father Duncan (John?) and their mother Flora Brown arrived on the ship *The Spencer* in 1806 from Colonsay Island, Argyllshire, Scotland. James had married Betsy (Elizabeth) McMillan in December of 1805 before emigrating. Older brothers Angus and Neil were also married before emigrating. Malcolm married soon after settling at Belle River. These four brothers and two sisters, Ann and Effie, were part of the 115 passengers on *the Spencer*. Betsy McMillan's parents also came to PEI on *The Spencer*. Malcolm McMillan and Graciel (Grace) McNeill settled with their children in Wood Islands, the community just east of Belle River. Ann Munn married James McMillan, Betsy's brother. So the James Munn children and the James McMillan children were double cousins and all grew up together with other Munn and McMillan children in one grand community of Belle River/Wood Islands. The families shared the same school and were all members of the Free Church of Scotland, as they were Presbyterians, one and all.

In 1806 when *the Spencer* was ready to leave Colonsay, one son of Duncan Munn and Flora Brown chose to remain. Donald Munn and his wife Sarah McLean were parents of twin boys, Neil and Alexander. The twins were born in 1798 and had probably started school. Sarah McLean was a young mother, perhaps age 16, and may not have been healthy after giving birth to twins. She may have died and the twins may have been raised by an aunt. (The family tradition is that an aunt travelled to PEI with the twins somewhat later.) Nevertheless, Donald remained in Scotland until the education of the twins was complete. Neil and Alexander then came to PEI in 1818. Neil Munn was educationally qualified to take a position as a school teacher and was hired to teach a school in Mermaid in Lot 48 of Queens County to the north and not too far from the Belle River Lot 62 where his uncles lived.

There is considerable uncertainty about Neil's family members. Some thought the twin brother was named Archibald, not Alexander as the Colonsay record shows. So searches for "Archibald Munn" were unsuccessful. Another possibility is that Alexander travelled on with "his aunt" to Upper Canada. (Coles and Harding, p. 19) Perhaps if the records searches looked for Alexander Munn and not Archibald Munn, evidences of Neil's brother may have been found.

Neil Munn did well at Mermaid as a school teacher. He married Elizabeth MacLeod, who is thought to be the first child born on Prince Edward Island, 1803, of Scottish emigrants who came on the ship *Polly*. These emigrants came from the Island of Skye. They were a part of Scottish emigrants called "Selkirk Settlers". They had occupied lands in Queens County, P.E.I., where the Duncan Munn and Malcolm McMillan families came in 1806.

Neil Munn and Elizabeth MacLeod are the progenitors of the genealogical book "From Island to Island", which records their descendants. Neil left school teaching and became a farmer. Their family is called the "Lot 48 Munns" or the "Mermaid Munns". Their first child was a daughter, Sarah Munn, born about 1832. Neil and Elizabeth raised 10 children on their Mermaid farm. The first son, Donald, is named for Neil's father, while the first daughter is named for Neil's mother, Sarah. By tradition, Sarah should have been named for Elizabeth Macleod's mother. There is a record of Elizabeth's father, Roderick Macleod but her mother is referred to as "Mrs. MacKenzie" whose first name is unknown.

The "48 Munns" and the "Belle River Munns" had considerable social contact. Thus Hector Munn (Belle River Munn) and Sarah Munn (48 Munn) were well acquainted and were married on 23 October 1851. They would be first cousins once removed. Cousin marriages were common in Scotland. Hector and Sarah had 9 children. The naming traditions of the Scots can be confusing. Hector's older brothers each named their first son "Duncan" for their grandfather Duncan. Hector and Sarah name their first son "Duncan Hector (Howard?)" to distinguish him from his cousins. Duncan Hector never married and died at age 23. Because of the confusion of first names, Hector and Sarah gave all their children middle names. Following Duncan Hector in order there are four girls: Elizabeth Ann (Libby Ann Compton), Mary Sarah, Flora Grace, and Dorothea Jane (Dorothy Jane), who is 2 ½ years older than James Hector. James is followed by another girl, Jessie Euphemia (Effie), then two more sons Neil Alexander, and John Daniel.

Scottish naming system was generally observed, but not always. The first son would be named for his father's father and a second son would be named for the mother's father. The first daughter would be named for the mother's mother and the second daughter would be named for the father's mother. If each son of four brothers followed this pattern, then there could be four cousins with the same first and last name and led to confusion. Though this is the general pattern Hector and Sarah used in naming their children, they added a middle name. Hector and Sarah used both names when referring to their children. Grandfather James Hector always referred to his sister as Dorothy Jane and his younger brother as John Daniel. On the other hand, there is no record that James Munn, child of Duncan Munn and Flora Brown or Hector, child of James and Elizabeth, had middle names. It should be added that after these first two names of sons and daughters were used, there were no further rules. Quite often, though, names of uncles and aunts and great grandparents were used. A good example is that Neil Munn and Elizabeth MacLeod used Sarah, Donald, and Roderick. Alexander, not Archibald, Charles, William and James were other sons, while Mary, Dorothea, and Ann were other daughters. They gave no middle names. Note how many of these names were used by Hector and Sarah as well as names of great grandparents and aunts and uncles on Hector's side, i.e. Flora, Grace, Euphemia, Neil and John.

Hector Munn of Belle River was a successful farmer. He farmed the 50 acres he was given by his father, and eventually inherited the other 50 acres. This was collectively called the "Old Farm". Hector owned neighboring farmsteads called "Hill Farm" and "Hemlock Hill Farm". He had a sizeable estate when he died in 1876.

HECTOR MUNN FAMILY AT BELLE RIVER "OLD FARM", P.E.I.

Duncan Howard (from left), Hector, James Hector (in front), Dorothea Jane, Sarah, Jessie Euphemia (on Sarah's lap), Flora Grace, Mary Sarah, Elizabeth Ann. (Neil Alexander and John Daniel were to come later). 1868.(Greg Munn Collection).

TRAGEDIES AT BELLE RIVER

Hector's death on April 21, 1876 at age 51 was the result of being kicked in the abdomen by a farm animal, a colt or mule. He lingered and suffered in pain before he died. This gave him ample time to direct a full, detailed will. Death in the midst of productive years and with none of the girls married and 4 children under age 12 was a stark tragedy. His wife Sarah was only 44 and lived only 6 more years. The oldest son Duncan Howard died 6 months after his father.

James Hector became the oldest male in the household at age 11. The three oldest girls found husbands in two years. Dorothy Jane married Alex Stewart at age 23, eight years later. The Stewarts moved to Boston were Alex entered engineering school. He and Dorothy Jane eventually moved to Seattle, Washington where he became chief engineer for Seattle Public Schools.

Two of Hector's three farms were sold with equipment. Sarah and the four younger children kept the "Old Farm". This farm was willed collectively to James Hector, Neil Alexander and John Daniel, with the stipulation that they could not settle the estate until John Daniel was 21 on 26 November 1889, a significant date to remember. When Sarah died on 15 December 1882, James Hector was 18 (b. 26 July 1864). It would be roughly 7 years before the estate could be settled.

The tragedies of Belle River, Prince Edward Island continued. On 1 February 1884 at the age of 21, James Hector married a cousin, Margaret MacLeod. (She is likely a second cousin, a granddaughter of Roderick MacLeod, James' grandmother Betsy MacLeod's father). "Maggie" was not well. She may have contracted tuberculosis in her teens. James Hector had taken her on a wintery sleigh ride. He had misjudged the thickness of ice on a pond and the sleigh broke through. In the rescue Maggie had fallen into icy water and took a chill that added to her weakened condition. James Hector was extremely guilt ridden by the situation. They were married regardless of Maggie's failing health. She clung to life for two years and finally died on 3 March 1886. James Hector remained at the Old Farm in Belle River long enough to see that his dearest wife was buried.

(Many young people contracted tuberculosis on "the island" in those days. In fact it may well have been the cause of death of James' brothers, Duncan Hector and Neil Alexander and sister Effie, all of whom died young. Cousin Edger, son of John Daniel Munn, said that a lad with tuberculosis had a harmonica and generously let his school buddies play it.)

A NEW PLACE AND A NEW LIFE

James Hector most certainly loved Maggie very much. He saw to her burial. Her illness and death only compounded the sorrow of the tragedies of the deaths of his father, his brother Duncan and his mother. Prince Edward Island had become a cold, bitter place of much death. He needed to get away. The first refuge was in the home of his sister Dorothy Jane and her husband Alex Stewart in Boston. His formal education had been cut short by the death of his father when he was 11. One thing he gained from his farm experience was a love of horses and how to train them. But that wasn't an adequate start for a career. So he apprenticed himself to the Boston carpenters' union and quickly earned for himself journeyman carpenter status. What could happen then? He learned that there was a ready market for carpenters in the booming Canadian and American west.

The Canadian National Railway was completed in 1886 with passenger service from Nova Scotia to Vancouver, British Columbia. James said good bye to his sister Dorothy Jane, to his younger brothers and sister Effie. The Canadian National Railway took James Hector Munn with his newly earned journeyman carpenter status as far away from Prince Edward Island as train locomotives could go.

It is unclear how long the apprenticeship was or when James Hector Munn arrived at Vancouver. His son George speculated that the carpenter's training was about 5 years long, as that is the length of such a training program in the United States. Yet James Hector had to have transacted official business in Jefferson County, Washington Territory in the fall of 1889. He spent enough time in Vancouver to become a soldier with the Salvation Army and purchased a uniform. He did not play an instrument, but he was a good public singer and had a strong baritone voice. So he may have been a participant of a street evangelism team.

Two factors directed his attention southward from Vancouver, Canada. Washington still held territorial status. Statehood was granted 11 November 1889.There was news of the construction of a major sawmill complex at Everett, Washington Terr. Carpenters were in great demand there. There is no evidence that he went there to take a job at that time. He was not the only person from PEI to come west. He knew that a cousin, Jim White, had gone to a place called Maynard in Jefferson County. To get there in those days there were small boats, part of the notorious "Mosquito Fleet" that took people and goods to the various ports of call around Puget Sound. He took such a boat to Port Townsend, the county seat of Jefferson County and the closest port of call to Maynard, which is on Discovery Bay to the west. Small boats went regularly from Port Townsend to Discovery Bay.

[Note: There were two settlements at the south end "head" of Discovery Bay. Maynard was on the west side on Salmon Creek. It was near the point fartherest into the bay that boats could dock at low tide. A wharf had been built there. "Cooper's" was on the south east side of the valley about a mile inland on Snow Creek. Eventually, a railroad was built on the east side of Discovery Bay. It went through Cooper's. "Cooper" is the name of a pioneer family that still lives there. "Cooper's" was the name of the settlement well into the 1930's. Yet when a post office and a school were started there, the residents began using the name "Uncas", the name of a character in James Fennimore Cooper's, "The Last of the Mohicans". Today, the name for the farming region at the head of Discovery Bay is simply "Discovery Bay".]

Mary Beth Munn Yntema recounts this part of James Hector Munn's journey in her family memoirs (unpublished).

"He (James Hector Munn) decided to find his friend Jim White, who had come earlier from Prince Edward Island who lived at Maynard, Washington. Jim went by small boat from Port Townsend around by Protection Island to the Maynard dock. Later it was rumored that he had jumped ship from a foreign vessel and was a fugitive sailor. James arrived at Maynard after dark and found his way to Jim White's house. He could see some sort of a party was going on. He pulled his cap down over his eyes, knocked on the door, and asked (in his best Scottish brogue) if there was

room for a beggar at this place. Jim White immediately recognized his voice and there was a grand welcome and reunion."

James stayed off and on with Jim White as he went back and forth between his land claim to the south of Maynard and Port Townsend, where he conducted business and explored the social life. While in Port Townsend, James usually stayed at the Seaman's Bethel. This was a hostel for single men, usually sailors. It was run by a Christian agency, probably the Salvation Army. At the time, 1888 to 1893, it was a building at 88 ½ Quincy Street. As the new city was platted, this was a location on the north side of the Quincy Street wharf, out over the water when the tide was in. The building and several neighboring buildings and the supporting wharf have long since been captured by the tides and rot. Seaman's Bethel moved in 1893 to a building at 230 Quincy Street. The building had been a house of ill repute and town fathers were much pleased that Seaman's Bethel took over the location. Today, 2010, the building houses the Courtyard Cafe. It is next door to the Leader Building. Both buildings date from the 1880's. (See Map 1).

During the late summer or fall of 1889, there was an orchestra group composed of two violinists, a trombonist, a B-flat coronet player and a bass violinist. They would go about town each Sunday giving performances. They played for Sunday school and church at the Methodist Church where they were joined by the organ. Then in the afternoon they performed at the Congregational Church at 2 PM and then at the Seaman's Bethel a 3 P.M. Finally they went to the YMCA for a 4 o'clock performance.

These were hymn sings as well as orchestral music. The audiences were generally small but much appreciated as there was very little culture available in this wild, '80's seaport. The base violinist was a young 17 year old girl. On several occasions James Munn was in the audience at the Seaman's Bethel. The room was small and James sat close in and could not help notice the young base violinist. She, in turn noticed his attractive baritone singing voice. Yet they were not ever introduced nor did they speak to each other.

THE ARCADIA HOMESTEAD

James Munn was busy proving up his new homestead claim. C.M. Ogden had filed a homestead claim on 120 acres (three 40 acre pieces) on 1 October 1890. This is located up the Snow Creek about 8 miles south of Cooper's at Discovery Bay. The relatively flat area around upper Snow creek was called Arcadia and was also the source of what is called Ripley's Creek today. Ripley's Creek flows southward toward the Little Quilcene River and Snow Creek flows northward to Discovery Bay. James Hector Munn purchased the 120 acres from C.M. Ogden for $150 according to the record filed 6 June 1891. The land is in Section 22 Township 28 Range 2 West Willamette Meridian. (See Map 2).

(The Homestead Act of 24 April 1820 of the U.S. government was enacted to encourage settlement of Ohio. It continued to be applied to lands in Kansas, Montana, and Washington, Oregon and throughout the West. To file a claim under the Homestead Act there were several requirements. The person making the claim for free land had to be a U.S. citizen, or one who **had filed "intent" to become a naturalized citizen**, and who was at least **21 years old**. The homestead was limited to one quarter of a section or 160 acres. Usually this was indeed adjacent land, but it could be composed of non-adjacent 40 acre parcels. A claim was to be "proved up" in five years. If not, it reverted to the government and could be claimed by someone else. However, one could sell an unproven claim for $1.25 an acre. The new owner still had to prove-up the homestead by the end of the original five year period. To "prove" a homestead claim, one must build a dwelling with a chimney and live in it over a period of two years. One could come and go during those two years. Local rules were sometimes applied as well. In Montana, a claim could be 640 acres or an entire section. In some areas the claim needed to have a water source, a well or be by a stream.)

James purchased his homestead instead of filing on a new plot. He also had to file intent to be a citizen and he had to live on the claim for two years. The 5 year time limit was already running when the purchase was made. Several dates need to be carefully noted.

Patent No. 16376 was filed by C.M. Ogden 1 October 1890. It was purchased by James H. Munn for $150. The transaction was dated 6 June 1891 and filed in Jefferson County record on 15 June 1891 as Patent No.15624.

Completed Patent No.15624 is dated with the Land Office 30 January 1892 and filed 20 June 1892. It grants to James H. Munn 120 acres: the E ½ of NE ¼ and the NE ½ of SW ¼ of Sec.22 Twp 28 N R2W WM. It was "signed" by President Benjamin Harrison. Note that the two year residence requirement is met with both the C.M. Ogden and James Munn occupancy.

James H. Munn filed Intent to be naturalized on 14 September 1890 in order to purchase property. He was granted citizenship on 23 May 1898. There was a required waiting period between "Intent" and "Declaration" of at least 5 years. He had to renounce his loyalty to Victoria, Queen of Great Britain and Ireland. (The "Intent" is by action of the Superior Court of Jefferson County, Washington, as recorded in the National Archives, Vol. 57, p. 3A, and #114. The Naturalization Declaration of Citizenship was also before the Superior Court of Jefferson County, Judge James G. McClinton. It is recorded in National Archives: Vol. 1, p.116, Row E12-8. 1898.)

In order for Patent 15624 to be granted on 30 January 1892, James had to have occupied the land for two years. Since we do not have the General Land Office data, it must be that James began his homestead occupation on or before 30 January 1890. These dates suggest that James Munn arrived in Jefferson County sometime in 1889, at the latest, in order to have had time to discover the location and come to agreement with Mr. Ogden on the sale.

Thus the Patent 15624 for 120 acres in Arcadia Valley was granted on 30 January 1892. (Volume 27a, page 477 of General Land Office records.) C.M. Ogden may have made the initial filing as early as 1887 and James needed to hurry to complete the requirements of the patent that he bought in 1890.He built a cedar house and lived in it off and on since October 1890 or before.

There is a story in Ana Munn's memoirs that at one point Jim had been away from his cabin for a month or so. Two neighbor homesteaders assumed he had given up on the homestead. The door and window(s) were locked. They had climbed onto the roof, removed shake roofing and climbed inside and removed most of the contents. They were aided by a horse and wagon to carry the meager belongings away. It had been raining before this theft occurred. When James Munn returned and discovered the theft, all he needed to do was follow the fresh hoof prints and wagon trail to where the goods were still being unloaded. James firmly asked them to put the goods back in the wagon and take them back to the cedar cabin. This they did. The men, George and August Thomas, were greatly embarrassed to have been caught in the act of theft. Later they were the source of several malicious rumors. One was that James Munn was a fugitive sailor who had jumped ship. And that he was an escaped criminal from Scotland who was serving sentence on the ship.

Of course James Munn made legal entry to the United States from Canada and had already filed for naturalization. He could not afford to accuse the men of theft or to continue bad blood with the neighbors. In the backwoods of the pioneer days you never knew when you needed to call for a neighbor's help. The matter was chalked up to be a simple misunderstanding and the Thomas brothers were neighbors of Jim and Ana throughout their lives.

Originally, access to Arcadia was by foot path or horse/wagon trail along Andrews Creek. This route eventually was used for a railroad for the McCormick logging operation into the hills from Crocker Lake. Later it became the route of choice for the Olympic Gravity Water Line between the Big Quilcene River dam and Port Townsend that crosses

Highway 101 just north of Crocker Lake. There were also trails that went between Lake Hooker and Arcadia. There was a primitive bridge across Lake Hooker where a trail continued west. That trail or wagon road was improved and rerouted up the hill to the west of the lake in 1892. This was officially known as Arcadia Road on into 1930's. By then the lake had been given a new name and the road began to be called "Leland Hill Road". Arcadia Road or Leland Hill Road ended at a stream near the farmstead owned by Mr. Ripley. Hence, Ripley Creek got its name. The name Arcadia fell into disuse sometime along the way.

The Arcadia Homestead, once proved-up, was never occupied as a home. It proved to be a valuable asset from time to time. The timber on the homestead was sold to Payne and Brown logging company. A 20 acre piece was sold to Ana's nephew, Bob Henderson. Bob returned it when he left to sign up for the Spanish American War. Eventually the plot was sold to McCormick Logging Company of Crocker Lake. The logging company operated a railroad logging company that clear cut the timber all along the Snow Creek, Ripley Creek and Howe Creek watersheds in the 1920's. The homestead could never have been a family farm. It was partly a swamp. The soil is rocky glacial till with shallow topsoil. There are today several home sites still in "Arcadia", none of which are productive farms.

THE COURTSHIP

During the time that James Munn was "proving up" his Arcadia homestead, he made many trips to Discovery Bay, where Jim White, his fellow PEI émigré lived, and Port Townsend, where business needed to be conducted. Travel between Maynard and Port Townsend improved when a family named Tukey began a ferry service between Maynard and the northeast shore of Discovery Bay. Today this is near Adelma Beach.

While in "town", Jim would stay at Seaman's Bethel. In fall of 1890 he began to realize that the town orchestra was no longer coming to Seaman's Bethel. He began asking about for information about the pretty base violinist and where he might find her. He was informed that her name was Miss Edwards and that she lived in a house uptown. He found the house where she had been living and was informed that she was teaching school at Discovery Bay at Cooper's. Well!! He had gone right by the school house many times and she was living right under his nose.

The school session at Cooper's was funded only for September through December 1890. At the end of the session, Miss Edwards prepared her students for a closing program at which the children would recite and entertain. The parents and the entire community were invited. It became the event of the season and of course James Munn came as he hoped to have more than a chance encounter with the school mistress, Miss Edwards. The children gave their recitations and then Miss Edwards invited everyone to join in a community sing. The room was crowded and James found a place quite close to the young teacher. He joined into the singing led by Miss Edwards with her bass violin. One can only imagine the looks and sparks that flew about at this fun occasion. It was the second meeting of Jim and Ana. Since the school session was over, Ana immediately returned to Port Townsend to start teaching a new class there in January 1891.

By January 1891, Ana Edwards had taken the teacher's examination the second time. The first time she only received a temporary certificate after her first testing as she hadn't scored well on the mathematics part. She had been allowed to take an elementary class at Port Townsend for the January to August session of 1890 before she took the school at Cooper's. Now she had a proper certificate for all grades and had a new class which she taught from January to June 1891.

Meanwhile, Jim was hired by the Dick Brown Logging Company to build a logging camp on the west shore of Lake Hooker. He was living at his Arcadia homestead about a mile and a half up the hill. The logging camp was being built on land rented from Edwin and Adelia Nichols. This was on Lot 1 of the Nichols Homestead. The camp was situated at the mouth of a small steam that had washed down dirt to form a small delta jutting into the lake. The Munn family later called this "The Point". Jim built a cook house, bunk house and assorted equipment buildings and a barn for the mules used to pull the logs. The job would be completed at the end of August. Jim had a team of horses and a dray cart at his disposal that probably belonged to the logging camp. (Map 3).

Ana Edwards' brother Grant, who was seven years older than she, had earned his teacher certification in Kansas and was qualified to be a county school superintendant. He was teaching in a school house near the Leland Post Office which was in the home of John Ryan at the north end of Lake Hooker. Grant needed to start another school at Tarboo, which was in the next valley to the east. So he assigned his sister Ana to the Leland School. Ana was to begin there in the fall of 1891. The school term at Port Townsend was over. Ana decided to move to her parents' house at Leland. They needed help taking care of several grandchildren. This whole back story will be told when we turn to Ana's part of this account.

Ana had her belongings, a bed, a dresser, her bass violin and a trunk loaded onto the Port Townsend Southern train that recently had been completed past Lake Hooker and as far as Quilcene. She sent word to have someone meet her at the Lake Hooker train platform at the bridge to Arcadia Road. She needed help to take her belongings another mile to the Edwards home. The oldest grandchild of G.W. and Matilda Edwards, Robert Henderson, had arranged for Jim Munn to come with his horses and a dray cart to meet the train to pick up Ana's belongings. Jim Munn and Bob Henderson were ready and waiting as the train came in from Port Townsend. Ana notes the date in her memoirs as 29 June 1891, a pivotal date for both.

The Edwards house was located on the east side of the hill that forms the east side of the lake. At that time there was a road, the Smith and Donnelly Road, which started near the train platform and snaked eastward up the hill. Then the road went down the other side past the Edwards house before proceeding over Tarboo Hill towards Tarboo and Chimacum. The small hill up from the lake had been cleared and even platted as a city by a homesteader named Rose. It had developed into a big patch of wild strawberries. So for many years it was called "Strawberry Hill".

This was not the first time Ana had made this trip over Strawberry Hill, so she and the younger Edwards grandchildren decided to walk over the hill. Jim Munn and Robert Henderson drove the dray cart with Ana's goods on a road that went around the south side of Strawberry Hill, past Ana's brother-in-law Thad Smith's house and around to the Edwards house on the hill. There was also a connection near the Edwards house with the Smith and Donnelly Road. This would be like going around by the Cutoff Road today as Thaddeus Smith's house was near where the Cutoff Road and Hwy 101 intersect. There are a few apple trees still producing in Thad Smith's orchard at the side of the road. The Edwards house was on the east of Highway 101 today near a recent Pope logging operation.

Ana and the Henderson children had just arrived at the bottom of the driveway to the house when Jim Munn and Robert Henderson came with the cart and luggage. Ana's parents had seen them coming and came down to meet them and to open the gate. There was a grand reunion and much chatter as Jim and Robert came up. Jim asked where the luggage was to go. Ana just directed him on up the hill. "Put things in the empty room at the top of the stairs," Ana said with a wave.

The Edwards house was newly built and the room for Ana was up stairs and empty. It was next to the room where the Henderson children had their beds, and Robert knew this was to be his Aunt Ana's room. Bob Henderson would have been 15 at the time. They proceeded to move the belongings to Ana's room. They set up Ana's bed that they had unloaded and even put blankets on the bed. As they were finished, Bob went down to get in on the homecoming chatter. Jim had a final thought. He returned up the stairs and tucked the bass violin under the top blanket of Ana's bed and left. He went back to his horses and drove them back down the hill. He waved good-bye and left without further ado. Later Ana Mae inspected the move in and noticed that the bass viol was under the blanket and quizzed Bob Henderson about it. But Bob knew nothing and Ana Mae put it out of her mind.

SUMMER OF 1891

After delivering Ana's goods, James Munn went back to his cabin up in Arcadia. But he came down to Lake Hooker daily to work on the camp construction job for Dick Brown Logging Company. Often on Sundays there was a visiting preacher that held services at the school house on the east side of the lake. Miss Edwards' brother Grant had assigned to her the task of directing the Sunday school as well as teaching. The Sunday school and worship service were in the afternoon as the preachers would come out in the morning and could catch the train back to Port Townsend in the afternoon.

One Sunday in late August, a pair of ladies from Port Townsend Salvation Army Post had come out to hold the service. James had joined the Salvationists in Vancouver, so he was on hand that Sunday to lend his fine baritone voice to the worship songs lead by Ana with her bass viol. It was a nice afternoon. After escorting the preacher ladies to the train, James, Ana and Ana's niece and nephews continued on their favorite walk over Strawberry Hill to the Edwards home.

It was dusk by the time the joyful company of Sunday worshipers appeared at the Edwards gate. James told the children to go on ahead to the house, as he wanted to visit with Ana Mae some more, alone. It may not have been the first time that James had escorted Ana Mae home. This time he hoisted Ana up on a log that was beside the gate. They set there as it grew dark. Jim began explaining to Ana that the summer was nearly over. He was finished with his job with Dick Brown. He had been able to complete the homestead requirements and had filed for the Patent at the General Land Office. He now planned to go to Everett, Washington where there was work at a big logging camp. He knew that there was need for a school teacher at the camp. Would she come with him? He was tired of being alone and they could get married.

Of course he knew that Ana had a contract to teach at the Leland School for the coming year. He was hopefully surprised when after a bit she replied that she would have to think about it and talk it over with her parents. About then there was sound of a door slamming and footsteps on the porch of the house above them on the hill. George Edwards began to call out asking what was taking so long and what was going on. Ana invited Jim to dinner the next night and said she would have an answer to his proposal at that time. Then she said as a matter of parting. "You can visit the house for the first time and see where we live." To that Jim replied, "Oh, but I've already seen the inside of the house. Don't you remember when I brought your luggage from the train, you told me to put your things in the upstairs bedroom? That is when I put your bass viol under the blankets. I thought that when you went to bed, you would reach over and cause the viol to make its deep sound and you would think of my voice and remember me."

By that time father Edwards was getting very anxious for the safety of his youngest and last unmarried daughter in the hands of some foreign criminal, who had jumped ship to squat on American soil. He had heard all the rumors the Thomas brothers had been spreading about James Munn. Soon Ana and Jim parted in the dark. Ana tried to go directly up to her room, but father and mother Edwards would have nothing of it. They wanted to know what was going on. Ana confessed that she had just had a proposal of marriage but not to worry. She had invited Mr. Munn to dinner tomorrow and would tell him then that she couldn't go with him and get married. She assured them that she had a contract to teach school and she was going to fulfill the contract.

Jim Munn spent the next day putting his cabin in order to be closed up and finishing his work with Dick Brown by cleaning up the horses and making sure the other animals were ok. It was with a hopeful heart that he came up the hill to the Edwards house for the meal he was to share.

It was a cordial evening though a bit strained. Jim had not really met George W. and Matilda Edwards in a formal sense. Yet it was with full reality of the situation that he heard and accepted Ana's answer to his marriage proposal. He left the next morning for Port Townsend and found the earliest possible transport to the east sound and Everett. He began his new job.

Before long, Leland School began for the 1891-1892 session. A new teacher, Miss Ana Mae Edwards, was at the door to greet the children. Actually, most of the children were her nephews and niece. People had gotten on about their business for the year.

III: ANA MAE EDWARDS, 1871-1891

Ana Mae Edwards Munn, age 34. (George Munn collection).

HARDIN COUNTY, IOWA

Ana Mae Edwards was born 24 September 1871 near New Providence, Iowa in Hardin County. Eldora is the county seat of Hardin County, northeast of Des Moines. Today the major town is Iowa Falls, which is near US 20 and on US 65.

Ana Mae was the first born before a twin brother, James Porter. They were born on a Sunday. Her mother, Matilda was unattended as the midwife came late (or Ana Mae came early). The arrival of Porter, as he would be called, was just a bit at hazard even though the mid-wife did come about an hour before he was delivered.

Ana Mae and James Porter were the second set of twins for Matilda and George Washington Edwards. Eldora (DORA) Parmelia and Viola (VILA) Almeda had preceded them by nearly 4 years (30 September and 1 October1867). Ana Mae became the sixth daughter and Porter the third son of Matilda and G.W. Edwards. Their first child was Louisa (ISA) (19 June 1855). The other children were: Veroque (OKA) (17 November 1856), JOEL (6 December 1858), ELVA Maude (25 March 1861), and Ulysses GRANT (Lyss) (20 December 1864). There was one more son born after Ana Mae and Porter. Lewis was born at Ackley, Kansas and was possibly bitten by a snake or spider and died at age of 21 months. (Elva Edwards-Cole, page35, claims he died of cholera.)

George Washington Edwards and Matilda Fitzgerald were married 3 September1854, as recorded on page 5 of Book 1 or Hardin County, Iowa. It is thought that theirs was the first wedding in the county even though the New Providence area of Hardin County was being homesteaded earlier by Quakers. G.W. and Matilda rented a farm from a Quaker family.

Edwards and Fitzgerald families were neighbors in Morgan County, Indiana where both families had homesteads near the White River not far from Indianapolis. G.W. was the youngest of three children of Jesse Edwards and Elizabeth Bryant. Elizabeth's mother was a weaver that worked in the Edwards' household in Adair County, Kentucky. Jesse's parents didn't approve of Elizabeth, so when Grandmother Bryant decided to go to Indiana, Jesse and Elizabeth with their two children, Sarah and John, went with her. Jesse did not take to the hard life of a pioneer. He left his family before his son George Washington Edwards was born. He went back to his family in Adair County, Kentucky and later remarried. G.W. never met his father. The White River flooded over the Edwards' and Fitzgerald's farms several times. The two families decided to abandon their homesteads and move to Iowa. When Matilda was only 9 years old, her mother Fitzgerald died leaving Matilda with the care of her three siblings: Joel (7), James (5) and Nancy (3). Relationships became complicated when Matilda's father married G.W.'s sister Sarah. Then Elizabeth Bryant Edwards remarried to Eli Ritesman (sometimes spelled as pronounced: "Wrightsman"). One of the Ritesman children married John Edwards as well, so that there were a host of double cousins between the Edwards children and the Ritesman children. (See Appendix II). The two families had neighboring farms in Iowa as well. Though New Providence was a Quaker community and they were renting from Quaker farmers, they did not become Quakers. George Washington Edwards was thirteen and Matilda Fitzgerald was twelve when they attended Baptist camp meetings in the community. They began attending Sunday school and church with the Baptists and preferred that connection the rest of their lives. It was during this time that they got married. Matilda and G.W. continued to care for Matilda's siblings.

(QUAKERS OF NEW PROVIDENCE, IOWA: A VIGNETTE)

The first formal record of Quakers in Iowa is at Mt. Pleasant in the S.E. corner of the state in 1835 while Iowa still had territorial status. Quaker groups followed that settled in Mt. Pleasant, Iowa City and Cedar County to the west of Davenport on the Mississippi River. Quarterly Meetings were organized there in 1858. When Iowa Yearly Meeting was organized in 1877, there were Quarterly Meetings in Salem (near Mr. Pleasant), in Henry County, at Springdale in Cedar County (where West Branch Monthly Meeting is and where the future Pres. Herbert Hoover was born.) There was also a Quarterly Meeting organized before this in 1853 called Honey Creek QM in Hardin County with concentrations of meetings around New Providence in the SE edge of the county. The people had started their homesteads much earlier. So it was here that the Edwards and Fitzgerald's were able to find established farms to rent from older Quaker owners.

Life was difficult as share-croppers. As they had not sold the homesteads in Indiana, they decided to return. They stayed for three more years. That is why Louisa was born in Iowa and Veroque and Joel were born in Indiana. The White River continued to flood, so G.W. hitched-up his team to the wagons and Matilda packed in all the quilts she had been making and they went back to Iowa and Hardin County. This time they rented a different Quaker farm closer to Ackley. Elva Maude was born there in March of 1860. They stayed at this farm throughout the Civil War.

GEORGE WASHINGTON EDWARDS AND THE CIVIL WAR

A year after Elva was born, the Civil War (aka the War Between the States) began, 12 April 1861. George Washington Edwards volunteered for service in the Union Army on 12 September 1861. His discharge document reads as follows:

> *George W. Edwards, Sergeant, Co. B., 11 Regiment Iowa Veteran Volunteers. January 1, 1864. For 3 years or until the end of the War. Discharged July 15, 1865 at Louisville, Ky. General Order #26 of (?) Dept. Born State of Indiana, 29 years of age, 5 foot 71/2 inches high. Dark complexion, blue eyes*, brown hair. Occupation farmer.*

He was 25 when he joined and 29 when discharged.

(Note: This discharge document describes the Veteran Volunteer duty from 1 January 1864 to July 18, 1865. It does not include his first 3 years from 12 September 1861 to 11 September 1864.)

*Elva Edwards-Cole, his granddaughter who ought to know, affirms that his eyes were brown.

The State of Iowa was required to raise 11 regiments by proclamation of Pres. Lincoln, 23 July 1861. The regiment had 922 officers and men when they "mustered" at Camp McClellan near Davenport, Iowa.

My sister, Mary Beth (Munn) Yntema, researched the details of the service of G.W. Edwards for her unpublished family story, "Head

Waters: Munn-Edwards, Maxwell-Bond". Here are highlights of Co B, 11th Iowa Volunteer Regiment.

November 16, 1861. They left on the river steamer "Jennie Whipple" for St. Louis and Benton Barracks. After receiving instructions and training in camp duties, they were "ready" for action.

December 9, 1861. They went to Jefferson City, then "up" the Missouri River to Boonville where Confederate parties were engaged. Most of the Missouri was in Union control by June 1861, but guerrilla bands were active.

December 23, 1861. They went by rail to California, Missouri.

March 12, 1862. Then they went by steamboat down the Mississippi and up the Ohio to Paducah, KY. They went up the Tennessee River to Savannah, Tennessee, which was 20 miles from Mississippi State border to the south. General Grant was in command when Ft. Henry was captured after a gun battle from ships on the Tennessee River.

The next U.S. Grant campaign was at Corinth on the Mississippi at Shiloh Church where Confederate General Johnston was prepared to make a stand. Grant's army with the 11th Iowa Volunteers moved to Pittsburg Landing on 23 March 1862. The 11th was under command of Maj. Gen. McLennan and Col. Hare. A Union charge on 6 April 1862 was unsuccessful. There was advantage to the Confederates. The next day saw the southern troops routed and the North in control. For the 11th Iowa Volunteers, there were 33 dead, 11 wounded, 1 missing. Over 20,000 men were killed at Shiloh counting both sides.

Following Shiloh, there was a reorganization to form a "Brigade" that included the 11th. They marched to Grand Junction, Tennessee and bivouacked until 28 November 1862 when it was apart of Gen. Grant's expedition down the Mississippi River to Lake Providence, Louisiana.

April 23, 1863. They were ordered to take Vicksburg. The 11th was involved in various aspects of the siege of Vicksburg that finally concluded with victory on 4 July 1863. The balance of the summer was in rest. In late summer, the troops were subjected to the hardship of heat and malaria.

G.W. Edwards claimed he was involved with Grant in the battles at Chattanooga, Missionary Ridge and Lookout Mountain.

G.W.'s three year enlistment would be up in September 1864. Well before that date, the opportunity was offered to the 11th Iowa Volunteers to re-enlist. Most men elected to reenlist. The discharge document states that G.W. reenlisted as of 1 January 1864 as a "Veteran" Volunteer. In March 1864, the veteran volunteers were granted a leave and G.W. returned to Hardin County, Iowa and his growing family. Matilda, as other wives of Union troops, had suffered through the support of the family without a husband and father. It just made the second parting that much more stressful. One result of the furlough was the arrival of a second son, Ulysses Grant Edwards on 20 December 1864. G.W. always referred to Grant as his furlough son, though he would not meet him until after the war was over.

The 11th Iowa **Veteran** Volunteers were reassembled on 22 April 1864 at Davenport, Iowa. They were augmented by new recruits for what turned out to be the final year of the war.

The Volunteers went back to Clifton, Tennessee and marched to the mountains of N. Georgia. They became part of Sherman's army formed at Ackworth, GA, 8 June 1864. There were 11,200 veteran soldiers. Sherman did a head-on assault on Southern Troops in the Battle of Kennesaw Mt. This was a mistake as many men were lost. In this battle, 24 July 1864, Fourth Sergeant Edwards was injured in the jaw and chin by a "spent" bullet that entered his left cheek, took out 2 teeth, ricocheted off the right jaw and was captured in his mouth. He spat it out and it became a reward of the Civil War that was kept in the family for many years and may still be somewhere in some granddaughter's memory box. G.W. said he was not able to eat well, so he knocked out matching teeth on the right side of the jaw so he could feed himself through the bandages. The wound healed well and seemed never to slow him down in later life.

In G.W.'s daughter Ana's memoirs she says, "He always went into the hospitals after battles, as there was a shortage of nurses and orderlies.

He had plenty of practice as a nurse and assistant surgeon." Atlanta fell to General Sherman's troops on 1 September 1864. This became the effective end of the War in the West. But the official end was 9 April 1865 in Appomattox, Virginia. The Union forces under Sherman took their time crossing Georgia to Savannah until 22 December 1864. **Sgt. G.W. Edwards and the 11th Iowa V.V. were in this march. From Savannah the troops marched up to Washington, D.C., where they became part of the Army of the Tennessee in the march down Pennsylvania Avenue.

Cpl. George W. and Matilda Edwards. 1864 while on furlough.
(George Munn collection).

The 11th Iowa V.V. was transported by rail and steamboat to Louisville, KY. Sgt George W. Edwards was discharged on 15 July 1865. There was transport to Davenport, Iowa where the Regiment was disbanded.

Having been away from his family for most of four years, understandably, G.W. needed to get reacquainted with his family. The new son, Ulysses Grant, could already walk. Grant called himself

"Lissa" as he learned to talk. His mother and older siblings called him "Liss". But his little sister Ana refers to him as "Grant" throughout her memoirs.

The farm near Ackley, Iowa seemed too small and G.W. was restless. He decided to move the family to Missouri to a farm near Cainsville in Harrison County. This is in northwest Missouri near the Thompson River. (Today it is east of I-35.) While there the twin girls Eldora Permela and Viola were born on each side of midnight (30 Sept 1867 and 1 Oct 1867). The climate was hot and humid. Some members of the extended family came down with typhoid fever. Matilda was sick and "unconscious for six weeks" according to Ana Mae's memoirs. Nancy, Matilda's little sister died. The rented farm was in the Missouri flood plain and flooded in the spring. G.W. became discouraged and loaded everyone back in the wagons and went back to Hardin County, Iowa. Matilda's brother, "Uncle Jim Fitzgerald" had not made the Missouri trip and they moved back to a farm near him, perhaps closer to New Providence.

SECOND SET OF TWINS

It was here, back in Iowa that the second set of twins was born 24 September 1871, Ana Mae and James PORTER. Ana (A-nah not ann-ah) was named for a neighbor friend of Matilda's at the time, Ana McDowell. James was named for his uncle, but was always called Porter. His mother called him "Portie". As develops in many twin births, there becomes a difference in the health of the two children. Ana Mae was chubby and precocious. Porter struggled as a baby. In fact, Matilda did not have enough milk for both of them. So Ana Mae was soon weaned to cow's milk so that Porter could have more of nature's best milk. Ana soon was drinking out of any bottle she could find, a skill that became her downfall. Porter continued to be growing slower and was less aggressive most of his life, though he was dearly beloved by his twin sister.

KANSAS CALLS

A provision of the military discharges following the Civil War was special consideration for homesteads that were opening in the West. The Homestead Act of 1862 had been meant for settlers in the Northwest Territories, Ohio, Michigan, Indiana, etc. But now, the Indian wars of Kansas were over and Kansas was open for homesteading. One provision of the Act was that homesteaders were to occupy the land for 5 years. War veterans could count their military service years against the 5 years. They still needed to pay filing fees, build a residence with a free standing stove, at least one window and a door. They could claim up to 160 acres and needed to occupy the land for two years. (The 5 years started when the claim was filed. The two years was for actual occupation of the property.)

George Edwards had never owned property and rented farms all his married life. He had taken his family from Iowa to Indiana. Then he went back to Iowa, to Missouri and back to Iowa. The family grew with each move. The horse drawn wagons received a work-out on the primitive roads of the era. Now was time for yet another mini-wagon train move, It was March 1873. Ana Mae and Porter were 18 months old. The oldest child, Louisa was 18 and had married Lewis Hall whose family lived in Ackley, Iowa.

So the older children and Matilda knew the routine well. Preparations went like clockwork. G.W. bought a second wagon and mule team. The two wagons were covered with canvas. Household goods, bedding, farm equipment and children were sorted out between the two wagons. The older four children, excluding Louisa, would be in one wagon. Joel could handle the team well. The parents and the two sets of twins were to be in the second wagon. Everything was arranged and they began sleeping in the wagons to get practice for the journey. Then an unusual and unfortunate event happened.

A GOING AWAY PARTY ENDS ABRUPTLY

Ana McDowell, Matilda's best neighbor friend and Ana Mae's name sake, decided to give a going away party for Matilda. The neighboring ladies were invited to a quilting bee, perhaps to finish off a quilt that the travelers could take. The McDowell house was large and well built with second floor bedrooms.

Ana Mae and Porter were too young to leave at home and Matilda brought them to the party. The quilters immediately busied themselves with the project. Matilda left the twins in a back room where harnesses were kept. She knew that Porter would surely be content playing there. Neither child was walking. But Ana Mae could scoot about quickly and soon found the stairs to the second floor, unbeknownst to her mother.

As the quilters were nearing the end of an afternoon of quilting fun, they heard a strange coughing coming from somewhere in the house. Upon inspecting the room where the twins were left, Porter was still there but Ana was nowhere to be seen. The coughing sound continued. No one had suspected the stairs. At any rate, the door at the top of the stairs was closed. Finally, as the sound continued, Matilda decided to go up and check. Upon entering a bedroom, the sound seemed to come from a little door to a closet under the eaves. Sure enough, there was Ana. She had found a bottle tucked way back in the closet and had tasted the fluid that was in the bottle.

One of the customs of the day was to swab down mattresses and bed posts with a weak solution of sulfuric acid as part of spring cleaning. Perhaps this was a treatment for bedbugs. The bottle of dilute sulfuric acid had been secreted back away from any child. But it didn't fool Ana Mae. She knew what to do with a bottle with liquid. This is how she had been feeding herself most of her young life. She had taken enough acid to cause her to cough up blood onto her special dress for the party occasion.

Mother Matilda immediately went into action as did Mrs. McDowell, who was a doctor's daughter. A doctor was called. In the meantime, Mrs. McDowell found an egg. The raw eggwhite was beaten and poured down Ana's throat. It was vomited up as black fibers. Then Ana was given cow's milk and that was vomited up. By that time the doctor had arrived and declared that the ladies had done just what he would have done. "If the baby lives for 24 hours, she will get well", he pronounced. But she could only "eat" milk for some time. The quilting party was at end. Ana had gone to sleep by then and Matilda took her home. But what about the Kansas journey that was to begin the next day?

Since all things were ready for the trip to Kansas, the two covered wagons left the next morning as planned. G.W. made some changes. He traded places with 13 year old Elva Maud. She went to Matilda's wagon to care for Ana Mae and Porter. The oldest child was Veroque, 17, the twin girls and the two boys, Joel and Grant were in G.W's wagon. They were able to buy milk along the way for Ana. The trip took about 30 days.

ANA'S LIFE LONG BURDEN

Ana Mae survived the prescribed "24 hours". The acid had burned her upper esophagus and seemed not to affect the voice box. Ana spoke with a rather high voice as did her sisters. The scaring left her food passage reduced in size and flexibility. In early years, Matilda and the older sisters carefully smashed her food. Meat, fruit and anything raw was dangerous. Even in later years she sometimes had a piece of meat or orange slice stuck part way down. There were "Heimlich Maneuver" events long before the term was invented. There were occasional trips to a doctor which were followed by days of "rest" as each event took its toll. Bread, cornbread or cake mashed up in milk was a staple diet for her. From Ana's memoirs, page 12, is her take on the burden.

"Early in the winter when I was three, I suffered a severe choking spell, the worst I ever had. It was early winter and the butchering had been done. Mother had cooked up some scraps of meat and pieces of back bone. One evening she brought in quite a bowl full of cold meats to cut up to make a big dish of hash. I was hungry for meat and it smelled so good. Mother seemed not to have quite enough so she stepped outside to bring in some more. I had been playing around the table and spied the meat. My appetite got the

best of me and when Mother stepped out, I stepped up and secured a piece of meat not very thick but quite large. I heard Mother coming back and I dodged under the table with my hunk of meat. I tried to swallow the meat in a hurry but it stuck in my throat and I coughed and gagged. Mother heard me, recognizing that choking sound, at once looked under the table. She pulled me out and started slapping me on the back to dislodge whatever was stuck in my throat but no meat came up. She finally laid me on the bed and went on with preparation of her meal. Of course, I could eat no supper and she took me to bed with her that night hoping the piece of meat would loosen. From time to time she offered me water but I could not get any water down. Nor could I get any meat up. This condition lasted several days until I at last developed a fever. I wanted water, water all the time, till at last on the fourth morning I started to have a coughing spell. Mother held me over the edge of the bed and slapped my back. After a long spell of coughing, the meat finally came up. I was so nervous and tired I started to cry like a little baby. Mother opened the door and let in a big hound puppy that belonged to Uncle John Fitzgerald. The puppy made a dash for the meat and Mother patted me on the back and said, "Now let the puppy get choked". I had learned my lesson the hard way and after that my Mother did not have to watch me so carefully."

When dairy companies began to make ice cream, Ana was truly blessed. Most any summer event called for a party for which she would order a five gallon container of vanilla ice cream. The order came in a cold pack with dry ice, so it kept solid until gone. The ice cream was available to everyone. Ana came with a serving dish that she filled to the brim. Actually, the five gallons of ice cream seldom lasted past a second day.

Any housewife who cannot enjoy food is probably a poor cook. Meat, bread, milk and potatoes became her main family menu. She always had a big kitchen garden and enjoyed raising vegetables. She tended to boil vegetables until they were mushy, as she required for herself she mashed them more with a fork before eating carrots or cabbage. She did not serve salads. Chickens were usually stewed until the bones could be lifted out. She made dumplings, not fried chicken. Breakfast was bread and butter, over-cooked cereal and always a big glass of milk. In self-defense, as her daughters grew up, they took over the cooking. In the years when Ana lived in the "office", she was served a plate of food to eat at the switchboard. When she was caring for her little grandson, she was ready to feed him the mashed up food she prepared for herself. No "Gerber's" for us.

In the years when she lived by herself her standard order from the "Limit" store, where she had a credit account, was 7 to 10 loaves of white Wonder bread. She crumbled the bread with milk and added sugar to taste. She had milk from her cows until her grandson Bob took over the milking. His contribution to her well being was a quart of milk from the morning milking. She kept chickens and had a kitchen garden from which she could find some vegetable most any time of the year, as Leland has such mild winters.

IV: KANSAS HOMESTEADS, TO 1889

〰

KANSAS OPENS FOR SETTLERS

The north central part of Kansas was open prairie that had been home for Pawnee and Kansa Native Americans. Pressure on the Native Americans to the east had pushed tribes into Kansas and Nebraska in the 1830s. The Europeans were not far behind. In Iowa and Missouri to the east, the best land had been taken up by the time that Iowa became a state in 1846. Kansas was given territorial status in 1854 as part of the Kansas/Nebraska Act that was leading up to the War Between the States. There followed a time of turmoil between pro- and anti-slavery factions known as the "Bleeding of Kansas" when Kansas suffered from outlaws and banditry. Statehood, as a free state, was achieved on 27 January 1861, just in time for the Civil War.

After the war, came the train construction era. From 1867-1885, cattle were driven northward to train railheads at Abilene and Ellsworth on the Chisholm Trail in Central Kansas just south of Ottawa County. The cattlecars were loaded and moved east to slaughter by packing houses of Kansas City and Chicago. At the end of each cattle drive, the cowboys would have pockets full of money and were ready for some good times after the rigor of the drive. That is why that area of Kansas became the epitome of the Wild West.

The settlers were arriving at the same time. So they were contending with bandits, train robberies, bank robberies and sheriff posies. Jesse

James robbed his first train in July of 1873. Most of the action was to the south of where the little two wagon train of the Edwards family were entering north central Kansas from Nebraska. They settled near Coal Creek in Ottawa County about 12 miles east of Minneapolis, the newly established county seat. They had the feeling that they were the first pioneers to arrive at the peaceful valley. They were naively unaware of the turmoil not far to the south. For George Washington and Matilda Edwards and their 8 children this was a dream fulfilled. They would have their own land and whatever improvements they made were to their benefit not a landlord's.

FROM ACKLEY, IOWA TO ACKLEY, KANSAS

One wagon carried G.W., the older boys Joel (15) and Grant (9), Veroque (17), and the twin girls Dora and Vila (5 ½). Matilda, Elva Maud (13) and the twins Ana Mae and Porter (18 months) were in the other. Chickens were hung in a cage below one wagon and there was a cat. Matilda was known for her homemade quilts and feather blankets. G.W. had accumulated farm equipment, harnesses and they had a supply of vegetable seeds and seed potatoes to plant as soon as sod could be turned.

What route did they take for the journey in March-April of 1873? We can only guess. As the crow flies today, the route from Ackley, Iowa across the S.E. toe of Nebraska and on to Ottawa County, Kansas is at least 375 miles. At a pace of about 12 miles a day, a maximum speed of mule-drawn wagons and with adequate time for rest and over-night camps, it would have taken them about 30 days as Ana suggests in her memoirs. (Of course a babe of 18 months would not be certain of the number of days. Perhaps it was a family memory told and retold through the years.) The first Iowa part of the trip was probably a repeat of the trips to Missouri and back. They probably crossed the Missouri River at Nebraska City where there were flat barges that could ferry westward bound travelers. They then entered Kansas at "Belleville" as other travelers report. Belleville is directly north of Ottawa County. After crossing the Republican River, it would be about a two day journey to arrive at the Coal Creek homestead. Coal Creek was a "nice flowing creek" between two low sets of hills. It flows southward to the Solomon River. Then there was yet another small stream that ran through their future homestead before reaching the larger Coal Creek. Later there was a neighbor family named Ackley. A name was needed for a post office and it was named Ackley. Matilda Edwards was the first post master of Ackley as she kept the mail desk and boxes in her parlor. There is a record of postal workers of the time that lists Matilda Edwards as postmistress.

They camped by the small stream and lived out of the covered wagons for several months as they set about "proving" the homestead. The boys immediately set out to break up the sod of Kansas blue grass that was also food for the mules. The boys planted corn and root vegetables. They opened up a potato patch as well. April was the perfect time to grow a crop for early summer as well as to harvest fall grain and winter food of squash and carrots.

THE ACKLEY HOMESTEAD

The homestead structures soon began to take shape. First was a sod house that was "about 18 X 20 feet." It was set 18 inches into the ground with two foot thick walls extending above ground. A double door entrance faced eastward. There were windows on the south and north sides. At the corner of the west side was a doghouse and a little room for the cat. She had a small door of her own. The cat had kittens soon after they arrived. All the kittens found good homes as all the neighbors needed a cat.

G.W. built a barn large enough for the mule teams and a horse or two that he wanted as soon as he could buy them. The barn was built out of sandstone rocks that were quarried from a hill nearby. There were cottonwood trees along the creek that supplied roofing beams that were covered with sod and then with shingles. Grass was cut as soon as mature to provide hay for the mules and future horse and cow. Hay was stacked outside the barn. A pole barn was built for a cow and her calf that were purchased from a neighbor. They would always need fresh milk for Ana Mae.

Inside the sod house they stretched the canvas wagon covers across so that there was a separate space for the parents and Porter who was still being cared for by mother Matilda. Ana had her gruel of crumbled cornbread and milk. A stove was set in the SW corner and in the SE corner was the kitchen area with shelves, table and chairs.

Soon the boys discovered that there were wild rabbits to be caught and wild grapes to be picked. The family diet was enriched with fresh meat and jelly. The nearest store was 10 miles south at Bennington. There they could purchase staples of beans, sugar, cornmeal and bacon. Before long the garden was offering up fresh vegetables. They were able to plant sugar cane and purchase meat from neighbors as well. There was more than enough butter for daily use, so the extra butter was salted down for use in the winter.

OTTAWA COUNTY, KANSAS

The Kansas Legislature of 1860 established Ottawa County along with other counties in the northeast corner of Kansas. It was named for a tribe of Native Americans. The county government was started in July, 1866 as the county then had the required population of 500. Voting in 1870 and 1872 designated the county seat to be Minneapolis, a central location, over the larger town of Bennington, to which a rail road line had been built.

The County was further divided into Townships, which of course are six miles square. The County has four townships north and south and five townships east to west, which makes the county twenty-four miles by thirty miles. Each township has a number designation and a name. The township to which the Edwards family came is Township 11 South and Range 1 West of the 16th Prime Meridian. Its name happens to be the same as the county, Ottawa Township. It is the third township east of Minneapolis and the second from the south boarder of the county. Roads were platted to be along the township lines, and then every mile along section lines. Sometimes the section lines are hard to follow with a road. To get to Minneapolis from the homestead, the Edwards travelers from Ackley went two miles east, then two miles north and then followed the Township Road named Limestone Road for fifteen miles to get to Minneapolis. To get to Bennington was actually only about 10 miles. At Bennington they could take a train to Salina, Abilene or Ellsworth.

LIFE ON THE FRONTIER

In 1874 there was a plague of grasshoppers. They were dense enough to block out the sun. Gardens had begun to produce and were stripped to the root tip. Though there was time to plant anew, the harvest was small and, as might be expected, the winter to follow was deeply cold, long and hard. Word of the difficulties filtered out to the east where good hearted people filled barrels with clothing to send to the "suffering pioneers". Ana remembers getting a black and white checkered petticoat which she was most proud to wear.

By the time Ana and Porter were four, the Edwards family was nicely established. G.W. had built the required structures for proving the homestead and then some. He was now the owner of a farm and never again did he rent. Yet his skills as a carpenter were much in demand. He contracted out to work on farm houses and barns. He bought Matilda one of the first sewing machines in the area. She took in dress making orders and sewed for neighbors as well as for her own family. She bought some geese and made feather-filled blankets and pillows that were in great demand.

The boys and Veroque took care of most of the garden and animal care. Soon, however, Veroque was hired out to a family about 20 miles away. She was able to attend school as well as do housework. Elva Maud took a similar housekeeping job with a family only 10 miles away. The wife of this family was too ill and old to do housework. Once when Elva came home, she brought a piglet that was part of her pay. This pig became the responsibility of Ana Mae and Porter.

Here is how Ana tells about another aspect of the homestead farm:

"My father built a spring house over the wonderful spring we had. It was built of stone up one story and the upper story was built of lumber as a granary for wheat and other grains. In the summer the older brothers slept there and a nice stone approach led up to the door. The spring house was built with a narrow hall way that took in the spring and a larger room that had a water way built all along two sides to hold the crocks of milk. This waterway flowed directly from the spring, ran through the building and out again and joined the pig yard that came up not far away. Mother also kept all meats in the spring house. Her washing equipment was there as was a small fireplace built under a tree very close to the spring house where she could heat water for washing milk things as well as laundry water." (Memoires, page 13).

Dora and Viola took on the inside tasks and did the house cleaning and gradually took on more and more of the cooking. The Edwards family became an economic and social force typical of pioneer families.

On 26 January 1876 Matilda gave birth to a son which they named John Lewis. He was named for Matilda's brother John Fitzgerald, but they called him Lewis or Louie. Everybody doted on this little fellow. As he began to walk, he pretty much had the run of the place. One day he was out in the yard playing and came into the house pointing to his foot that hurt. His mother couldn't see anything wrong, yet the leg became swollen and he lost consciousness. He died that afternoon in his father's arms. That was 27 October 1877. He was just 21 months old. The whole family took the loss very hard. The only conclusion made was that he was bit by a snake. (Elva Edwards-Cole says that he had cholera. (Page 35)

In 1877 the woman for whom Elva worked died. Her husband was so distraught that he died so soon after his wife that the community held a double funeral for them. The farm became the property of the farmer's nephew, Edwin Knight. He had been a frequent guest of his aunt and uncle, so before long, he proposed to Elva and she accepted.

Meanwhile, Veroque, who had been working for her board in town while she went to school, had a suitor as well. Dave Henderson was a railroad engineer and manager. A few weeks after the Knight wedding Dave and Veroque showed up at the sod house with the proper papers and George W. Edwards, who was a Justice of the Peace, performed their wedding. This left the two older boys and the two sets of twins at home. The Edwards tribe was soon added to, however, with the birth of Henry Granger Knight (21 July 1878) and Robert Henderson (18 October 1878). Ana was only 7 years older than her two new nephews. They both figured largely into her future, but of course they were just novelties at that time.

Twins James PORTER and Ana Mae Edwards. 1878. At nearly 7 years old.

It should be noted that today the area is farmed for wheat, corn, soy beans and other field crops. These first homesteaders, or sod busters, did raise some grain, but mostly opened limited areas of grassland for pasture, family gardens, small dairy and horse operations. George Washington Edwards was an accomplished carpenter and supported the family working off the farm.

In the spring of 1878 after G.W. had had some good paying carpentry jobs and Matilda had earned some money with her sewing and by selling quilts. They decided to build a frame house and not to go into debt building it. It was not a large house, but much more room than the sod house. As Ana put it, "It was a decent house." It was a two story house. The entry was into a large room that was living room, dining room, and it had the stove center rear. There were two back rooms. One was G.W. and Matilda's bedroom and the other a pantry. The stairs at a side angled up to the center of the upper floor. The girl's room was at the front and the boy's room at the back. The chimney from the stove came through the girl's room to the roof.

When the new house was finished, the community decided a school was needed. What was the start of Ackley School was held in the girl's room until the community could build a school about two miles away on land contributed by the Kibler family. Ana started school on the opening day and it became her joy of every day. She chided her brother Porter for his willingness to be outside as much as possible. He was never a dedicated student and as soon as he could he stopped going to school.

There was need for postal service for the growing community, so Matilda placed a dedicated desk just inside the door to her parlor and accepted the mail that was brought by from the train from Bennington two or three times a week.

The Ackley School became the social center for the Edwards family and the entire community. Spelling bees and recitation programs and music sings were held in rotation. The Edwards children liked to recite poetry. One type of poem they enjoyed was the nonsense rhyme. One

such learning challenge was called "Up Jumped Old Mother Jackson".
It is as follows:

Up jumped old Mother Jackson,
Round the round-top and down fell the cagement.
Smack Michael three stoble ditches
The dead man kicked the blind man's eye out.

Once upon a time, the pig was in the swine;
The swallows built a nest in the old man's beard.
There I bit buttermilk, saddled my house and
rode round the world
Ten miles yon side of the moon.

There I met Old Johnny Kerwhimple.
You know the old rogue as well as I do.
I asked him to grind me nine yards of steel,
Nineteen times finer than either meal or flour.
He said he would not, which I believe he could not.

So I put spurs to my shoulders
And bolted over hills and ditches and old barn doors.
At last I fell down and broke my neck
Over an old bag of rusty moonshine.

The other day down at Sandy Bull's
I met an Irish lad; he was unlike a man,
He had an old bone of a hat,
with nothing like the crown of it.
Hand on iron shoes with wooden buckles
and linen shirt with woolen ruffles.
How he who sees this lad and will not take him up,
His reward will be a half pint of pigeon's milk

churned in a green cat's horn.
Eighteen hundred and ninety four,
sitting in the corner fast asleep,
With his eyes wide open, and his bosom full
of hot sweet Irish potatoes.
(Anon)

THE HOUSE FIRE

All seemed to be going extremely well for the Edwards family until April of 1881. There came a day of intense activity. A meal was cooking in the oven. Matilda had heated enough water on her outside stove to wash nearly all of the everyday clothing of the family. She was hanging the last of the laundry on the line when she noticed smoke coming from the girls' bedroom window. There was immediate and total action from everyone. A fire had started in the floor of the girl's room where the chimney came up through from the cook stove below. When G.W. opened the door of the bedroom, it was completely filled with smoke and fire. He closed it immediately and turned to the boys' room where he was able to throw the beds and most of the contents out the window. Downstairs, the Post Office desk and mail was first out. Then nearly all the furniture and the contents of the other rooms were carried out in time. They even saved the cookstove with its roast for dinner. The nice dresses, beds and everything the girls had in their room was a total loss. Fortunately, the laundry drying outside had most of the everyday clothing.

The nearest neighbors, the Ackleys, had recently moved to town and their house was vacant and had room for everyone. G.W. set at once to rebuilding a house on the foundation stones of the burnt down house. The spring house, the dugout house, the barns and pig house were all unscathed by the house fire. However, that very fall, a prairie fire came through the region and burnt the roof off the barn and the hay stacked at the side.

Thereafter the Edwards family referred to the area of the homestead as the "Ackley's". This is confusing, as the community from which they had come in Iowa was Ackley, Iowa and Louisa and Lewis Hall continued to live there. For several years, the Coal Creek Ackley's continued to be the center of the Edwards clan. Ed Knight sold the farm that he had inherited and he and Elva moved into the Ackley house. Ed decided to set up a store in the spring house on the Edwards homestead and would go to Bennington from time to time to purchase merchandise for resale.

Following the house fire and a prairie fire, a cyclone hit nearby. G.W. became disenchanted with pioneer life in Kansas. Grant and Ana showed strong intellectual inclinations and needed educational opportunities not available in the country. Grant wanted to be a school teacher. Matilda had studied up on midwifery in books while in Iowa and would sometimes take Ana with her on a delivery. Also, G.W. had had significant experience as a medical aid in the war so that he was often called upon to set broken bones and to sew up wounds. Her father's stories and her experiences with her mother lead Ana to decide she wanted to become a doctor. Knowing this, G.W. and Matilda decided it was time to sell the homestead and move into town.

TIMBER CULTURE ACT OF 1873, 1874 AND 1878, (AND 1891).

U.S. Congress was concerned about the healthy development of the prairie lands the Dakotas, Nebraska, and Kansas. The environmentalists of the day predicted that the destruction of the grass lands would bring erosion and soil loss. (They were right, of course. It took another thirty years to figure out what to do about it.)

The "Timber Culture Act of March 3, 1873" was made law. It was amended on March 10, 1874 and again June 14, 1878. (It was repealed in 1891.)

By this Act a family could obtain 160 acres in addition to the land obtained under the Homestead Act of 1862. The family was required to plant 40 acres of trees. The 1874 amendment lowered the planting area requirement from 40 to 10 acres. They were to live on the land for five years and pay a $30 fee to file the Certificate.

The Timber Culture Act was an open opportunity for a huge land grab. Claims were made that were never properly earned. They were immediately sold to speculators. Thus the Act was repealed after just 13 years in play.

George W. and Matilda Edwards took advantage of the Timber Culture Act and filed a claim on the quarter of land directly north of their homestead quarter. And of course he completed the claim. It appears that he did build a house and members of the family lived there. As for so many claims, it is probable that few trees were ever planted.

The Certificate is dated 12 December 1883. Matilda Edwards had started her personal diary in February 1881. Her entry for December 11, 1883 reads: "Nice day. G.W. went to Salina to take a deed timber C." (i.e. Timber culture).

December 12, 1883: "G.W. and I went to Minneapolis to take a deed to Joel. Warmer to gather corn. Sent letter to Media."

George W. Edwards with his family had earned the addition "quarter". The property was immediately transferred it to Joel, his oldest son. It thus appears on an 1884 map of Ottawa Township.

The legal description of the homestead claim is: SW1/4 of Section 18 of Township 11 South of Range 1 West 6 Prime Meridian, containing 154.80 acres, under the Homestead Act of 20 May 1862 of U.S. Congress. It is Homestead Certificate No. 3157, Application 17821. Dated 9 September 1878 "by" *President R. B. Hayes* and by W.N. Crook, Secretary. It was recorded 11 Dec 1880 in Ottawa County, KS. Book F Page 636.

The Timber Culture claim is: NW1/4 of Section 18 of Township 11 South and Range 1 West 6 Prime Meridian, containing 155.60 acres, under the Act of March 3, 1873, and March 13, 1874 and Act of June 14, 1878 'to encourage the growth of timber on the Western Prairies. This is recorded December 12, 1883 at 3:30 PM at the Salina, Kansas Land Office. $4.00 final payment receipt. Recorded at Ottawa County in Book H page 406. The actual Certificate 77, Application 720 is dated fifteen May 1884. ." Signed by the President, *Chester A. Arthur,* by Wm. N. Crook, Secretary, and S. W. Clark, Recorder. (**Map 4**).

MINNEAPOLIS, KANSAS YEARS

Ottawa County, Kansas is a neat rectangle of 30 miles east and west and 25 miles north and south. The Solomon River angles from the NW corner of Ottawa County to the SW corner past Minneapolis, the county seat. The city is laid out in a modified square along the Solomon River. The main businesses are on Second Street. Concord Street intersection with Second Street is the "center" of the town.

On 1 May 1885 G.W. moved the family to Minneapolis, possibly sharing a house with Joel and Alice, who had moved to town earlier. Ana and Porter started school immediately. On 17 June 1885, G.W. purchased a house on a large lot, Lot 5, on S. Spruce Street, not far from where a right-of-way was preserved for the future railroad. The house was within easy walking to businesses, churches, schools and most town activities. The house had a second story and a basement. There were four rooms plus a pantry downstairs. There were porches, a well with pump, coal shed and out house. There was even a small stable and chicken house. They brought their cow and chickens. The house had all the niceties of the day and ample room for the whole family and visitors. In fact, there was room for boarders to augment the budget when the older children began to move away. Matilda bought a washing machine right away, as washing clothes for such a large family was a serious problem. (**Map** 5)

G.W. worked out all of the time they lived there. The railroads were busy building stations, landing platforms and the like. There were new companies building stores and warehouses. There was always employment even though it meant that G.W. was away from Minneapolis except on weekends. The family immediately tried out every church in town. G.W. and Matilda eventually joined the Baptist Church, but the young people liked to go to the African Methodist Church that featured lively southern singing for the evening services. It was at Minneapolis that Joel and Alice became lifelong members of the Baptist church and continued to attend Baptist Churches where ever they went.

As soon as he could, Grant began extending his high school classes with Teacher Normal school in the summer. When he finished high school and had passed the teacher's examinations, he began teaching in small country schools.

Ana, now age 14, was examined for placement and told she could enter high school in the fall except for a weakness in mathematics. She spent the spring and summer studying math make-up courses. She took the 8th grade exams in the fall and was able to receive a grade school certificate and stand with others who had finished grade school. She claimed that she made her own graduation dress. Porter was tested as well and was placed in the 5th grade with 11 year olds, much to his sister's dismay. Before long he quit school. He was able to apprentice himself at a barber shop and Matilda recorded that he began professional work at Cooper and Mills barber shop on 15 January 1887. Later he moved to Bennington to work in a shop there.

Porter and Ana Mae as teenagers in Minneapolis, Kansas. Circa 1887.
(Munn Family collection).

Lewis and Louisa Hall had tried earlier to farm in the Coal Creek area, but had not done well and moved back to Ackley, Iowa where Lewis went into business with his brother in a butcher shop. Later he bought a small hotel.

In September before the move to town, Dora had visited a neighbor family in Ackley. The oldest son of the family and Dora took to each other almost on sight. They came one day to Dora's father with a wedding license. G.W. officiated with the vows of matrimony. Dora and Hiram C. Ruggles were married on 28 September 1884. Hiram Ruggles was an engineer and was working for the railroad on bridge construction. They moved about a good bit as the railroads worked west. They were living in Denver in April of 1889.

Joel married Clarissa Alice Morse in 1881 in Minneapolis. They first lived in the Ackley house when the Edwards moved back into their rebuilt Coal Creek house after the fire. Alice, as the family called her, was one of the early school teachers at Ackley. They moved into Minneapolis for a while and then they went to Decatur County in northwest Kansas where Joel tried his hand at farming.

The summer of the move to town Viola met John Merrill in Ellsworth, Kansas. John was a talented musician. They were married 14 January 1886.

Ed and Elva Knight also bought a house in Minneapolis. It was at 506 Clay Avenue between 8th and 9th Avenues. It was in easy walking distance to the South Spruce Street Edwards house.

VAROQUE HENDERSON DIVORCE

Dave Henderson's railroad employment also took him out of the home. He had a long contract in Denver. A rumor filtered back that he had been unfaithful. Ana was visiting in the Henderson home in Ellsworth when Veroque and Dave confronted each other with their problem. Veroque declared a formal separation. She moved with her family to her parent's Minneapolis home. The Henderson children at the time were: Robert (Bob) (9), Elva (7) and John ALLEN (5).

There developed a very nasty divorce situation that went to court in Ellsworth County. Dave filed a counter suit claiming that Veroque had invited a man into her house. That man was in the courtroom and was identified by Dave. The man turned out to be Veroque's Uncle John Fitzgerald, Matilda's brother, who indeed admitted to visiting his niece as he travelled through town. The judge ruled in favor of Veroque, giving her custody of the three children, Robert, Elva, and John Allen. Dave was ordered to pay support until the children were through high school. Dave was very remorseful and apologized. The damage was done. Dave honored the court order and supported the children as required right on until Allen was through high school in Port Townsend. Veroque remarried to a Civil War veteran friend of G.W.'s, Thaddeus Steven Smith, on 3 February 1887. They moved to another house in Minneapolis for a time. Thad Smith was most instrumental in the decision to move west.

Veroque had been employed at a milliner's shop in Minneapolis. She also took work at a dress shop, as all the Edwards sisters had learned sewing from Matilda. So it was with this skill that Ana joined with Veroque as a seamstress in the dress shop when she had free time. The dressmaking skill came in handy several times in Ana's future. Ana claimed that she never bought dresses but always made her own, though as the years went by, the style of dress she made did not change much. In later years Ana's daughters generally saw to finding dresses for her.

MARRIAGE PROPOSALS

Ana recounts several times she received proposals to marry. One suitor was Little Willie. Ana was 13 and in school at the Ackley school. Little Willie was 16 years old. He came to the school and knocked on the door and asked her to come out. He was on his way to Texas. He proposed that she wait for him until he came back in five years. Well, that was hardly a possibility in Ana's mind and she gave him no encouragement even though he gave her a bag of peppermint candy and a blue ribbon to "match her blue eyes". Puppy love can be strange.

When Ana was taking music lessons, still 13 and going to Ackley School, a dance was planned for the music students and everyone was assigned a partner. Hans, a six foot one Scandinavian lad, was assigned to Ana. The couple did have a good time as Ana said he was a good dancer. Later he came to the Post Office at the Edwards home and asked for Ana to come outside. With little ado he proposed to her. This time she was ready with a stock answer that she was preparing to be a doctor and couldn't consider marriage. "He was a good fellow", she added.

In Minneapolis a young Catholic fellow took a shine to Ana and asked her to marry him. She again used the "I'm studying to be a doctor" excuse but added that she was a protestant. He begged her to reconsider and try out his church by attending Mass for a year and then decide. She agreed and went to Mass faithfully. Meanwhile another fellow had noticed her. He was aware of her commitment to the Catholic fellow, but would come to the Edwards house to visit Porter. Ana thought nothing of it. Then, as the year drew to an end, the Catholic priest asked Ana for an interview. He asked her if she were ready to join the Catholic Church. She had made up her mind and told the Father that she had learned that she did not need to make confession to a Catholic Father but that she could go directly to Jesus with her confessions. This made the priest angry and he then accused her of breaking her vow to the Catholic suitor by seeing other men. He was referring to the visits by Fred Rose. At that time Ana simply thought Fred was visiting Porter as Fred had not talked to her at all. So the affair with the Catholic lad was over. But as soon as Fred E. Rose heard that, he became more forward and began to find ways to talk with her. But the rest of that story must wait while the Edwards family goes to Port Townsend, Jefferson County, Washington Territory.

Central School, Minneapolis, Kansas. Circa 1885.
Ana Mae Edwards attended here for her high school year.
(Ottawa County Museum).

V: THE MOVE WEST

ON TO WASHINGTON TERRITORY

Since George and Matilda were married in 1855, they had moved seven times if the move after the house fire is counted. Each time they started pioneer farming all over. Yet the public tone of the post Civil War period was the desire to move west. The construction of the railroads had added to the westward fever as the railroad companies provided well paid jobs. The jobs were moving west as well and the railroads were advertising for people to come and live "out" west so that there would be an increase in railroad passengers and commerce. Towns and cities in Oregon State and Washington Territory were advertising the availability of "Free Land" that was covered with virgin forests and fertile valleys ready to make men rich.

George Edwards was naturally caught up with the fever. Though he had his home in Minneapolis, he would be gone more and for longer times as his jobs building railroad buildings kept going farther away.

THADDEUS STEVENS SMITH

Added to the excitement was Veroque's new husband, Thaddeus Stevens Smith. Thad Smith was a veteran of the Union Army. (Corporal, Co. E, 6th Penn. Reserves, 35th Penn. Volunteer Infantry.) He had distinguished himself in a heroic charge up a hill to capture a Confederate gun position on the 2nd day of Battle of Gettysburg, July 2, 1863. He was awarded the Congressional Medal of Honor. After the heroism, he had been captured and sent to the notorious Andersonville Prison. He survived the experiences but was left with a gimpy leg that became his banner thereafter. He was a strong minded man that became an organizer for Republican political ideas. He held meetings for every election campaign and was always ready with a speech in his pocket to proclaim the glories of the American life of freedom and productivity.

Thad Smith was George Edwards' best friend before Thad married Veroque on 3 February 1887 after her divorce was final. Thad received a sizeable one lump pension payment that recognized his time in prison without pay. He knew what to do with the largess. He had written to the Land Office in Washington Territory and had decided that Port Townsend was where the greatest opportunity was awaiting. The city was poised to become the "San Francisco of the Northwest", as soon as rail service reached it from the south. The excellent harbor would make the city and surrounding country-side the largest city on Puget Sound. He had also convinced Matilda's brother, John Fitzgerald, of the excellence of his decision.

Thad Smith left for Washington Territory in July 1888. John Fitzgerald left on 8 August 1888 to meet him. Thad located a 40 acre plot near Hooker Lake (at that time) that was on the sunny side of a hill (south side of 'Strawberry hill'). It overlooked a willow flat that could be easily cleared. It had a clear brook for water and a nice stand of cedar trees to cut and split for building material. (Today the location is at the intersection of Highway 101 and Cutoff Road.) John Fitzgerald located a site on the Little Quilcene River about three miles to the south. (John's wife Meda came west about the time that Veroque came. John and Meda did not like the raw pioneer life, sold out and went back to Kansas after a short year.)

Thad sent money for Veroque to come with the children and he set out to build a house for them. Veroque left from the Bennington train station on 8 October 1888. She was nearly 32. Robert was 10, Elva 8, and Allen was 6. Porter Edwards Smith was born 9 Jan 1889 after they were settled in Leland. Matilda was most displeased to see the family leave as Oka was soon to give birth to "Little Portie", as Matilda would call her grandson. This was not the first nor the last time that folk met at the train station to wish loved ones farewell as friends and neighbors headed west.

THE REST OF THE FAMILY

John Merrill and Viola sold their home in Ellsworth and came to Minneapolis as well. They made their home in Matilda's parlor. Porter quit his barber job in Bennington. The men folk began to go on ahead. Ed Knight left Kansas on 24 February 1889. He had sold his house in Minneapolis on 29 January. Elva and her three children moved in with Matilda. Henry has been mentioned. Chandler Knight was born a year after Henry and was 10. Charles was born in July of '81 and died after only 4 days. Claude Everett Knight was born in 1882 and was now 7. Chandler Knight, or "Channie" as he was called by the family, was born with a heart defect and was never strong. He took much special care and needed to be carried about as a boy. He died at the age of 15 when his heart gave out. Today a hole in the heart or a heart with weak valves would be fixed. He was born two generations early.

John Merrill and George W. left together on 14 March 1889. When Ed Knight arrived in Port Townsend, he found there were no houses to rent, so he bought (rented?) a lot and began to build a house. When G.W. and John Merrill arrived, they set about assisting him. This house is at 806 Fillmore Street and is still occupied.

Matilda was left to close up business and sell the house in Minneapolis. Life in Minneapolis was getting complicated. The house was heated with coal and the winter had been extremely cold. Coal was increasingly expensive as it had to be brought from the train at Bennington. The water in the well was not only inadequate in amount but was found to be contaminated for drinking. The well was covered and sealed. Water had to be purchased by the barrel as the city had not yet developed a new water system using Solomon River water.

THE JOURNEY OF ELEVEN PLUS ONE

Matilda sold the old cow and chickens. The stove was sold separately from the house. Much of the household goods were packaged and shipped on 6 April 1889. They boarded the train in Bennington on 11 April 1889. There were 11 of the Edwards' family in the party and a good friend, Cora Smith was riding with them. She had a fiancé, Will Brown, waiting for her in Port Townsend. They were married immediately on arrival. The "eleven" were: Matilda, Grant, Viola and her new-born baby, Leroy Fredrick Merrill as well as her two year old, Ana Delores Merrill, Elva Knight and her three sons, Henry Granger, Channie and Claude, Ana Mae and her twin Porter. They held up the departure until little Leroy was born.

They were met in Denver by Dora Ruggles. Matilda states that the train left Denver at 10:45 on April 29th. They reached Portland, Oregon on 2 May 1889 but were delayed enough when crossing the Columbia River that they missed their intended connection to a ship that was to take them from Tacoma to Port Townsend. They had to stay overnight in Tacoma, but caught the side-wheeler, the *Olympian*, a ship of the notorious "mosquito fleet" that plied the Puget Sound. At 1:15 P.M. on 3 May 1889 the *Olympian* reached Union Dock in Port Townsend.

The men had expected them the evening before and had waited on the dock over night. But they joyfully escorted the travelers to Uptown Port Townsend to the yet unfinished house that Ed Knight had started. The wood shed had been fixed up for the men to sleep in and the women and children all found beds inside Ed's house until other arrangements could be made.

The Edwards Clan, except for Joel and Alice's family and, of course, Louisa and Lewis Hall's family, had essentially reached as far west as anyone wanted to go. The new pioneering adventure had begun.

(TRAINS, TRAIN FERRY AND BOATS: A VIGNETTE)

As the Civil War began, the railroads had been built through the Eastern States to the Mississippi River. By 1860 the "National Railroad", for example, had been declared to be the road from Baltimore, through

Cumberland in the mid-Allegany Mountains to Wheeling, WV. It went on to Columbus, OH, Indianapolis, IN and ended at East St. Louis. The migrants heading west needed to cross the Mississippi on boats and form the mule and oxen wagon trains on the west side as they began the long trek to California or Oregon.

As the Civil War came to a close, there was great enthusiasm to build train lines on across the Great Plains. The federal government had given the train companies land grants so that the sale of land could finance rail construction. Financiers of the East were eagerly investing great sums as well. The Union Pacific Company began the straightest route out of Chicago to Omaha, NE. From there it headed west along the Platte River through Nebraska to Cheyenne, WY and west toward Ogden, Utah, purposely avoiding Denver. From San Francisco the Central Pacific RR was being built westward. These two systems connected on 10 May 1869 at Promontory Point, Utah not far from Ogden.

The Northern Pacific received its commission in 1864 to build from Duluth and St. Paul across the northern states: Bismarck, ND to Billings and Missoula, MT, to Spokane, WA thence toward the Oregon-Washington border at Walla Walla.

Meanwhile, construction had started on the Oregon Railroad and Navigation Co. in 1874. It built a short line around the Columbia River rapids between The Dalles and Celilo Falls. This was extended both ways from Portland to The Dalles and from Celilo to Walla Walla to connect with the Northern Pacific. This was completed in 1882.

Nebraska and Kansas were opened up for settlers and homesteading, but folks from the East preferred Kansas and began clambering for rail service. So in 1863 Congress authorized the construction of the Kansas Pacific railroad to go from Kansas City to Topeka, KA. By 1866 the KPRR was working its way on to Denver. Then it was pushed on to Cheyenne in 1871. From there, of course, trains could pass into the UP-CP system to Central California.

Construction of the Oregon Railroad and Navigation Company continued southward from the Columbia River through Baker valley towards Huntington, OR on the Snake River. The Union Pacific had built northward from Ogden and met the OR&NC (some parts were called the Oregon Short Line) at Huntington. This junction was completed in 1884, which some say completed the first transcontinental road because the U.P. used bridges over the Missouri and Mississippi. There was still no bridge over the Mississippi at St. Louis.

The North Pacific RR constructed a line from Tacoma WA south to Kalama on the east (or north) side of the Columbia. NPRR built a line northward from Portland on the south (or west) side of the Columbia River to Goble. The Columbia River valley narrows between Hunter's Point (near Goble) on the west and Kalama on the east. At this point the system used a train-ferry.

A train ferry or barge, the *Tacoma,* was built in Portland and launched on 9 August 1884 and immediately put into service. It could carry three locomotives, 23 freight cars, six passenger coaches and a caboose. The river velocity could run at eight or nine mph. The barge had square ends and pushed a lot of water ahead. In the spring the Columbia was subject to flooding. So the barge was slow and often delayed. The *Tacoma* was in service as an integral part of the NPRR until 1906 when railroad bridges were built across the Columbia and Willamette Rivers to connect to the railroad on the south side of the Columbia River. Subsequently, NP built a railroad on the north side of the Columbia from Pasco/Walla Walla area to Portland and thus to Tacoma.

To complete the story as it concerns the Edwards clan, a branch of the Kansas Pacific RR was built into the Solomon River valley from Abilene. It reached Bennington KA in 1878. The settlements of Bennington and Minneapolis had contested for the county seat of Ottawa County. Minneapolis won out perhaps because it was geographically central. But the railhead head made Bennington the commercial focus of the county until the railroad was extended to Minneapolis and beyond. For a time a railroad was in existence that entered Ottawa county from the east and came by Ackley and Wells to Minneapolis. It had a short life.

Railroad ferry *Tacoma* brings Northern Pacific train across the Columbia River between Goble, Oregon and Kalama, Washington. Circa 1900.
(Columbia County, Oregon, Museum)

The fall of 1884 marks the opening of a rail system from the Atlantic coast cities to Puget Sound at Tacoma. This also marks the beginning of the reality of travel to the west. The events of the Edwards family were also coming to a focus. G.W. and Matilda had decided to move into town so that the children could experience better schooling. Work was available for G.W. as the railroads were in full construction of train stations, warehouses and the like to support the local commercial aspects of train systems. Also people continued to flood in from the east to open businesses and to try their hand at farming without having to start from pioneer status. The sale of homesteads on the prairie and houses in town was relatively easy as well. Then when Thad Smith got his pension in 1888, all was ready to begin that next move west.

One more transportation factor needs to be added. The population of Washington, and specifically the Puget Sound, had been largely water or boat directed travel. The future cities around the Sound, from Olympia in the south to Everett in the north and all the communities, small and large, between were entered and serviced from the docks on their shores. The upland was heavily forested and not immediately available for agriculture as were the lush valleys of Oregon. So the organization of Washington State came 30 years after Oregon (1889 vs. 1859).

Commerce and people were moved around Puget Sound with a fleet of private ships and boats of all sizes. They were not too large or very fast, but there were many. Thus they were called the "mosquito" fleet. Between the major ports of Seattle, Tacoma, and Everett on the east side and Bremerton, Port Townsend, Port Angeles on the west side, as well as Victoria and Vancouver, BC, there seemed to be daily visits from one boat or another. The smaller ports would have weekly visits to bring people and mail in and out.

The passenger ferry *the Olympian*

The *Olympian** and her sister side-wheeler the *Alaskan* were just two of the many ships travelling the great inland sea of the Puget Sound. (Puget Sound, with all its bays and inlets, is now being called "Salish Sea"). Most ships used wood to power the steam engines. Wood for fuel was readily available at water's edge. Cutting the wood was a labor intense job for the first emigrant settlers that were hacking their way into the upland and clearing farm land as they went.

---

*   (The Olympian and the Alaskan were built in Wilmington, Delaware for the Oregon Railroad and Navigation Co. They were 261 feet long with 73 foot beam. They never were efficient and lost money. The Alaskan sank off Oregon with loss of 30 lives in 1889. The Olympian was being towed to the east coast in 1909 when it ran aground in the Straits of Magellan. Its bones on the rocks were a reminder to ships of the treachery of the Strait.)

Finally, as a close to this essay on the opening of rail and boat transport in the west, it is appropriate to mention that the Canadian Pacific Railroad also was being constructed. Like the Union Pacific-Central Pacific to the south, it was being pushed west from Vancouver, BC at the same time as the construction across the Canadian prairie was under way. The two roads met in the Canadian Rockies on November 7, 1885. By about 1888, James H. Munn, who had just completed his apprenticeship in carpentry in Boston, was able to travel by CPRR from Nova Scotia to Vancouver to start life anew as did Ana Mae Edwards and her family. Jim and Ana first met each other, casually, in Port Townsend in the fall of 1889. But there is more of the Edwards story to tell.

VI: THE EDWARDS FAMILY IN PORT TOWNSEND, WASHINGTON TERRITORY

PORT TOWNSEND, THE VICTORIAN CITY ON THE BAY

Port Townsend, in May 1889, was a boom town. It is located at the northeast end of Quimper Peninsula which in turn is at the most northeast end of the Olympic Peninsula. This makes it a port town located at the east end of the Strait of Juan de Fuca and at the edge of Puget Sound. Its bay was a natural stopping place for the ships coming into Puget Sound and leaving to the orient or San Francisco. The U.S. government needed an official location as an entry point. There had been a struggle between Port Townsend and Port Angeles to the west as to which port was to have the U.S. Customs House. Port Townsend had recently won the contest. A three story sandstone building was being constructed in uptown Port Townsend. The building seemed to peer over the bluff at the edge of the uptown. Today it is a historic, one of a kind Post Office. George Washington Edwards was immediately employed in its construction.

The shore of the bay and its docks and port facilities of downtown of Port Townsend was almost a different city from the uptown. There were several docks reaching out over the tide flat to meet ships that needed to dock at low tide. The docks became extensions of the streets which were named for early U.S. presidents or famous founding fathers. Taylor, Quincy, Adams, Monroe are a few. Taylor Street extended to Union Dock, which was well built with an extra extension for larger ships. The street parallel to the bay edge was Water Street. The bluff base permitted just enough room for Water Street and with buildings on both sides of the street. The parallel street to Water Street is Washington Street and it makes an angle up the bluff to the Customs House/Post Office. The intersection of Taylor Street and Water Street became the center of downtown. Quincy Street had its dock extension as well. The early businesses made good use of the edges of Quincy Street dock for several buildings. There was a men's boarding house, a restaurant and some stores. The fact that the tide came in and out under the buildings simplified sanitation issues for the downtown businesses. One such building was 88 1/2 Quincy Street or the Seaman's Bethel, a boarding house run by the Salvation Army for single sailors waiting in town for their ship to sail. (Map 1)

Downtown and uptown were two different cultures. Bars, "boarding" houses, and honky-tonk halls catered to the transient men and shipping activities of this wild era. The fact that bars were often poised out over the high tidal waters made it possible to "shanghai" the young lad who thought he was in town for a good time only to find he had been "slipped a mickey finn", passed out and lowered into a waiting skiff. By the time he knew where he was, he was well out on the "strait" headed to the Pacific Ocean and the orient. Wise people and nice people didn't go downtown after dark.

Uptown was completely different. Homes and even fancy houses were being built as fast as possible. The Methodist and the Episcopal Churches that were being built were the oldest west of the Mississippi. A school was located on the uptown intersection of Lawrence Street and Taylor Street. This crossing became a second center of commerce. There was a Marine Hospital. The Uptown Theater and the Baptist Church was situated among the grocery, hardware, and dry goods shops. A grand brick county court house was built with a four faced chime-clock tower. It is arguably the showiest court house in the State.

The city had a street car system. Water Street was cut off by a slew at the north and a tidal basin to the south. The street car tracks were built over the south tidal basin and then brought along the base of the bluff to a block or so before Taylor Street downtown center. The street car line went out to the hills to the south called the 5th Ward so that homes could be built out beyond the two central areas. It went on to the North Beach area.

Not only was Port Townsend seen as the entry port for all of the developing Territory of Washington, soon to be the State of Washington, it also was touted as the future western terminus of the railroad system connecting to all points east. Plans were in hand, construction funded and dirt was being moved for the Port Townsend Southern Rail Road. The construction was heading southward past Discovery Bay to Quilcene, at that time the county's second city. At the same time in Shelton, in Mason County to the south, construction was heading northward toward the Hood Canal. The hope was that Port Townsend would be the San Francisco of the Northwest. In fact, Northern Pacific had already decided that its western terminus would be Tacoma. Puget Sound water provided a much cheaper passage than trying to blast through the foot hills of the Olympic Mountains and bridge the three major rivers flowing off the Olympics into Puget Sound. It would take the eastern bank crash of 1896 to end the speculation for PTSRR. Until then, jobs, especially construction jobs, were abundant in Port Townsend and the Edwards men folk were experienced and ready workers.

THE EDWARDS SETTLEMENTS

Ed Knight had a good start on a house on Fillmore Street uptown when G.W. Edwards and John Merrill came to join him in February of 1889. As soon as the latest group of the family was situated, Ed Knight, who operated a store in Kansas, began partnership with a downtown store. He soon found his way into other activities and was a major clerk or organizer for the 1890 census of Jefferson County. That was the first census after Washington became a state. He reported that Port Townsend had just over 10,000 people for that year.

There was an immediate opening for a county school superintendent for which Grant was qualified. At that time the task was mostly the organization of local school boards and assisting in decisions of funding, teacher procurement and school location. He ended up being a teacher as well. He was the teacher of the Leland School in 1890.

John Merrill, Viola's husband was a capable carpenter and construction worker, but his love was instrumental music. He immediately set about organizing an orchestra. He needed to have a bass violinist, so since Ana had music training in Kansas, he recruited her and taught her to play what she called a bass viol. The group practiced during the week and then spent Sundays going from the Methodist Church in the mornings, to the Seamen's Bethel in the afternoon and a youth program in the evening. John Merrill eventually took the job of conductor on the tram system that had a round house off Discovery Road at San Juan Avenue. He built a house not far away from the round house.

In September of 1889, Joel and Alice Edwards decided that farming in Decatur County, Kansas was not going to be successful. They decided to follow the family to Port Townsend as well. They arrived September 12th with 4 children: Lola (5), Ray (4), Elva (2) and Guy (1). A third son, Schuyler Bricen, was born in Port Townsend (19 April 1897). Alice's mother, "Grandma Morse," came as well as she was a fundamental part of the family. Joel bought a lot in the Fifth Ward, as Ana put it, and built a fine Victorian house that is still there at 25th and Gise Street. He found ready employment as a carpenter. He and Alice were founding members of the Baptist Church (Conservative) that is also still on Lawrence Street in the Uptown business district. The family members were solid Christians. The children were all excellent students. The four older children went to the University of Washington at the same time. One way Joel and Alice financed their education was to rent a house in Seattle and the family lived there during their university years.

Ulysses Grant Edwards built his house across the street from Joel. After his years as County School Superintendant and teaching in country schools, he enrolled at Central Washington Normal School (Central

Washington University at Ellensburg) and obtained advanced teaching and administrative credentials. Later he was a customs inspector for the U.S. Government.

Eventually, G.W. and Matilda bought a lot at 2554 Gise Street a few steps from their son Joel's house and built their last house. The back fence of Joel's house was the fence of the Laurel Grove Cemetery. Joel's house is currently owned by a great granddaughter.

Porter Edwards, Ana's barber brother, immediately got a "chair" in a downtown barbershop when the family came to Port Townsend. Unfortunately he was not able to work very long. Men wore their hair short in those days. The barbers cut hair by snipping off little ends of the hair with scissors. An occupational disease of barbers was called "Barber's Pneumonia" caused by inhaling the hair bits. Whether that was Porter's problem or if he had contracted tuberculosis, no one seemed to know. He became very weak and had a hard time standing to do his work. He spent more and more time resting as he could not breathe well. He suffered a year and then he died 4 July 1890.

The loss of Porter was preceded by even greater tragedies, if that is possible. According to Matilda's diary, Ana received a letter on 27 May 1889 from Fred Rose's mother in Minneapolis, Kansas. Fred was dead from a gunshot to the chest. Ana has no time to absorb the news of Fred's death as the next day Elva gets sick. Six days later, Elva is dead as well.

Just a month after arriving in Port Townsend, Elva Maud Knight died at age 28(4 June 1889). Ana describes her symptoms as "high fever, deliriums and stomach pain." No certain cause of death was identified. One account suggested that she died of malaria. It is possible that while she was a child and the family was living in the swampy part of Missouri that she was infected then. But it seems unlikely, as malaria has ongoing symptoms and none seem to have been reported. The family, understandably, was devastated. Matilda simply fainted away, as often happened to her in stressful times. The stress of closing out in

Kansas and organizing the travel west and now the suddenness of Elva's death just put her out of the picture for nearly two weeks.

Ana was the only one who was functioning. Viola and John Merrill had two little children and John was building his house. G.W. was trying to provide support with a new job at the Custom's House. Veroque was living twenty miles and a day's journey away.

Elva had come with her three sons. Henry was eleven, Channie was ten, and Claude was seven. Strangely, their father, Ed Knight, was not much help. According to Ana, who did not like him much, he cared little for his children. In fact he was quite selfish in that he resented that Ana and his sons were living in his house. He couldn't live there if Ana were there. His solution was to have Ana marry him, which was a very scary thing to her along with the other tragedies. Ana was nearly as distraught as her mother. She was still trying to handle the news about Fred Rose and now her brother-in-law, Ed Knight, expected her to marry him just days after his wife had died!

Ana relates how great this crisis time was for her. She had Viola take the two smaller boys and Ana went into seclusion to a bed room and began to pray fervently. It finally came to her what she had to do. She found an apartment she could rent. She could have the boys stay with her until Matilda was better. Matilda eventually took the smaller boys. But Henry, who was only seven years younger than Ana, slept on a cot in Ana's apartment. School was soon to start and children would need clothing, so she went about the neighborhood soliciting sewing jobs. She had no respect for Ed Knight after that, even if she ever did. She actually blamed Ed for Elva's sickness as Ana claimed that Ed didn't want any children after Henry was born. He had given Elva something to abort their second pregnancy. The child was full term but died a few days after being born.

Elva Maud had been Ana's special sister. Elva was 12 years older and it was Elva who took major responsibility for Ana following Ana's accident with the bottle of acid. Elva was her caretaker on the wagon trip to Kansas and on into Ana's childhood days in the sod homestead house. It was Elva, more than her mother Matilda, who was Ana's model to be a young lady. Elva and Ana would go on shopping ventures in Minneapolis and talk about young men and what it was like to be married. Elva had been Ana's confidant as the Fred Rose affair heated up that last year in Kansas.

Fred E. Ross of Minneapolis, Kansas. Circa 1888.
(Munn family collection)

FRED E. ROSE

In Minneapolis on Saturday afternoons, Elva Maude and Ana Mae made an occasion of going shopping. They would dress up and visit the stores but never buy much. They were just having fun. Unbeknownst to them, they were quite the attraction for the young men, two in particular. One managed the drug store and the other was a writer and type setter for the town paper the Solomon Valley *Democrat*. They both knew about the Catholic suitor and Ana's testing of the Catholic Church. The news that Ana had not accepted the Catholic boy's offer was noted especially by Fred Rose's mother, a friend of Matilda's, as well as by other single and available men of the town. Fred Rose had an office that looked out over the main intersection of the town and he noted Ana's comings and goings, but his courtship remained mostly in his imagination. The drug store attendant was even more subtle with his courtship and plans. He never once spoke to Ana about his imaginations. The two young men belonged to the same men's lodge. They would verbally poke at each other. The drug store lad, whom Ana never names, is said to have claimed that he would marry Ana no matter what.

Fred saw his opportunity one Saturday when Ana and Elva were shopping. He invited them to visit his office. Fred had actually purchased the printing business and the shop was across the street from where Ana and Elva had been. During the walk about the print shop, he asked Ana if she was aware of him and his new shop. She couldn't say she was aware of him. Fred then went on to say that he had been "noticing" her come and go for a year or more. Ana couldn't deny all that, but was glad Elva was with her to help cool the situation.

On another day Fred invited Ana and her brother Grant to visit and hear a new music box he had purchased. After this Fred asked to come and hear Ana play the organ at her house. There followed several casual meetings of this type. Both Fred and Ana were busy. Ana was in her last year of school and she had received the news that her family had decided to go to Washington Territory. She was pressured to finish school early. Fred was involved in various lodge and business interests. Then in October 1888 Fred invited Ana to take a buggy ride in a new buggy and pulled by a new team of horses that he had purchased. He took her out of town to Rock City, a park with an unusual formation of large rounded rocks that are called "sandstone concretions". The park like setting was a popular tourist and a local trysting spot. Ana had made a new gown for Sunday wear and wore that. She simply expected a nice autumn outing.

Instead, with little fanfare, Fred Rose proposed to Ana. She thought it was a joke, but soon realized that Fred was in dead earnest as he seemed to tear up. Then she told him, "Don't cry Fred. I wasn't going to say no. I was going to say yes." "Do you mean it?" he almost shouted. He put one arm around her and kissed her. "He smashed me right on the mouth, good and hard," was how Ana writes about the event.

The next time Fred saw her, he had a ring that he put on her finger. It fit well. It was of silver, set with a center garnet and two side opals. He presented the ring to her and hurriedly left to go to a Lodge meeting. Ana would have liked more time with him then.

Ana really was busy with school. She had decided that in order to make the expenses of medical school, she needed a way to earn some money and that she would do this by teaching school. So she took extra week-end teaching methods seminars that were offered and she asked the school principal if she could observe in school rooms at the elementary level. All this in addition to taking double assignments of her regular classes as the departure date was set four or five weeks before school was out. There was no time to be gadding about Minneapolis shopping. Fred seemed to be equally preoccupied with his news writing and Lodge activities. He had come to the Edwards house before Christmas and left gifts of several dolls of different sorts and a Christmas banner.

Matilda had been taking in boarders to augment the cash available. So when Fred did come by, the parlor was full of men and there was no place to visit let alone "spark" a bit. Even before the train left, Fred had grown depressed and unhappy. Ana visited him in his office to say good bye. She had no idea at the time that it would be their last meeting. All she knew was that Fred was obviously not excited that the girl he had chosen to marry soon would be leaving Kansas. Ana's attitude was simply that people often had to be separated for a time before getting married and things would eventually work out.

Before they knew it, the Edwards family was ready to board the train to go west. The trip distracted Ana from the affair, but as soon as she got to Port Townsend, she sent a letter to Fred. She continued to write a letter each week. Each week a letter would come from Fred. Fred letters were positive at first but then he asked why Ana had not written at all. For some reason Ana's letters were not reaching him. The fourth letter was strange. Ana grew concerned but was busy getting settled so put it all aside.

Here are some excerpts from that fourth letter:

Minneapolis, Kansas. May 14, 1889
"Dearest Ana: Poor little false hearted girl, why don't you write to me? Sixteen long days have passed since you left 'beautiful valley of the Solomon'—I have written with this –four letters—not even a line have I received, I do not know whether you arrived in Port T--- in good health or not. What have I done, Ana to be treated this way you must know I long to hear from you. If you received my letters and had much regard for my feelings, a few lines telling me of your safe arrival would have demonstrated it much better than this peculiar silence. But Ana, I love you yet so much as when you were here------

Then this from the ending, page 7:

"I promise to smoke no more after tonight. I have not chewed a particle since the night I promised you not to---the only time I even kept my word in regard to the weed, and "Virtue has its own reward'(?) in copious doses of the 'cold shoulder" Well, fare thee well. I am yours most affectionately, Fred E. Rose."

Though somewhat dark, it hardly sounds like a letter written five days before shooting himself in the chest. It was undoubtedly the last letter Fred Rose had ever written.

Then on May 27 the letter came from Fred's mother with the news that Fred was dead!! The news dismayed the whole family and Matilda was careful to report it in her diary.

According to Fred's mother, Fred had been sending letters to Ana, but had not received a single letter in return. The last time Fred's mother had seen him alive, he had hurriedly came into the house near dusk, found his pistol and left mumbling something about "getting to the bottom of this". The next morning, Fred's body was found near the new water pump station that the city was building. He had one shot in the chest. His hand gun was at his side. The officials examined the situation as best they knew how. They asked around and learned that Fred had last been seen leaving the Lodge meeting with the fellow from the drug store. They had seemed to be angry with each other. There was no additional evidence to suggest anything to the officials other than that Fred was said to have been distraught concerning some young woman that had gone west. In his depression he had shot himself. Suicide was the conclusion. "Death by his own pistol" was all that was reported for the final record.

From the *Solomon Valley Democrat*, Minneapolis, Ottawa County, Kansas. May 24 (Friday) 1889:

"Fred E. Rose: Last Friday at half past eleven, Mr. Groom of the Water Works saw the body of a man lying on the grass near the works. Upon close inspection he found that the party was dead and saw a revolver in his hand. He immediately notified the coroner and sheriff. They went there at once and found the body of Fred E. Rose who was formerly foreman and local editor of this paper. An inquest followed at which a verdict of suicide was rendered.

"In looking back over his career in this office we can recall numerous instances that go to explain this insane development. What seemed oddity and curiously sensitive traits were undoubtedly the workings of a deranged mind. For days he would keep absolutely quiet, answering necessary queries with monosyllables. He would go to the case, set up a well worded local, read the proof and the first thing we knew of it was when we read it in this paper.

"Upon the suggestion of a companion last Thursday (May 16)he gave up his revolver, saying significantly that he didn't

want to hurt anybody. The evidence is quite plain that he took the weapon from home with a suicidal design. Other evidence of a mania for self destruction exists. On several occasions the river bank has attracted him and he has been known to inquire whether the body of a person falling into the river near the dam would ever appear. His mother divined the cause of his death before the particulars had been told her.

"Some months ago, in one of his moody, brooding periods, he caused a notice of an imaginary marriage of himself to appear in one paper--carefully excluding it from the balance of the issue. When it turned up afterward in the Commercial, was first angry, then distressed, but finally allowed it to pass as a joke.

"On two occasions for months at a time he refused to speak to other compositors in the office, the reason for which action was a complete mystery to everyone but himself"

"The report that a 'love affair' had any part in his moody feelings is not well based. He was engaged to a young lady who moved recently to Washington Territory, and a letter from her reached his address the night after his death. There was no rupture or quarrel, and while the absence of his friend may have encouraged solitude and gloom, there was nothing extraordinary about it.

"Some months ago, he voluntarily severed his connection with the *Democrat*, and to induce him to remain we suggested higher wages, but he took offense, and stated that he would not be guilty of so indirect a method if more pay was his object. It was a sudden whim which he regretted after his successor had been employed.

"There are dozens of rumors connected with his suicide, but the *Democrat* freely pronounces them false. Rose was not a drinking man. He was a teetotaler, if he drank much that day it was after five o'clock, for he worked in our office until that hour helping us out on the report of the editorial convention. If he drank that evening it was a part of his premeditated death, and not because of habit. Other rumors are absurd. It was a plain case of suicidal mania which invariably takes its victim sooner or later. It was a misfortune – not a crime. No blame can be attached to anybody.

"The funeral occurred at his mother's residence last Sunday at 2 o'clock and was largely attended. The A.O.U.W., of which he was a member, took charge of the body. Perhaps the most perfect illustration of his sensitive and curious make-up is that he neglected his last dues in the A.O. U. W., thus losing the insurance of $2,000, which would otherwise have been paid. If he owed a dollar, he was unhappy until he paid it. If he put a small local in the Democrat, he would insist on paying it. He sent a paper to a friend who we wanted to mark 'complimentary,' but he would not have it that way. We believe that he deliberately neglected his dues, intending to die, and deeming it dishonest to allow the lodge to pay his policy. In brief our obituary would read: Scrupulously honest, well read, scholarly, and a thinker, he enters the future with less wrong doing toward his fellow men, than any young man we ever knew."

Strangely, the day after the body was found, Fred's mother picked up the mail. There were Ana's letters!? They had been opened and showed wear as if having been opened and closed often and having been carried about in a pocket.

Fred's mother asked Ana to come back to Minneapolis as soon as possible and go with her to an attorney and make an appeal to the officials with what she thought to be the true story. By this time, Ana was deeply involved in the circumstances surrounding Elva's death, funeral and the care of Elva's children. She had neither the time, money or will to make the trip back to Kansas to try to gain justice for what may well have been a legal gun duel in which the most distraught contestant had gotten the worst of gunshot(s) in the dark. Ana just had to put the matter out of her thinking as yet another tragic memory about which there would never be resolve or recourse.

Both Ana and Fred's mother were in agreement about what happened. The post office in Minneapolis was a service of the drugstore where Fred's nemesis worked. The fellow had access to the back of the glass fronted mail boxes and when Ana's letters arrived, he stole them and they never got to Fred. Instead the thief had opened the letters and studied them. He would taunt Fred with bits of information they contained. Fred suspected what was going on and had begged for the letters, but the fellow continued taunting Fred to say that Ana would not come back. Instead he, the thief, would go the Washington Territory and win her hand himself. At this Fred put out the challenge to a duel.

Considering the state Fred was in, it was indeed suicide—suicide by gun duel. Ana reasoned that a person does not commit suicide with a shot to the chest, but to the head. Fred's gun had indeed been fired, as the officials claimed, but he fired amiss purposefully or was unable to make a clear shot in the semi darkness. In those days there was no comparison ever made as to whether the bullet came from Fred's gun or some other gun. Most duels usually have witnesses, but Fred seemed not able to think of engaging a "second".

Three out of four of Fred's letters are still in family possession. A thorough search to subsequent news papers has been conducted, but no reports of further hearings or official inquiries were made.

The official record stands that Fred killed himself in a depression over a girl who had left him to go west. Ana's unofficial record is that a very nice, but a bit strange, young man was sorely used and killed as a result of a possibly legal but ungoverned duel. Fred deserved better. Ana never names the other fellow. Today it might be possible to find out who the other duelist was. What satisfaction would be gained from knowing who the true killer was, now that all parties involved are long gone?

Fred was raised by his mother after his father had died early leaving them well supported. Fred was well educated and valuable to the newspaper for which he worked. He had two sisters. Fred's mother and sisters became ill not long after the loss of Fred. They all died and there is no part of the family left. The *Solomon Valley Democrat* ceased publication in1891. Its competitor, the *Minneapolis Register,* is still publishing and has an office on Concord Street across from the building that housed its competitor, the *Democrat.*

Ana kept the ring, of course. She wore the ring and kept Fred's letters in a special box that she let her daughters open, read and cry over. One day Ana had placed the ring on the window ledge of the "orchard house" while doing dishes. A daughter picked it up and accidentally dropped the ring out the window. It was not discovered until the house and barn had burnt up in the hillside fire of 1901. In going through the ashes, the partially melted metal ring was recovered but the gems were forever lost or possibly destroyed completely by the heat. The twisted ring is still a precious keep-sake along with the love letters. None of Ana's letters to Fred were kept. Fred's letters were moved out with other papers when Jim and Ana moved into the Nichols homestead log cabin by the lake in 1900. They were saved from the fire.

ANA MAE EDWARDS, THE SCHOOL TEACHER

In those days in Kansas, a person could earn a certificate to teach elementary school upon finishing high school and that might be as early as age 15. Ana Mae had decided to follow the example of her brother Grant, who was 7 years her elder, into teaching. At first she saw teaching as a way to earn tuition into a women's medical college. School teaching paid more than house-keeping or sewing as her sisters had done and provided more intellectual stimulus for an alert person like Ana Mae.

But the announcement that the family would move to Washington Territory before Ana was through high school put her into a "pickle", as she put it. A departure date of April 29, 1889 meant trying to finish all the required work a month early. She had previously gone to two summer sessions of "Teacher's Institute". Her school superintendent allowed her to double up on her assignments. He also allowed her to observe or even substitute teach at the elementary level. She needed to take examinations as well to earn a teacher's certificate. Testing would have to be done when she reached Washington Territory. Unfortunately, all this activity shortened the time she could spend with Fred Rose.

In Washington Territory the minimum age was 18 in order to take the teacher's certification examination. This meant she needed to wait to after 24 September 1889.That was fine as she could not be given a class to teach until January 1890. Washington was granted statehood on November 11, 1889 and Ana took the examinations in December. She qualified at every level and subject except mathematics. To gain certification beyond the 3 grade level, she would have to study and retake the examination a year later, December 1890. Her brother Grant had been certified in Kansas and his certification was accepted by Washington State.

Meanwhile, Ana received word about the closing exercises for Minneapolis High School She had ranked first in the class and had won a scholarship to a college for women doctors. Life had drastically changed for her in those few months. She began to realize that ever becoming a doctor was unlikely.

When the school clerk of the Port Townsend schools learned of the scores of the examinations, she came to Ana and said that the woman who was to be the Deputy Superintendant of the school had failed the very same examination that Ana had passed. The position was open and needed to be filled immediately. The position also involved teaching a class. Since there was no other job available, Ana agreed to take the class, much to the dismay of the Superintendant who had been away and didn't know about the teacher who had failed.

Ana started teaching the first Monday of January 1890. There was a minor room mix-up the first day that put Ana's class in the only classroom. The Superintendant had to teach his class in the assembly room. He was only 22 years old and known for his sharp tongue. But Ana claimed she got along well with him.

Ana had no more than started with the class in Port Townsend when word came that there was a school at Discovery Bay that wanted to hire her. That was going to work out alright as the school would not start until summer. She promised the school director that she could come just as soon as the Port Townsend School was over. At the time she understood that the Port Townsend position was only an emergency position. Ana doesn't say much about this first position other than "everything went well" and that the school closed in July without a graduating class.

During the time after the Edwards family had come to Port Townsend and while Ana was recovering from the trauma of Elva's death, she had begun practicing with the small orchestra that her brother-in-law John Merrill had organized. They practiced during the week and would perform in churches and halls on Sunday. On one occasion in the fall of 1889, the orchestra was performing in the lobby of Seaman's Bethel, the boarding house on Quincy Street wharf (88 ½ Quincy Street). It was there that she noticed a nice looking fellow and, as the room was small, when the audience joined in the singing, she noticed that the young man had a fine baritone voice and enjoyed singing out. They did not meet or exchange names, but as she remembers the occasion, it was the first time she noticed the man who would become her husband.

Ana lived in her own apartment during this time after Elva had died. Her nephew Henry Knight shared the apartment so he could be closer to school. He was an unusually industrious fellow. He liked school as Ana did. They were kindred spirits. Henry found employment at a store for afternoons and Saturdays. Following completion of high school, he went to Seattle and studied the science of agriculture at the University of Washington. From there he was qualified for a federal job with the Department of Agriculture and was a career government employee in Washington, D.C.

KANSAS CLOSURE

When Matilda Edwards left Minneapolis, she sold the Spruce Street house on a contract. The same was for Ed and Elva Knight's house on Clay Avenue. Then by 1894, both properties were lost by their respective buyers for non-payment of taxes. Matilda bought them both back by paying the back taxes to Ottawa County. She paid $3.45 back taxes for the Spruce St. property and $6.66 back taxes on the Clay St. property.

As a result of the untimely death of Elva Knight and the assumption of care of the Knight children by Matilda and G.W. Edwards, Ed Knight had agreed to deed the Clay Avenue property to Matilda. The transaction was not filed until 1900 when Elva's estate was settled. Also as Elva would have future rights to the Spruce Street property, Ed Knight then filed a Quit Claim deed on that property as well. Finally, since by 1900 Henry Knight, Elva's son, was then 21 years old and would also have inheritance rights to the Clay Avenue property, he also filed a Quit Claim deed in favor of his grandmother Matilda. (**Map 5**)

A competent buyer was found for the Spruce St. property. It was sold to Elizabeth Lee on 31 March 1903 for $40. The Clay Avenue property, once Ed Knight's, was sold to Thomas Tibbits 20 March 1906 for $25. It is a small, narrow lot. Neither house has survived time. Both now have buildings that appear to have 1940's style. The Spruce St. property stands alone with vacant lots on each side. The empty lots are marked with 100 year old cottonwood tree. So ends the Kansas story.

THE UNCAS SCHOOL

When the Port Townsend school session was over at the end of June 1890, Ana got her things together and hired a fellow with a horse drawn cart to move her. The school superintendant noticed the activity and inquired as to where she was going. She explained that she had already made a verbal contract to teach at Discovery Bay. The superintendant was dismayed and felt she was leaving because of him, which was somewhat the case. But she told him that in order for her to continue at Port Townsend, she would need to take the certification exams again and that in the meantime, she was verbally committed to teach at Discovery Bay. Also, she would receive the same pay at Discovery Bay as she did at Port Townsend.

She went out to Discovery Bay by way of "Tukey's" at present day Adelma Beach. The road bed for Port Townsend Southern RR was being cut along the east side of Discovery Bay but the tracks were not in nor service started. Tukey's boat ferried people across to the southwest corner of Discovery Bay to the area called Maynard. The grade school had been built on land given by the Cooper's family who lived up Snow Creek at the southeast corner of the Discovery Bay flats. The Cooper family decided that the little house the directors had prepared for the teacher was too dangerous for a young single lady, as it was in among tall trees. So they invited Ana to live with the family. That suited the gregarious young teacher better. Besides, part of the class she would be teaching would be the Cooper children. (Descendants of the Cooper family still live on that farm in 2010.)

The school was called the Uncas School. It was a one room building with a wood stove (what else). The community men had constructed student desks, a teacher's desk, chairs, coat racks, etc. They also supplied adequate wood for the little stove. There were students from first to eighth grades. There were 14-16 children including George Andrews from Crocker Lake at the southern edge of the district, Horace Sims, a brother of Ed Sims for whom Sims Way in Port Townsend is named. There was also Billy Munn. Unknown to Ana at the time, Billy Munn would be a future cousin-in-law. He had come from Murray River in Prince Edward Island, Canada and was living with his cousin Ed White, another relative to be discovered later. Billy Munn would eventually be an employee of the Leland Sawmill Company.

Ana Edwards truly enjoyed those five months at Uncas School. The children were exceptionally eager and energetic. On Saturdays Ana visited the homes of the children. So she knew the community well. When the train was completed to Uncas, passing near the school, on alternate Saturdays she would take the train to Port Townsend or eventually go south to Lake Hooker to visit Oka Smith, her sister. That story will come later.

As the final fun event for the children, Ana organized a closing entertainment program. The entire community was invited. Mothers brought coffee, cakes, sandwiches. It was an evening event and everyone in the community came, whether they had school children or not. The children prepared recitations at all levels. At the end of the program Ana had planned a community sing for which she played her bass violin.

There was a bachelor homesteader in the audience who had seen the girl with the bass violin at the Seamen's Bethel in Port Townsend. On one of his trips to Town he had asked around as to who the bass violinist was. He had been directed to Ed Knight's house and had been told that she was teaching at the Uncas School in Discovery Bay. He was surprised at that information as he had also been staying with his cousin Jim White at Maynard, not far from the school. So on this occasion of the closing exercise of the school at the end of November 1890, he was sure to attend. Again, there was not a lot of room as nearly everyone in the community was there. He found a place at the front. When it was time for the community sing, he sang out with his strong baritone voice and Scottish brogue. "Isn't that the voice I heard at the Seamen's Bethel?" said Ana. He shook her hand and said, "I sure am the same man." Ed White, who was also there, chimed in and said, "He's been looking for you all over Port Townsend and here you were right here under his nose all the time." This was the second meeting of Jim and Ana. At that time it was more than the Scottish burr in Jim's singing voice that made her heart skips a beat.

The next day Ana took the train with her belongings, including the bass violin, back to Port Townsend. The teacher certification examination was given again that December. She was the only test taker this time. The results soon came that she had superbly passed the mathematics portion as well and was now qualified for a full eight grade certification for 5 years. Classes in Port Townsend had not yet closed for the fall. She was told that a teacher was near a nervous break-down and the school board wanted Ana to take her class when school started in January of 1891.

The class had been poorly managed. She had many problems getting the class organized as she thought proper. One problem was that there were 63 pupils and 60 desks! There were three older boys who were simply behind for their age. She had the janitor fix extensions to her teacher's desk where they got special attention. Then she bargained with the teacher of the next higher class to accept them if she could get them ready for that level. The teacher agreed. The boys eagerly took the challenge and soon were ready to advance and did.

The class was poorly disciplined as well. Ana was quickly able to put some ruffians in their place. A girl always came late and was dreadfully dressed in torn and dirty clothes. She was the butt of jokes from the ruffians. "Miss Edwards" went to the girl's home and found a mother whose husband was away most of the time. The mother depended on the girl to go to the market each morning. The errand was what was making her late. Ana simply suggested that the marketing could be done the night before, an idea the mother hadn't considered. Then Ana introduced the mother to a dress maker and laundry lady that lived nearby. A new dress was ordered and the older dresses washed. By the next Monday, the girl came to school with a new, clean dress and her hair washed and in curls. She looked like an entirely different person. The mean boys never teased her again. Ana was a teacher who was not afraid to teach the parents, if needed.

Ana's classroom became a show place for visitors. One fellow came in and sat in the back for several days. It turned out that he was the Superintendant's brother and Ana's class had been recommended to him by his brother as an example of a properly taught, well disciplined class. After a time the man complimented Miss Edward and said he was now ready to take his own class.

Here is how Ana dealt with a boy who had been pestering the girls. In her own words (Memoirs page 76):

"It was a Thursday after the morning singing. I told the school I wanted to make a correction of a pupil who had a bad habit of pulling the girls' hair and pinching them. I called the boy by name and asked him to please step up to the platform by my desk and he started to cast his eyes about the room. I said, 'Now will the girls whom he has been habitually pinching and pulling hair please come up to the platform and pinch his arms and pull his hair and see how he likes it.' Nearly every girl in the school came forward. When he saw the crowd, he just laid his head down on my desk and started to cry like a baby. 'Oh, I'll never do it again; I'll never do it again.' I signaled the girls to keep quiet. Then I asked him why he had been treating the girls like that for so long. He sobbed out that the girls always made fun of his crossed eyes and that hurt his feelings. That was why he punished them. I waited a few minutes and then explained that having crossed eyes was like having a broken arm in a sling. Then I asked, 'Is there any girl here who now wants to shake hands with Johnny?' They all did and all came up crying to shake his hand and told him they would not make fun of his crossed eyes again. I talked to Johnny's mother. As soon as school was out, she took him to Seattle and had the needed surgery done and bought him glasses. There never was a problem of teasing in the class again."

MORE TRAGEDY FOR THE EDWARDS FAMILY

As already related, Elva Maud Knight had died at just 28 years of age. She had left three children. Then after a year of weakness and illness, Porter, Ana's twin brother died 4 July 1890. He was not yet 19 years old. In April 1891, Veroque Henderson Smith became suddenly sick and died at age 35. Here is that back story and the consequences:

Thaddeus Smith was the first of the Edwards family to come to Washington Territory. In 1888 he had taken up a 40 acre piece of land overlooking Hooker Creek south of Lake Hooker (now Lake Leland).

In early 1889 his wife of a year or so came to be with him. She brought her children Robert, Elva and Allen Henderson. A new child Porter Edwards Smith was born shortly after she arrived. Thad had prepared a cedar shake house for his family and the family was well established when the rest of the family came west in May 1889. The south side of his forty acres overlooked a willow swamp and had a sunny southern exposure. He had cleared a nice home site and had set out his orchard and built a barn. The rail line had been extended past Lake Hooker and was within a short walking distance from his acreage via a buggy road. The family had visited many times, so the trips were more frequent with the train service. While Ana was teaching at Uncas School she was able to include a visit to the Smiths on some Saturdays.

In the spring of 1891 when Ana was busy with her Port Townsend elementary class, there was a flu epidemic. Veroque had come to "town" on business, but before she could get home she got very ill. She stayed in town for ten days with her parents. She had her two year old baby Porter with her. She felt she needed to get home even though she still had head pains. She felt that her husband, three children and brother had been long enough without her. Her brother Grant was the teacher of Leland School that was a mile away from the Smith home.

She didn't get any better at home. Just at that time a neighbor, August Thomas, came to say that his wife had gone into early labor and asked Veroque to come to his house and stay with his wife while he went for the doctor in Port Townsend. The man did not have a buggy and Veroque rode with him on his horse to his house up on "Leland Hill". She was there for the live birth of the baby, but she became sicker and sicker. Her head ache was so bad that she just had to rest on a bed. A doctor finally came. At least he was in time to affirm the health of the new born (Lewis Thomas) and to examine Veroque and proclaimed that she had "mastitis" and left!! Veroque went into a coma and never recovered. She died Monday, 19 April 1891 in the home of Mrs. Gus (Mary) Thomas.

As soon as Grant could get out of school, he arranged for the care of little Porter. Thad was in total shock and incapable of decision making. Grant went into Port Townsend with the news. There was a funeral. On Monday, April 26, George W. and Matilda Edwards had their things together. They caught the morning train and moved out to Thad's house to take care of the children. Now there were 6 children: the three Henderson children, Porter Smith and they brought Elva's sons Channie and Claude Knight with them. The new arrangement would be that Thad would deed G.W. and Matilda the north half of his "40" in exchange for the care of his children. G.W. immediately set about clearing a home site and building a new house. Once again he was starting over. G.W. and Matilda were practiced pioneers.

Ana needed to move as well and she found a room where she and her nephew Henry Knight could stay. He was now thirteen years old and working in a clothing store afternoons and Saturdays to support himself.

Edwards/Cummings Place at Leland. Circa 1920. (G. Munn Collection)

A COUNTRY SCHOOL

By the time that Ana had finished with the spring elementary school class in Port Townsend, she had been teaching continuously since earning her provisional certificate in December of 1889. She was ready for something different. Her brother Grant had been teaching at the school donated to the community by John Ryan who lived on the northeast side of Lake Hooker. Grant was also the county School Superintendant and he had been asked to organize a new school for the community of Tarboo. Tarboo was in the next valley east of the Edwards Place. He asked Ana if she wanted to take the Leland School. It meant that she could also live with her parents and help with the six children, her niece and five nephews. The next session would not start until September 1891. There was no question in her mind as to her next move. She had already gone out on the train several times and was gaining a sense of belonging to the area.

On 29 June 1891 Ana had her luggage packed up and taken to the train. She had sent word ahead for help moving bed, trunk, dresser and baggage from the Lake Hooker train landing near the east end of the low bridge over the lake. They were to be taken to her parents' new house on the land that Thad Smith had given them to the east and over a hill from the bridge. When the train arrived at the landing, Robert Henderson, now a thirteen year old lad was waiting with a young man who was working for the Dick Brown logging company. The waiting gentleman had a horse drawn dray wagon. It was none other than Jim Munn. Ana was in a hurry to get settled in so she just left Robert and Jim take care of loading the wagon. The other children were there also and they decided to take their aunt on the scenic short route over the hill on a curvy steep road called "The Smith and Donnelly road". It started at Lake Hooker, went up over the hill that the family called Strawberry Hill, down past the Edwards house and on over Tarboo hill, past Tarboo Lake and to Tarboo valley and on north to Chimacum or south to Quilcene. Meanwhile, "Bob" Henderson and Jim Munn took the longer gravel road that paralleled the railroad to the south and then curved east past the Smith house and on to the Edwards' new house.

The walkers arrived only minutes before the horse and wagon. There was a grand welcome going on by the big log at the bottom of the hill where a road went up to the house. Jim Munn stopped briefly to ask directions and was quickly told to put the things upstairs in the empty bedroom. So Jim and Bob proceeded up around to the back of the house and took the things up the stairs. They set up the bed and its mattress and even put on a blanket. Bob was on his way down and Jim decided to go back to the room. He took the bass viol case and placed it on the bed under a blanket and left.

At the bottom of the hill, the Edwards family was still talking excitedly, as they usually did. Jim just waved himself past them and went back to the Brown Company horse barn and took care of the horses before going to his homestead up the Arcadia Road, later the Leland Hill Road, to his Arcadia cabin.

Eventually the welcoming was over and Ana and the family went up to get settled for the night. Ana noticed the strange location of her bass viol and asked Bob Henderson about it. He had no idea and she simply put it out of her mind as she began to think about how she was going to help her mother and have the children show her around the lake and the community.

That summer of 1891 was very special to Ana and her parents. She immediately pitched in to plant a garden. She took over the heavy laundry task and helped with the cooking. When the work was done, the children would walk with her all over the community. They explored the lake on boats and met the neighbors on up "Leland" Hill. One of the tasks of the school teacher was to be in charge of the Sunday school program that met in the school house. So she began leading the Sunday school the next Sunday with the encouragement of G.W. and Matilda. Some Sundays there would be a visiting preacher. Matilda was always the host of the preachers who may come on Saturday afternoon and stay overnight.

On one Sunday late in August a team of ladies from the Salvation Army were the guest speakers. Though Jim Munn was usually at the Sunday meetings, he did not miss this one as he had joined the Salvationists in Vancouver BC as well as having been a guest at the Seamen's Bethel in Port Townsend that was managed by the Salvation Army. Afterwards he walked home with Ana and the children. When they arrived at the big log at the bottom of the Edwards hill, he told the children to go on up to the house as he wanted to visit with their aunt a bit. Jim neatly lifted Ana up on the log and he sat beside her. After a few exchanges of banter he got down to business. He explained to Ana that he had completed his requirements to claim his homestead. His job with the Dick Brown Logging Co. was completed. The next day he was going across the Sound to Everett where he had a job waiting for him at another logging camp. He knew that Ana was going to start teaching at the school soon, but said that there was a teaching position at the boarding house where he was going. She could teach there.

Ana did not immediately turn him down as she had begun to find him more than a nice voice and a comfortable friend. It was getting dark and father G.W. began wondering what was going on down on the big log. He went for his rifle as he had heard some disconcerting rumors about this foreign fellow that spoke with an accent. Ana called up that she would be right up and turned to Jim to tell him that she would need to discuss the proposal with her parents, but that he was welcome to come back to dinner tomorrow and she would have an answer for him then. She added that he could see where she lived. Jim laughed and said, "I've already been to your house and seen your bed room." Ana acted surprised until he explained about the bass viol under her blanket. "I thought that when you reached out during the night and as you strummed across the strings that the sound would remind you of me and my baritone singing voice." Ana said no more as she was sure her voice would give her true thoughts away.

They parted and Ana went into the house and had a big talk with G.W. and Matilda. When Jim came the next night he had no idea what to expect. G.W. and Matilda were gracious and accomplished hosts and the evening went well. Ana explained to Jim that she had a firm commitment to be the local school teacher. She must fulfill that obligation. She didn't give him a flat out rejection.

Jim went back to his cabin on Arcadia hill. His pack was ready and he left the next morning on his way to the job in Everett. In a few days,

Ana began teaching school. Teaching the class was hardly work. Five children were actually her relatives. The days went by quickly.

Leland School picnic 1892.
End of school picnic with a neighboring school. From left: Bob Ryan, Charlie Andrews, Claude Knight, Jack Ryan, Henry Knight, Malcolm O'Dell, Mrs. Haus, Arnie Hunter, a driver of visiting school children, Winnie Andrews, Frances Tookey, Elva Henderson, Thad Smith, Porter Smith, Channie Knight, Ana Edwards, U. Grant Edwards, Allen Henderson, Bob Henderson (standing). (Allen Beach Collection in Jefferson County Historical Society archives.)

ANA'S VISION

One pleasant afternoon that summer Ana was alone and walking over Strawberry Hill. As she was coming down toward the lake, she paused and sat down to take in the view. It was a clear, sunny day. The lake was especially calm. From that point she could see to the south end of the lake and nearly to the end of the north end. The forested hill rose from the lake and the neat little farm of Edwin and Adelia Nichols lay before her. There was a rounded, sugar loaf shaped hill in the background. The high ridge of Green Mountain had virgin trees nearly to the top and Mount Townsend rose up further back above everything. The mountain still had patches of snow where the ridges shaded the snow the mountain seemed to fill the sky to beyond the horizon. As she took the she took the whole scene in, she came to the self realization that this was the most peaceful and wonderful place in the whole world. Then and there she decided that this was the place she wanted to live the rest of her life.

AND SHE DID.

GEORGE WASHINGTON EDWARDS AND MATILDA EDWARDS IN LELAND

Veroque (Oka) Edwards Smith died in Leland on Monday, 19 April 1891, at the home of neighbors, Gus and Mary Thomas, where Oka had been attending the birth of their child, Lewis. Following her burial in Port Townsend, on the next Monday, 26 April, G.W. and Matilda Edwards took the train out to Thaddeus Smith's farm to begin the care of the children, their grandchildren. James PORTER Smith was only two years old. Robert (Bob) Henderson was thirteen, ELVA Henderson was ten and John ALLEN Henderson was eight.

Thad Smith's 40 acre piece was on the southeast slope of "Strawberry Hill". Today, 2010, it is at the intersection of U.S. 101 and Cutoff Road. It belongs to Pope and Talbot Lumber Company, except for a home site at the SW corner of the intersection that belongs to a family named Cherry. This is where the last few apple trees of Thad Smith's orchard still produce apples.

Thad Smith gave his father-in-law the north half, 20 acres, for caring for his son, Porter. The Henderson children were receiving money from their father, Dave Henderson, and that support continued until each had completed high school. Now that payment went to their grandparents. George Edwards received a pension for his Civil War service. G.W. and Matilda brought with them Channie Knight and Claude Knight, also their grand children that they were raising following the untimely death of Elva Knight two years before.

Thad Smith grew increasingly discontented following his wife's death. He decided to deed the "South 20" to G.W. as well as continued payment for caring for his son. Thad then moved into Port Townsend. He lived and worked in various places in Port Townsend. When he died, 14 March, 1933, he was buried in the Port Townsend Laurel Grove Cemetery. It was noted more recently that he is the only person buried in the cemetery to have received the Congressional Medal of Honor. His Leland house was gradually torn down and recycled as G.W. found use for the boards and shakes. The remains were gone well before the highway was built over the location. But a log access bridge over the creek remained on into the 1930s and as a marker of the home site.

As soon as George W. Edwards arrived in Leland, he began to build a house on the north half of the Smith homestead. G.W.'s house was northeast of Thad's on the side of the hill above the draw from which the stream came. The meadow and home site are still clear of trees today. A Pope and Talbot logging road has taken place of G.W.'s road to his house.

The house sat on a small bench above the meadow. There was a dug well to the rear of the house. Eventually a well-house and wood-shed was built to cover that area. To the south of the house on a higher bench, G.W. built a barn and a shed for equipment. The privy was to the north of the house on the side of the hill. Matilda planted ivy by the privy and long after everything else was decayed or burned up, an ivy mound the shape of a mushroom remained for many years.

There were large red cedar trees in the meadow. G.W. cut these down and split out the timber, beams, siding and shakes with which he built the house and barns. The house had two stories with the dormers for the roof facing east-west. There was a porch on each end. The front of the house had several steps going up, but the back porch had only one or two steps.

As the years went on, much of the twenty acres to the south was cleared. There was a hill pasture to the south above the barn, the meadow pasture, and the hill side between the house and barn was a pasture or was cultivated for a kitchen garden. A horse chestnut tree was planted at the bottom of the hill in front of the house. It grew to be quite large and rounded. Eventually cars would be parked under the tree.

There were two access roads. One was an extension of Thad Smith's road that skirted the south end of Strawberry hill that came from Leland Road and the railroad. For a time a logging spur of the railroad went along that road. The rails were taken up after the logging was competed. Thad Smith's road went on toward the Edwards home site and connected with the Smith and Donnelly Road that went eastward over the top of Strawberry Hill from the lake bridge and continued on over Tarboo Hill to the east of the Edwards' Place. That road was placed along the north property line between the Edwards Place and what was eventually Kawamoto's farm.

George and Matilda's house was just finished enough in June 1891 for daughter Ana and the grandchildren to occupy the bedrooms upstairs. George was a good neighbor and helped others to build their homes. Neighbors would help each other with hay making. As mentioned before, George Edwards was a registered Justice of the Peace as well as a notary. The several deeds that were needed to settle his daughter Elva Knight's estate and the deeds of sale of the Minneapolis properties were all hand written by him. His hand writing is very neat and perfectly readable.

Matilda was a mid-wife for the community and was present for the birth of all the Munn children. As mentioned they kept a home for 6 grand children. Channie Knight had a poor heart and was never strong. He died at age 15 in the Edwards house. The three Henderson children each completed grade school at Leland School and went to live with Uncle Joel and Aunt Alice to go to high school in Port Townsend. Porter Smith was shot and killed in an unfortunate accident in 1904 at age 15. This was a terrible tragedy for all but especially for Matilda. Both G.W. and Matilda began failing after that and they decided to move into "Town" in 1907.

G.W. purchased a lot near 25th Street in Port Townsend. The house he built still stands at 2554 Gise Street, though it has been modified. Louisa had been able to come west for a family reunion at which pictures were taken on 15 March 1914. All the Edwards children were present. Later on 3 September 1914, there was celebration of their 60th Anniversary for which Matilda reports "Thirty persons were present". But Louisa had gone home by then and was not in the anniversary pictures. G.W. took sick soon after the anniversary party. He died on 26 September 1914. Matilda lived on and was a parent for Dora Ruggles' youngest son. Matilda has many entries in her diary about grandson, John Ruggles. She seemed always to have had a grandchild under her wings.

Matilda's last diary entry is 31 December 1918. She was ill then. She died 8 February 1919 and is also buried in Laurel Grove Cemetery in the family plot just a few steps through the back gate of son Joel's house next to the cemetery.

As a benediction to two pioneers of the frontier, here is George Washington Edwards' table blessing:

"Sanctify these blessings to our use, Heavenly Father,
Pardon and pass by our many sin and short comings.
Guide us through life, and be with us in death,
For our Savior's sake.
AMEN

George Washington and Matilda Edwards by their Leland house, circa 1893. The view is from the "barn hill" looking NE. G.W. split all the material from cedar trees that grew on the land, except doors and windows. The gabled second floor had two bedrooms. (Munn family collection.)

VII: JIM'S UNFINISHED BUSINESS

~~~

RETURN TO PRINCE EDWARD ISLAND

There is a census taken in Canada every 10 years as is the law in the United States. But the Canadian census is taken a year after the US census. It happens the first year of each new decade. For 1891 Canadian census, James Hector Munn and John Daniel Munn are registered as living in the Munn farm house at Belle River. That is a fact. The exact timing and circumstances are uncertain. This is how and why it must have happened.

The estate of Hector Munn had never been finalized. He had willed the Old Farm to his three youngest sons, James Hector, Neil Alexander, and John Daniel, to be divided between them, but not until John Daniel was 21 years old. John Daniel was born 26 November 1868 so now, 1891, he was 22 or 23 and the estate could be settled. He had been living in Boston with his sister Dorothy Jane and her husband Alex Stewart, just as his brother James Hector had done. In fact he had found a wife there and had gotten married. His first child was soon to be born. His wife was not with him at Belle River, perhaps because the baby was soon due at any time.

Another event had brought James Hector and John Daniel together. Their brother Neil Alexander had died. Now there were only the two of them to finalize the estate of Hector Munn and the disposition of the Old Farm. It was a simple decision. James Hector was no longer a Canadian citizen. At least he had declared his intent to be a naturalized citizen of the United States. Even more, he had bought rights to a homestead and had completed the requirements to prove it up. Not only was he a land owner in his newly chosen country but he had set his mind on marrying a young school teacher from Kansas who was now teaching school in the community where he had chosen to live. Probably without much fanfare, James Hector signed over his rights to the Old Farm to his younger brother John Daniel. It would become the place for John Daniel to raise his big family of seven boys and three girls. (A last child, a boy did not live out a year.)

James Hector had another duty to fulfill. He needed to pay his final good-byes to his beloved wife Maggie. When she died James was only 22 and in great sorrow. He had essentially fled as far away as he could from the memory of the sickness and death that surrounded that marriage, as well as the loss of his father, oldest brother and mother. He had not the time, money or emotional health to complete Maggie's burial. Now he was healed in spirit and had money to bring closure to his Prince Edward Island youth. He found one face of a pair of stones used to grind grain. He had it engraved and put in place to mark Maggie (Margaret) McLeod's burial place in the Wood Islands Presbyterian Cemetery. It reads:

"In Memory of ----Maggie----Beloved wife of James H. Munn----Died----March 3, 1886----age 23----Gentle reader as you pass by----As you are now so once was I. ----As I am now you soon shall be---- Prepare for death and follow me."

James Hector Munn was now ready for his new life in Washington State. He returned to the carpenter's job at a logging camp east of Everett, Washington. Here he spent the year to come in profitable work. Not only did he do construction, but he was responsible for the camp's horses.

We do not know much about that year. In early September of 1892 he received a special delivery letter from Ana. In the letter she explained that a homesteader at "Leland" had contacted her by letter from Port Townsend to say that he was very sick and needed money to see a doctor. He offered his 40 acre unproven homestead to her. She knew the homestead well. It was on the west side of the lake above and adjoining the Nichols' Place. She further said that though she had the money, $150, she was not yet 21 and thus not eligible to purchase a homestead.

James wrote right back to tell her to meet him in Port Townsend the next Saturday morning. He made his way to Port Townsend and arrived well before the train from Quilcene arrived in the afternoon. He had located "Mr. Mudgett" and paid for the property and they signed the necessary papers. Mr. Mudgett was able to catch a boat out of Port Townsend that day for Tacoma and left his past and the homestead dream behind. He had died of tuberculosis a few weeks later.

After seeing Mr. Mudgett off, James went to the Port Townsend and Southern railroad station on Water Street in time to lift Ana Mae off the passenger car. (The railroad came across what is now Kah Tai lagoon/pond and along the shore front of the bluff to about where the Washington State Ferry dock is. Water Street had not been extended through as yet.) Ana was pleasantly surprised that the transaction was done. Jim handed her the signed deed to be recorded when county offices opened.

There were a few hours before a boat was to leave for Everett. The train would not leave for Leland until the next morning. Jim had arranged with a hotel in town for a nice dinner for two. He had asked for the meal to be served in a room where they could be alone and able to talk things over. It was a very pleasant afternoon. They said their good-byes and Jim caught the boat to return to Everett. Later, Ana had the papers filed with the General Land Office. More than the tryst at the Edwards family gate, this was the occasion that James Hector Munn and Ana Mae Edwards emotionally agreed to become "Jim and Ana Munn" for the rest of their lives. How would this come about?

THE ORCHARD HOMESTEAD

Here are the particulars of the purchase of 40 acre homestead from Mr. Mudgett. Fortunately, James Hector's Arcadia homestead was only 120 acres. He was eligible to own another 40 acres and not exceed the allotment of 160 acres. Mr. Mudgett had started the claim in 1890, probably about April. Jim had five years, until March of 1895, prove-up the claim. Out of the five years, Jim (and/or Ana) needed to occupy the property for two years. There was a cabin on the property which Mr. Mudgett had built. They lived there temporarily. Jefferson County had built an improved road up the hill from the Hooker Lake Bridge. The road gave access to a plateau between two creek canyons. This was a better home site. As soon as possible James built a new house, a barn, and some other buildings. As was the custom, he set out trees for an orchard. About six years later, the house and all the buildings burned in an "accidental" fire, but the orchard was intact for many years hence it has been referred to as the "Orchard Homestead." The homestead was deeded to James H. Munn, 13 March 1895. The Land Office Certificate is No. 16926 and "signed" by President Grover Cleveland. (NW1/4 of NE1/4 Sect 26 TWP 28 R2WWM 40 acres). (**Map 3**)

Leland Hill west of Munn barn. The Orchard property is center right where there is a newer stand of fir on the upper side of Leland Hill Road that angles to the right. Note Lookout Tree. (G. Munn collection).

VIII: TOGETHER AT LAST

―――

LELAND SCHOOL AND EVERETT LOGGING CAMP

Ana Mae Edwards had taught school at Leland for one complete year, which technically completed her obligation to the community. But she soon began the second year in September of 1892.

Meanwhile, James Hector Munn had been working for a logging camp in Everett for a year, excluding any time he had taken to travel to Belle River, Prince Edward Island. He was employed in part as the stable hand in charge of the horses used by the camp. Jim enjoyed horses and considered himself a groomsman and trainer of first order. Basically he was up early in the morning to prepare the teams for the day by feeding them and harnessing them for their tasks of the day. Then at the end of the day he would remove and dress the harnesses, rub the horses down and feed them again before they bedded down for the night. He put in long days with much of the work in partial darkness. Housing was scarce so he bedded down in the livery stable. There was a boarding house nearby where he took his meals.

He was well paid and his days were full and except for Sundays and some Saturdays. He was very busy now that his life in Canada now closed behind him. He was increasingly anxious to get on with the life he had started in Leland. Following the events with Ana Edwards and the purchase of an uncompleted homestead, he could visualize life other than being single and caring for horses. He and Ana had been exchanging letters weekly and his letters were strongly urging that Ana could just as well come over to Everett. Everett was booming with many new families with children. There was a school located in the boarding house where he took his meals. The lady who was the teacher was quite ill and had told people that she could not go on. If Ana came to Everett, she could have the teaching job in this boarding house.

Ana still felt a responsibility for her Leland School, her parents and assisting with the care of her niece and nephews. She rather enjoyed teaching and especially teaching at Leland School. She was increasingly attached to the community and now even had the start of her own home on the hill above the west side of the lake. In fact, it had become a bit of an obsession with her that the lake should not be "Lake Hooker" but "Lake Leland". She claims responsibility for the name change. After all, the post office was "Leland" and the school was "Leland School". Why should the lake be named for someone who was no longer around?

NEGATIVE RUMORS

There had been nasty stories spread in the community about Jim Munn concerning a gold watch that a neighbor claimed Jim had stolen from him. The watch was indeed Jim's. Perhaps he had purchased it recently in Canada. George W. and Matilda believed the accusation until the truth was clear. But the damage had been done and the neighbor and Jim were never really good friends. They were neighbors thereafter and often worked cooperatively on their farms. A number of other issues divided the two. Jim and Ana considered themselves to be republicans and were against secret societies. They were members of Washington Grange, instead. The neighbor, George Thomas, was a lifelong democrat and an active member of the Masonic Lodge.

Ana and her brother Grant were much alike in their ways of doing things. Ana respected Grant. Grant had modeled the way into the teaching profession. He had made sure that Ana was given teaching positions. However, they had a running disagreement about marriage. Grant was a typical male chauvinist. He felt that marriages were contractual, legal and convenient. He felt that men were wiser and that the women in his life should respect his judgment. Ana, in contrast, insisted that marriage was an emotional and romantic relationship. Ana felt that women had capable minds and should be given more place in society. She had been an active campaigner for women's suffrage. When Grant got wind of this "foreign thief" that was courting his sister, he wasted no time in telling her that she was making a regrettable mistake and would be throwing her life away. What's more is that he considered her far too young to make a commitment. He wrote disparaging letters to all their sisters to inform them of Ana's intentions and to try to gain their support in his effort to discourage their little sister from the wrong course she was on. At first the sisters and Joel went along with Grant's rants. Each wrote to Ana to discourage her from doing anything rash.

Ana for her part was approaching 21 years of age and was several years older than any of her sisters when they got married. Ana could see more of her future in the land and place she had come to love. Grant for his part was still not married though he did get married shortly after Ana and Jim did. His children and Ana's children were closer in ages than any of the other Edwards cousins and eventually formed some lasting friendships. Later when Grant and the other siblings actually met Jim Munn, they wrote to express their sorrow for having harbored ill thoughts concerning Ana's choice. It is hard to have negative words removed. A breech in family unity had been made. In reality, Jim never seemed to have felt comfortable with his in-laws. He was not present at G.W. and Matilda's 60th anniversary family reunion. At least he is not in the family pictures taken then, or for that matter, none of the Munn children were in the pictures. Only Ana is in the pictures with her parents and sisters. Much later, after Ana had lost her husband, the twin sisters came to visit Ana and pictures were taken.

THE WEDDING

Ana had kept her parents informed about the "Orchard" property acquisition and of her decision to marry Jim Munn. G.W. and Matilda had grown cold toward her as they had believed the bad rumors about "Munn", as Matilda would call Jim in her writings. On 26 November 1892, a Monday before Thanksgiving Ana took the boat to Everett.

The fall session of Leland School had closed at Thanksgiving and would not open until January 1893. The Everett school was to continue right after Thanksgiving. Ana was conflicted. She could continue with teaching at Leland, but she felt that this was the time to make the break and go to her intended husband, regardless of the opinion of her family. The job offer seemed to clinch the move.

Jim met her at the boat dock and picked her up with her baggage that included the bass viol. He took her to the boarding house operated by his Salvation Army friends. There was a fine second floor room available. And yes indeed, there was a school room set up in the large parlor of the boarding house. Ana said that she was very tired from the trip and went right to bed. She was up early and had breakfast with Jim before he left with the horses. They took Thanksgiving dinner with friends of Jim's.

The day after Thanksgiving, the teacher had learned of Ana's arrival. She had second thoughts. She realized that without the teaching job she would have no income. She decided that she had to keep teaching and would not give the job to Ana. Without a job, how would Ana pay for her room?

Jim, of course said he would pay the board and room. Ana would have none of that. She would not be a "kept woman". She put an advertisement in the paper to get a sewing job and received an immediate offer from a dressmaker on Main Street. The shop was swamped with Christmas orders. Ana went to work the next day. Jim did not appreciate the situation and rather demanded to get married right away. Ana claimed that she already had paid for a week and he would need to wait for a decision until then. Even so, she said that if they got married, she would still work for the dressmaker. But the next day was a Saturday and Jim had taken the day off. He obtained a marriage license. It was too late to contact the best man.

The next Saturday, 3 December 1892, they went to a Minister's home at 8 PM and tied the knot. Ana was twenty-one and Jim was twenty-eight. He wore his Salvation Army uniform and she wore a green silk dress that she had made herself. They were in bed by 9 PM. Jim was up to care for the horses at 4 AM and she was at the dress shop by 7 AM. "Those were days when working people put in long days," Ana adds to her account.

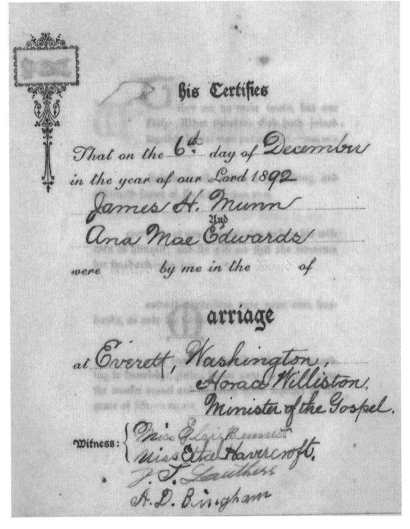

Wedding certificate.

MATILDA'S COMMENTS IN HER DIARY

September 30, 1892, Thursday: "Very nice day. School closed today." (Ana seems to have remembered that she closed the school the Friday before Thanksgiving. This date implies that it was at the end of September. The date is more consistent with the fact that Robert and Elva Henderson finished grade school with that session and started high school in Port Townsend in mid November 1892.)

November 21, 1892, Monday: "Cloudy. Ana went away to Everett, Wash." (Matilda's consternation is expressed with the words, "went away".)

December 14, 1892, Thursday: "Received a sad letter from Ana." (This was news that her last daughter had married that foreigner, Munn!)

EVERETT, WASHINGTON. 1893

Ana kept working up to the day before Christmas. The shop keeper wanted her to continue working after Christmas, but by then Ana felt she needed to get herself and her husband cared for. They had Christmas dinner with the folks who took them in for Thanksgiving, but this time Jim and Ana furnished the turkey, pies and trimmings.

Ana Mae Munn spent the week between Christmas and New Years getting her "home" in order. She washed clothes and cleaned things up for the two of them. One can imagine the state of Jim's wardrobe, since he had been single all his life. Drying clothes was a battle as well. The boarding house had a parlor with a big stove. Ana could put her wash out to dry in the parlor after folks left for the night but had to have everything clear by the time the residents came for breakfast, which was 4 AM. She began doing the laundry for the boarding house in exchange for rent.

Starting New Year's Day Jim's job shifted to the logging camp out of town. It would then be necessary to stay at the camp all week and return to Everett on week-ends, even though the camp was only three miles out of town. Days are short in January. Again, Ana had her own solution. The camp had not hired a cook and she decided that could be her job and the manager thought it was a good idea. The young couple cleaned up a space off the kitchen for their room. This was good, as the kitchen stove was kept with a fire at all times. The weather was very cold in the Everett area that year. In fact there was an unusually heavy snow that stopped all commerce so people could scrounge for wood to keep themselves warm. Many were living in tents.

A new crisis came upon them when Ana got the flu. The area not only had four feet of snow and little fuel to heat homes, but was struck with an epidemic that included Ana. Jim found some medicine that helped some. Ana became unconscious with very shallow breathing. What could be done now? Jim Munn was a man of faith and he knelt by Ana's bed and began to pray. Soon he was joined by his boss and another man, both of whom were Salvationists. After the men had prayed for two hours, Ana says she began to hear voice afar off. She said, "Jim?" The men leaned in and exclaimed, "Praise the Lord". Ana adds in her memoirs, "I will always say that the prayers of these men brought me back to life. These three men believed their prayers did it, so then I'll believe also."

Jim decided the logging camp was no place for his new wife. In a week she was back at the Havercroft boarding house and the camp boss had found an oriental cook. In two weeks she was as good as new and back at the sewing and house work, which was more to her liking even though she was not with her new husband except on week-ends.

CABIN HOME IN LELAND

Jim realized that they were on a limited time line to fulfill the Mudgett Homestead contract. They needed to live two years on the property before the five years was up since the homestead contract was registered with the Land Office. So they must get back to Leland.

Matilda's diary reads for March 15, 1893, Wednesday, "A very nice day. Ana came home from Everett. Lissa set out the pieplant." (Of course

'Munn' came as well, but wasn't mentioned. ('Lissa' was her name for Grant. It is short for Ulysses). On March 27, the entry reads: "Rain. Munn started back to Everett." Matilda was brief, but to the point. She was very slow to get used to her new son-in-law.

Jim and Ana had stayed with G.W. and Matilda at first. Jim learned of someone in Discovery Bay who was moving away and had offered a good price for all their furniture. They had more than enough furnishings and cookware to fill the corners of Mudgett's little one room house. There was a large bed in one corner, a couch in another, a dressing table, 2 rocking chairs, one arm chair, a dining table with six chairs, dishes and a Chinese mat to put on the floor. Then as Matilda reported, Jim went back to Everett.

To keep Ana company Channie Knight came to be with her. He slept on the couch. She said he wasn't doing anything at the Edwards house and he could help her get her garden in. He was only able to collect rocks which he placed around their yard as a border. Years later the grandchildren saw those stones placed strangely out in the woods and wondered why they were there. Every Monday, Ana would carry her laundry over to Matilda's, about a mile away. Matilda would have water heating and Ana would do all of the Edwards' laundry as well. "Just as in old times!" adds Ana.

There wasn't room for the bass viol in the little cabin. Ana took the viol back to John Merrill in Port Townsend. The instrument really belonged to him. Now that the courtship days were over, the symbol of those days was no longer needed.

Zuckerman's cabin on the hill west of Lake Hooker (Lake Leland). The Mudgett cabin where Ana and Channy Knight lived while proving the homestead claim would have been much like this. The men in the picture, except Odell, are relatives of Ana. (From left: Bob Henderson, Ulysses Grant Edwards, Malcolm Odell, and Henry Knight.) (Jefferson County Historical Society)

A REAL HOME

On 4 July 1893, Jim came home to stay. Earlier in that year the County had built a road from the west end of the Leland bridge through the Nichols farmstead, up the hill to the west and right across their "orchard forty" and on "up" and west to Arcadia. The steep part up has always been called the Leland Hill and though the road was labeled "Arcadia Road" on maps, it became known to locals as "Leland Hill Road". There are two major streams that cut deep canyons from the upper plateau down to the lake. This left a ridge between the streams on which the road was cut. There is a sizeable flat bench on this ridge and that was a much better place for a house. Jim immediately began to build a real house, with a drying porch, on this home site. Every board, nail and bucket of paint had been paid for in cash or sweat. He also built a barn, chicken house, a spring house and a root cellar. There was a clearing for a garden and still enough "flat" for a hay field/pasture. Actually the site had not been difficult to clear as the large fir and cedar trees had been logged off. They just needed to live on the place for the remainder of two years. Then, of course, Jim planted the "orchard".

HERE COME THE CHILDREN

As soon as there was time free from building his own buildings, Jim Munn began accepting contracts to build barns and houses for other folk. Toward the end of August, 1983, he was on a work assignment for Jefferson County. Able bodied men were asked to work on road construction in place of paying land taxes. It was called "poll tax", though had nothing to do with the right to vote. While Jim was away and while Ana's nephew, Channy Knight, was keeping her company, Ana began to have her first child. She sent Channy with a note to her mother, Matilda, who lived across the lake and over the hill to the east.

Immediately on reading the note, midwife Matilda knew what to do and she hurried back to the Orchard Farm with Channy. Two hours after she arrived, the baby came, Viola Dorothy, named for a sister on both sides of her family. (31 August1893). When Jim arrived home, Matilda had both dinner and a baby ready. Jim was surprised to see his mother-in-law as the cook but more surprised that she brought a daughter into the little family. Poor Channy, he was now out of his job as Ana's "company". Little Viola took his job. In two weeks Ana was up and about. Never-the-less, Matilda came every Monday morning with her laundry and did Ana's along with hers. Doing laundry and bringing babies in the world were special bonds between the two women.

The next several years were joyfully productive for Jim and Ana. Jim found regular work with the Port Townsend Southern Railway. This was during the railroad's most useful time as a business and travel connection between Port Townsend and Quilcene. The original plan for the railroad was to build on southward from Quilcene. On reaching

Quilcene Bay, the rails were to be placed on a bridge-causeway along the beach. This way the road would avoid cutting through the wall of rock where Walker Mountain came down to the water's edge. The rock was a formidable barrier but setting the pilings for the causeway was not much of an answer. The company ran out of money. Though the railroad was never completed, until 1926 or so, the PTSRR was a vital part of South Jefferson commerce.

As the Munn farm progressed they bought two cows for $10 each and Ana had plenty of milk for her family and even made butter to sell to the logging camps and in Port Townsend. One year Jim saw a young bear in his orchard which he shot. He took the bear flesh to the creek and cooled and washed the wild taste from the meat. The family was well fed that winter. Ana would bake bread for a neighbor and did laundry for the logging camp at the edge of Lake Leland.

Life was good. The children came along about as fast as possible. Son Hector John (named for grandfather Hector and Jim's brother John Daniel) was born 19 January 1895. Daughter Margaret ALICE (named for Jim's first wife and Ana's sister-in-law) was born 29 March 1896 and daughter SARAH Matilda (named for her two grandmothers) was born 29 August 1897.Sarah was her birth name, but for most of her life she used "Sara" as her signature name.

CALL OF THE YUKON

In 1893 there was a national economic depression caused by banker speculation in New York banks. The Port Townsend Southern Rail Road was already on a financial slide. Daily runs continued for a time to Quilcene. But Quilcene alone never provided financial justification for the rail road. The route was turned over to logging concerns and was an efficient way to get logs from the Pope and Talbot camp at Crocker Lake to terminals in Quilcene Bay or Port Townsend. When the logs were gone, the metal tracks were taken up.

Jim Munn worked with the maintenance crews as long as he could. They were glad for their cows, garden and summer berry pickings.

Channy Knight became weaker and weaker and his heart gave out. He died 30 August 1894 at age 14. John Allen Henderson followed his brother and sister to school in Port Townsend. George and Matilda Edwards were left with grandsons Claude Knight and Porter Smith.

News came to the region that gold had been discovered in Alaska. Actually the gold was in the Canadian Yukon or Klondike River area. Klondike Gold Rush would have been a better name. To get to the Klondike River in 1897, men went by way of Skagway, Alaska, a town at the end of a long fiord.

When there is little cash in the pocket, the possibility of easy money is a temptation that few young men can shake. Jim was down to 2-twenty dollar gold pieces, one for him and one for Ana. He packed a bag with a few clothes. Since he was a jack of all trades he felt that once in Seattle he could find work on a boat that was transporting horses and mules to "serve" in Alaska. Once he got to the gold country, he was sure he would strike it rich. From such dreamy thoughts are many disasters made. This was no exception.

Matilda wrote in her diary, "January 26, 1898, Wednesday, Jimmy Munn started for Skagua (sic) or Dyea gold fields." He wrote a letter to Ana from Seattle that he had found a horse transport boat and was working his way to Skagway as he had hoped. Fortunately he never went through to Dyea.

Ana Mae Edwards Munn was quite perplexed. Her four children were under five years old and the last one was only 5 months old. Not only were there tales of fortunes gained but there were tales of lives lost. Jim was not to be argued out of a great adventure as well as the possibility of a great fortune. There was no further news until 10 March 1898. Matilda reports in her diary: "Thursday, Quite a frost. Sent a letter to Lissa (Grant). Ana had first letter from Munn." The letter was written from A **JAIL HOUSE**!

Everything Jim had with him had been stolen except the clothes on his back and the $20 gold piece in his shoe. Ana's worst suspicions were realized!!

KLONDIKE GOLD

In one single week in mid-August 1897, 2800 people left Seattle for the Klondike. By September 1, 1897, 9000 people and 3600 tons of freight had left port. (Benton, p.123). They had no chance of reaching the Klondike gold field before the next summer. West coast cities were all struggling for a piece of the shipping and transport money. Seattle was in the best position, of course, to make the most of the economic windfall.

The gold field was a point of land between the Klondike and Indian Rivers, both tributaries of the Yukon River and deep in northwest Canada's Yukon Territory. There were two main ways to get to Dawson, the final bit of civilization at the edge of the Klondike fortunes. One was a 2200 mile (+/-) boat trip through Alaska starting at the Bering Sea. The trip took several months from Seattle and had to wait for the spring melt to come. The Yukon River was open to boats from July to September, in a good year.

The overland route was to cross Alaska's Panhandle. The route went north through the Inland Passage of British Columbia to Taiga Inlet that led to Dyea or Skagway. Dyea was fartherest up the Tiaga Inlet on the northwest side. The ships anchored at a landing from which there was a very long tide flat that had to be crossed to reach the beach. Dyea was on a narrow beach with snowy mountains rising immediately up to Chilecoot Pass. The climb that men and beast made was a 30 degree slope up which men carried enough supplies to last for a year. Canadian guards waited at the Pass to check every man's pack. Many were turned back for a second load, if they were not already done for.

Skagway, on the southeast side of Taiga Inlet, was an entrance to a longer route over White Pass. Promoters began claiming a rail line was going to be built from Skagway over White Pass. It eventually was. In the meantime men began waiting in Skagway to go by train. There was a long tidal flat at Skagway as well, though shorter than the one at Dyea. Enterprising promoters built 4 wharves on pilings out to permanent water where ships could unload. It was to Skagway that Jim Munn and his fellow boatmen came in January of 1898. What happened next has as many versions as story tellers. The following is an attempt to gather the most likely story.

PIRACY!?

The arrival of the ship loaded with horses was during a storm. As the ship neared the wharf, the crew noticed that there was another boat that was floating unattended in the bay. The ship's captain ordered Jim and other crewmen to board the vessel. By the law of the sea this would gain them ownership of the unattended ship. Jim Munn and buddies made a successful boarding and steered the prize ship to shore. As they arrived at the wharf with their potential fortune, they were greeted by a crowd of onlookers that included the local constable and the "former" owner and captain of the recently rescued ship. As the men stepped off "their" ship, they were immediately put in shackles and accused of PIRACY! Instead of capturing a prize, THEY were captured as a prize. The men, including Jim Munn, were marched to the city jail and charged as CRIMINALS!!

A court hearing was scheduled, but as fate would have it, the judge got sick and could not ever get up to hear the case. Instead a new judge was ordered to come north from Seattle. That took time to get the message down to Seattle and time to get a new judge up to Skagway. The "criminals" languished in jail all this time. Well, not quite. Of course they had shelter and food of a sort. Then it was discovered that Jim Munn was a journeyman carpenter. What booming Skagway most needed were carpenters. He was released each day to work at his trade at the construction of downtown structures. (When granddaughter Mary Beth Yntema visited Skagway in the 1980's she was sure she recognized some of the window and door treatments of some of the buildings that were a match to the Post Office that Jim Munn built at Leland.)

To make matters worse, the jailers thought they could make a bit of Klondike gold by making a public display of the captured Pirates. The men, including our Jim, were chained together and lead into the bars and put on display. The show netted no gold as the drunks in the taverns immediately dismissed the pirates as just a bunch of sheepherders and farmers, which they were.

When the judge became sick and the court was delayed, Jim did become anxious and began to realize the seriousness and dangers of the situation. It was then that he wrote the letter to his equally anxious wife. Ana by then had suffered through two months of worry. When the letter arrived and she read, "I'm in jail. I've lost everything as my suitcase was stolen. There is no judge and the case is set off indefinitely." What was to happen to her and her four babies? The youngest was now only 7 months old!

True to her strong character, Ana began making plans to go back to teaching at the Leland School. No teacher had been hired for the coming year as yet. But until May she could utilize the resources at hand. She had her two cows and was selling milk and butter. She began making bread and cakes to sell at the logging camps. She had plenty of wood for her cooking stoves. Spring was coming in a few days and she would put in a larger garden this year. She would get by somehow.

Back in Skagway a judge had arrived from Seattle. Then, just as the case was to go to court, the two ship captains got together, in a bar and after several drinks, perhaps, they decided that there was not enough evidence for either side and they dropped the case. The "Pirates" were freed. Jim took the first available boat back to Seattle.

Jim Munn arrived in Leland on 30 March 1898. This was twenty days after his letter from Skagway had arrived with the news of his incarceration and twenty days of Ana's worst worries. The entire Klondike Gold venture had taken 4 months. What a welcome Jim had! What contrition he felt! Ana writes that he knelt before her and put his head in her lap and cried. Maybe it was weeping for joy. Maybe both were crying. Ana doesn't choose to add her emotional state. Then Jim reached into his vest pocket and pulled out the $20 gold piece and told Ana he had come back with everything he left with. She went to her money drawer and came back with her $20 gold piece and said she didn't ever need it. All was well once more at the house on the orchard homestead.

Actually, Jim had been paid for his carpentry work and after paying jail housing and purchasing some new clothes, he had a tidy sum left. He immediately put a stop to any school teaching job for Ana. They set about talking a lot and making up for lost time. There is no place like home and there is no home like one with a father and husband present.

The "Pirate-Jail" story surely contains all the merits of pathos, injustice and final reconciliation, with relief and promise of future good things. Over 110 years later, who could object to the story?

It seems that the Jim Munn story is only one of many scam stories that are told about the Alaska Gold Rush times. It is reported that boat captains conspired together many times to scam their own crews with the "loose ship" ploy. In most cases, the novice gold seekers were bilked for legal fees charged by corrupt judges who were also in on the scams. The police, judges, sea captains and jailers all took a cut of the money bilked from the families who were desperate to free captive loved ones.

In this case, we would like to think, the scam seems not to have the scamming details. There was no "get-out-of-jail" bounty paid. Jim never asked for money from Ana and in fact arrived home before any money could have been sent, even if there were some. Jim was spared any climb over snow covered mountain passes or loss of serious outfitting gear. He had meals and a roof over his head the whole time. Jim learned important lessons about what is really most significant in life ---his wife and family. After all, the adventure of the story and the tensions of possible horrible outcomes but with miraculous, joyful endings, all makes for a great story for the children and grandchildren.

A fourth daughter was born to Jim and Ana on 16 February 1899. Jim wanted to name her "Klondike". Ana would never agree to such a handle for her child. Evangeline was named for "Evangelina", a heroine of the Spanish-American war which had started in April 1898 and was over by December 1898. Vangie, or Auntie Van, was the only child not given a middle name. She understood this and would say that "Evangeline is a strong name that needs no helping name."

In hindsight, Ana remembers her separation from Jim as nearly a year, not four months. And in reality, the Klondike Gold Rush was brief as well. The "city" of Dawson was started in the summer of 1897 and most people had left by December 1899.

NO PLACE LIKE HOME

Jim and Ana's 40 acre "orchard" homestead began to be too confining. The farm animals multiplied as did the family, now five children. The economic depression of 1893-97 was easing in the Puget Sound region because of the gold rush. Failed farms were being bought by new owners. One in particular in Chimacum Valley was being reinvested and rebuilt. Jim Munn took on work building a new house, barns, a creamery and a store to market dairy and general merchandise. This new business became Glendale Creamery.

The farm was large enough in its own right, but the creamery began accepting cream from smaller south county farms. The cash from sale of cream became a boon to the small farmers and homesteaders who had land and animals but were short of cash flow. For Jim and Ana, the regular employment at Glendale Dairy brought them a return to financial well being. The only problem was that the road to Chimacum was difficult and Jim could only come home on week-ends. He began looking around Chimacum for a place to which he could move his family.

THE NICHOLS HOMESTEAD

Captain Edwin and Adelia Nichols were among the very first to homestead the edges of Lake Hooker. Captain Nichols was a Civil War veteran. The *"Quilcene Queen"* reported that he had a $12 a month pension. That was a goodly sum for the time. Edwin and Adelia Nichols had filed and had earned the patent on 157-1/2 acres along the western side of Lake Hooker. It was composed of four lots that were partial "40s" along the lake edge and one full "40" that angled up the side hill to the southwest. Except for the hillside 40, the homestead was on the flat delta of five streams that flowed into Lake Hooker from the west and south. Over time the streams pushed soil into the lake so that what might have started as an oval lake had become shoe shaped with a narrows between a smaller south end and a larger north end. Actually the lake angles to the northeast. (See Map 3)

Where the lake narrowed is a natural place for a crossing. There is evidence that the Native American travelers had a trail on the northwest side coming from Crocker Lake. They fell large cedar trees from both sides of the lake whose top portions overlapped across the narrows. This would make the first bridge. Then earlier settlers, probably Capt. Nichols, had set pilings and timbers to give a bridge. There were also row boats available on each side near the bridge. During the rainy season, the lake level would lift the bridge deck off the pilings making the bridge unsafe. This was the bridge that was in use when the second band of settlers came. It was in use when the railroad was built and when the Edwards family and Jim Munn came in the 1890s.

Ed and Adelia Nichols had put together a lovely homestead for the time. They built a house of hewed logs (i.e., squared logs). It had an upper story with two bed rooms. There were two rooms downstairs. At a later date, a pantry/kitchen was built on the west side toward the creek. The house was set on a low ridge between the creek and the lake front. The front door opened to a "lawn" that ran down to the lake. There was a well between the house and the creek and in the "L" of the kitchen and parlor. The well was deep enough to tap water below the lake level so it was not creek water and was well filtered. The well casing extended above ground and had a cover and a turnbuckle to lower the well bucket down. Buckets were also hung over the side that held milk cans, butter and fresh meat to be kept cool.

A narrow buggy road came from the bridge and through the farm yard to the south of the house. Ed Nichols had a two part barn. On the side toward the lake was a lower roofed horse barn and a lean-to shelter for the buggy. Behind that was a taller cow barn with a hay loft above the cow stalls. There were additional sheds for chickens, pigs, and wood.

Behind (south of) the cow barn was the omnipresent orchard. All the structures are gone except several trees of the orchard. In 2010 the orchard would be at least 120 years old. There were about four pear trees of two varieties, plum trees, Italian prune and yellow prune or green gage prune trees. There was a grand variety of apple trees from early ripening Transparent, to late ripening King. There was a crabapple, a sweet cider apple, a Gravenstein tree and apples no longer named. To the north of the house were four or so cherry trees that included Queen Anne and Bing as well as pollination cherry trees. Also near the cherry trees but at lake side was a Greasy Pippin apple tree and a Russet apple tree. The inner farm and orchard were set off from the rest of the farm by picket fences. The buggy road between the house and barns was lined with picket fences as well. Along the south side of Arcadia road toward the hill there was a wooden sidewalk. Split cedar was abundant and often went to waste. Most of the construction of barns and fences and sidewalk was split cedar.

The garden area was also south of the barns and between the orchard and the lake. The creek angled in from the hill, passed under the road and curved to the north past the barns and the house. On the side of the creek on a bench below the main field there was a root house. It was cut into the hillside and entered from the creek side. It should have had stone walls, but didn't, so that the extension above ground was wooden walls as below. So the little food storage shed was one of the first structures to decay. Perhaps if one looks closely, here is still a strange depression at the creek edge where it was.

The main hay field extended to the south below the orchard. However, the "flat" area was split into a field cleared of stumps and a "field" with many old cedar stumps. This was called the creek pasture. The stumps provided fun castles for children to play on and in. If the bracken fern could be burnt off in the spring, about Easter time, the creek pasture sprouted with morel mushrooms in magnificent numbers.

To the north of the buggy road or Acadia Road there was another pasture that paralleled the creek and also had a stump field extending to the hill. Then the cleared portion narrowed to the north until one came to a smaller delta formed by another winter-time creek. A flat area there, called the Point by the family, was where Dick Brown had his logging operation where Jim Munn had been employed to build a bunk house, cook house and mule barns.

Finally, the Nichols land extended to the south and was pretty much uncleared wet land except for the most southerly Lot 4 that held another "delta" with some dry, flat ground as well as treed upland. This Lot was not worked until well into the 1920s when a Japanese family, the Tanamaras, built a house and barn and cleared a garden area. The side hill "40" to the west has remained in timber as it is cut by stream canyons and is quite steep. The timber has been harvested at least three times and has been a valuable component of the total farm stead.

The Nichols Place beside Lake Leland. Drawn by James P. Bury, a great grandson.

THE NICHOLS PLACE BECOMES THE MUNN PLACE

The entry in Matilda's Diary for Thursday, January 4, 1900 reads, "Mild and cloudy. Munns move on the Nichols Place." This is how that came about.

Captain Ed Nichols died about 1895. They had no children. His wife Adelia moved to Buffalo, N.Y. to live with her niece. Adelia rented the farm to logger Dick Brown who kept his horses there and may have planted the garden. Otherwise he had not occupied the farm or house. Adelia wanted to rent the property to Ana and Jim, even though Dick Brown had offered to purchase the land for a good price.

The Brown logging operation was winding down. Dick Brown had been cutting only high grade clear lumber trees. He would skid the logs down to the lake and float them to a landing directly across the lake where he could load them on rail cars. He sent them to a mill in Port Townsend that produced high quality, knot-free lumber. Not only was the log resource running out but Dick Brown was ageing. He died a few years after he had shut down his operation.

Jim Munn had steady work for Glendale Dairy in Chimacum. The company was doing very well with production and sales of fresh milk and butter as well as the general store. People would bring in fresh eggs and other farm products and exchange for chicken food, beans, flour, sugar, clothing, tools, etc. But Jim was not comfortable with the travel needed to get to Chimacum over the poor roads of the time.

A letter came to Ana from Mrs. Nichols' niece. Adelia Nichols was quite ill and in the hospital. Money was needed immediately. Could Jim and Ana buy the homestead right away? Even though Dick Brown had offered $4000, she would take $1500 for the property. For Ana the offer was a dream to come true. She had resisted any suggestion of moving to Chimacum and felt that the offer was too good to turn down. Jim went to the owner of Glendale Dairy, who was a banker, and asked for a loan. Jim Munn's reputation as an honest worker and budding businessman suggested that Jim should not take a bank loan, but to take the money out of the monthly pay he was earning. Jim and Ana immediately sent Adelia Nichols $300 and the bank sent the rest of the money. According to Ana in her memoirs, the loan was paid off in less than two years. The deed for the property, interestingly, identifies the title as for "Ana M. Munn and her husband James H. Munn". The adjacent Orchard homestead 40 acres was deeded to James H. Munn, alone. Now the two had a total of nearly 200 acres of land between them, in addition to the Arcadia homestead of 120 acres.

J.H. Munn home at Lake Leland, circa 1910. (G. Munn collection).

(THE LELAND BRIDGE: A VIGNETTE)

With the growing community up on Leland Hill and Arcadia, there was increasing need to replace the "low" bridge with a higher, wider and stronger bridge. The contract went to August "Gus" Thomas. He worked on the bridge from April to November 1900. Since the location of the abutments was not changed, he was able to use the older structure as a platform and transitional base. People were able to walk across the bridge all summer.

The bridge building process was creative. Gus Thomas pounded in a row of three fir pilings for each rank. A derrick held a pulley at the top. Each piling was moved under the pulley system. A rope went over the pulley and held a heavy wood block. A team of horses was hooked to the lead from the pulley and they were driven out to pull the block high into the derrick. A trip catch would release the block to fall on the top of the piling to drive it into the lake bottom. The top of the piling was protected from crushing with an iron cap. The horses would be lead back, re-attach to the rope and draw the block up again. Again the block would fall—kerplunk. Again and again would be raised and let fall until the piling was driven down as far as needed. No doubt this method had been used over and over for the driving of the pilings for the many railroad bridges for the PTSRR.

Lake Leland "Low" bridge. It was replaced in 1900. The shelter at the west end of the bridge is a boat house. Boats were kept handy for the winter time when flood waters made the bridge dangerous if not impassable. The Nichols homestead has a tight cluster of buildings. Yet Arcadia Road runs between the house and the barns. Note the tree on the right "horizon." It is the "Lookout Tree" that survived past the time of the Crown Zellerbach logging in the early '50s. (Jefferson County Historical Society).

As the three piling ranks extended out over the lake, they would were cross-braced with planking. Then each rank of three pilings would have a cap beam. Longitudinal beams were placed across the spaces between the ranks of pilings and then the bridge planking set across the beams. The longitudinal beams extended beyond the planking and a railing upright was set at the plank edge and braced back to the under beam. The railing appears to be about four feet high. That is not the five foot high rail of later replacement.

The **Leland Bridge was a great setting for any picture.** One of Jim's prize horses, circa 1910. Note lower railings. (George Munn collection).

Since the new bridge was four or five feet higher than the old bridge, the end abutments were raised with gravel fill. On the east side this made the bridge at the level of the railroad grade. On the west end the fill made a level road between the Munn house and the barns from the bridge all the way back to the "Nichols" creek. Later the edges were filled in even more so that today the roadway seems level with the adjacent yards.

The bridge decking is most vulnerable to wear and rotting from the weather. But the 18 inch diameter pilings, even fir pilings if immersed in water, will last a long time. The decking was first replaced with sawed dimensional planking and bracing with construction starting 6 August 1915 as reported in the *Port Townsend Leader*. Mr. Webster was the contractor. Lumber for the project was milled at the Munn Mill. The bridge deck was replaced again in January 1931. This didn't last long as in the summer of 1938 starting in April an entirely new bridge was set onto the pilings. That is, cross bracing, all beams, the deck and railings. The cross arm that held the telephone lines was removed as well. The contractor on this project left a big raft to the community children.

The big raft was anchored in the middle of the lake and became both a place to swim to and a place to stretch out in the sun. The fir bridge decking took a lot of wear and tear. In August 1941 a layer of black-top was spread on the surface. That was the last repair work done before the structure was abandoned as a bridge.

Leland High Bridge with new 1915 deck and bracing. No center cross arm for telephone wire. This is a view from the south east shore. Note the tracks of the Port Townsend Southern Railroad. (Munn family collection).

On 30 November 1939 after leaving the school children off at the post office turn-around and returning over the bridge, the driver misjudged the edge of the road on the east side of the bridge and rolled the school bus on its side. This accident was not because of the bridge, but it brought about a reevaluation of the need for the bus to cross the bridge. It was decided that the bridge pilings were unsafe for modern, heavier traffic. A bus turnaround was built near the George Thomas drive way. Later the Cutoff Road was put through across the old Currier homestead at the south side of Strawberry Hill. Then the school bus would not have to turn around and could drive by on Leland Valley Road with a major stop at the bridge from Leland Hill Road.

As logging equipment and trucking using the bridge became heavier and heavier, it was concluded that either a new bridge with new pilings would be needed or some other access to Leland Hill would be needed. That was when Snow Creek Road was built on the west side of the lake from Highway 101 as it is today.

Through the years, Leland Bridge had become a choice place for fishermen to stand to drop their lines down into the shadows of the bridge. The shadows and living plants and worms growing on the pilings made the waters below the bridge a collecting place for trout and bass. So the fishermen campaigned to leave the bridge for fishing. A compromise was reached and the west 30 feet were removed. The "fishing pier" was accessible from the east side. The pier was left until 1977 when locals appealed to have it all removed from being a visual and liability hazard.

The Leland Bridge was more than a way to get across the lake. Fishing off the bridge was superior, as mentioned. It was also a great trysting place as it was both a public place but distantly private. Young men would carve special initials on the railings. There were some special markings and notations of vows placed there over the years. But the bridge was also the best swimming hole ever. As the children grew and the grand children grew, the Munn lawn and shore was a welcomed location for swimmers. Neighborhood boys built platforms at various levels out from the pilings. One could dive from the bridge deck, the railing, or a "high dive" platform that was rigged above where the water was deepest. At low water in the summer when swimming was at its peak, the lake depth was 12 to 15 feet deep. If one jumped off the bridge feet first, it was possible to feel the soft, cool mud about the feet. A forward jack-knife dive or swan dive might end just above the mud. But no one ever was hurt from a dive off the highest diving position. A challenge of underwater swimming was to kick down from the surface and to come up with a handful of mud and raise it high as proof of "touching the bottom".

Finally, it must be mentioned that the bridge was in its day the best ever place to set off fire-works on the Fourth of July. Few people even remember Roman Candles flares. They have been banned as fire hazards of the highest order. But when aimed out over the lake from the bridge, they made a glorious display of colored balls of fire in the sky like shooting stars. The spent ashes fell harmlessly into the water. Neighbors also had launchers from which rockets could shoot over the water and end in a brilliant explosion. They were amazingly spectacular. The rockets would be sent up one at a time and thoroughly enjoyed before the next rocket was lit. There is nothing like shooting off a rocket for oneself.

Leland Bridge and PTSRR train, circa 1914. George Munn says that he was the "mid-jump" swimmer. (From *P.T. Leader*, unknown publication date).

FIRE ON THE HILL

Ana and Jim's sixth child was born 16 June 1901. He was named George Edwards Munn for his grandfather. He was the only child born in the log house by the lake. He always felt special because of that and the little triangle of land where the house stood was to be his one day. He liked to call it the homestead but it was purchased and not proved up as a homestead as was the Orchard 40. Viola was eight years old at the time

131

and became like a second mother for the little boy. Viola was always the little mother even for her sister Alice.

The summer of 1901 was ending with a hot, dry August. The logged of land on the hill above the lake had a healthy crop of bracken fern and the stand had dried up sooner than usual. Bracken fern has a special attraction for children. No one cares what happens to ferns and they make wonderful construction material as they can be pulled up and arranged into imaginary houses and castles to encourage childhood make believe. Neighbor girls who lived on the hill up Arcadia Road were having a grand time building a regular city of dry bracken fern. Their older brothers thought it would be great fun to tease and scare their little sisters by setting the city on fire. The "city" exploded! There was a northwest breeze blowing down toward Lake Leland. Before anyone knew what was happening, the whole side hill was in flames. In no time the line of fire reached the vacant homestead from which Jim and Ana had moved the year before. The house, the barn full of hay, the sheds and all were involved. The streams were dry, even if they could be reached for water. The fire kept heading down the hill through the stump pastures toward the "Nichols" homestead buildings.

Everyone jumped to do what they could. Ana got up on the roof of the log house. Someone brought buckets of water from the lake into which burlap sacks were soaked and thrown up to Ana and she beat out any embers that came her way. Bracken fern was whipped by the wind and broke off in pieces of leaves that continue burning in the air and then fall to the ground to spread the fire. Jim and others were doing the same wet burlap sack technique up on the roofs of the barns. The fire warden was called but by the time he arrived, there was nothing he could do. The men remained on the roof tops all night. Ana had to stop fighting. She was utterly exhausted from the effort and stress.

The lake side buildings were all saved. But there was nothing left of the buildings on the hill. The Orchard was scorched and survived for many years until the pilfering of apple hungry bear ripped them down and the shade from towering new growth of fir trees left them light hungry. Fortunately all the important materials that the family had accumulated had been moved to the lake side buildings. Since the summer's crop of hay had been lost, most of the cows and extra horses had to be sold. The one fortunate result was that Ana's ring that Fred Rose had given her was found near where the kitchen window had been. The ring was bent and had lost its gems. It remains both a reminder to Ana of a former life and a reminder to her family of the destruction of a dream that had started with the original homestead on the hill.

The 1901 fire was a disaster to the Munn ranch. But fires were common on into the 1930s. In 1935 there was an especially extensive fire that swept to the south across the Little Quilcene River valley and as high up on "Green Mountain" as there were trees. The flames could be seen from the Leland Bridge. The mountain was no longer green. In the days of the Civilian Conservation Corp (CCC), that area was replanted with seedlings and today it is really a Green Mountain again.

The Munn Family, 1907. James Hector, Ana Mae (Edwards), Viola Dorothy, Hector John, Margaret ALICE, Sarah Matilda, Evangeline, George Edwards. (G. Munn collection)

The Munn farm about 1910. Looking northeast from the hillside "40". There is no new "red" barn nor sawmill. The skimming station is at the end of the bridge. The south pasture is newly cleared. The creek pasture to left center is full of stumps and logs. The high bridge would be about 10 years old. (Munn family collection)

IX: MUNN FAMILY BUSINESSES

THE SKIMMING STATION

Glendale Dairy was a very successful business. Whole milk was being brought in from nearby farms where the cream was skimmed off to make butter. The skimmed milk was returned to the farmers. To expand the production the dairy decided to establish skimming stations in outlying locations and then bring just the cream into the creamery at Chimacum. Stations were set up in Quilcene, Leland and Discovery Bay.

Jim Munn built the skimming station on his newly acquired farm in Leland. He later bragged that the building was the first building in the valley made from sawed lumber. He built it at the edge of Arcadia Road just at the west end of the newly built "high" bridge and at the grade of the new road. Thus the building was at graded in front but set up several feet elsewhere. There never was plumbing to the building, so one presumes water was carried from the Munn well across the "street". According to Matilda's diary, G.W. Edwards began taking milk to the skimming station on 3 May 1903.

Farmers would save the evening milking and add the morning milk to it. Then they came with the horse drawn wagons with their full milk cans to the station. A milk sample was taken to spin in a hand operated centrifuge to test the butter fat content. This number and the number of gallons of raw milk were used to calculate what the farmer would be paid. The milk from the various farms was mixed together in the same large vat. Skimming milk need time for the cream to rise to the surface. The cream would be skimmed off with a large ladle. The farmer would take back the skimmed milk from the previous day's production. By the time the farmer reached home, the calves and pigs would get sour skimmed milk. The children would get fresh milk kept out from the shipped milk.

Before long the skimming process was upgraded by the installation of a steam-driven separator. The steam separator made a great improvement in the time and freshness of the product. The farmer could wait until his milk was processed and take his "skimmed" milk, as it still was called, back home the same morning. The time waiting became an important social event each day as the men, usually, would exchange news and tell farm stories. They could leave the milk and go the ¾ mile on to get their mail, if that was not on their way home. So the wife and children would keep up on community happenings at lunch time.

It was Jim Munn's job to see that the cream was taken on to Chimacum and Glendale Dairy. Again at first this meant driving a cart over the Smith and Donnelly Road to Tarboo and on to Chimacum. Later a road was built over Eagle Mount from Discovery Bay. Then Jim, or a hired hand, would take the cream to Cooper's or Uncas where the cans were added to those from that area and all taken to Chimacum from there. The workers got quite a workout taking the full cans from one cart to the other and getting the empty cans in exchange. Since Glendale Dairy was operating the store as well, it was possible to place store orders and the drivers would bring back staples and butter for the farmers to pick up the next day. All sales profited the dairy but also made life out on the farms a lot more civilized and livable. Of course just having a cash source was a boon to the entire community.

The next commercial development, however, was better for the dairy than the farmer. Glendale Dairy noted that the skimmed milk had more than animal food value. They decided to purchase whole milk to process into cheese as well. Then the skimming station at the Leland Bridge became a collection depot for the whole milk. The skimming building with the steam separator was no longer needed for processing. It stood idle for several years.

Then before long, the DeLaval hand separator was added to the progressive inventions. Every farmer could do his own cream separating of the fresh milk after each milking time. The cream was then taken to the "Skimming Station" depot for transfer on the same routes. Eventually when the quality of the roads improved and with the use of trucks rather than horse carts, it was possible for the cream to be collected at the farm one or two times a week. However, the Leland Bridge collecting point was used well into the 40's as it still cut down on the time of the cream trucks to make their circuit. Some of the farm yards were quite impassable for the heavy trucks in the wet months. By then the Leland transfer station was the Leland Post Office as well. Folks needed to make a daily run for their mail and would bring the cream cans for the scheduled pick-up. The Leland Post Office porch was still a gathering place. A five gallon cream can is just right height to be a seat while waiting for the mail to come. More about the Post Office will come later.

MR. KAWAMOTO AND BUSINESS EXPANSION

The skimming station was a worker intensive process. A person was needed on hand at the station to be ready to accept the milk, take the samples, do the testing, record the incoming volumes, set up the skimming vats, skim the cream off, collect the skimmed milk back into the cans, clean up the vats and the equipment, transport the product on its way to the dairy, etc. Then start all over for the next day. So Jim needed help. Ana was busy with the young family, as the oldest child was only eleven years old.

Jim reached back into his Vancouver, BC days and the friends there and he made contact with a young Japanese man. There was an embargo against people coming from Japan and China into the United States at the time. But with proper health clearances, Japanese could enter the U.S. through Canada. Thus contact was made with Kaichi K. Kawamoto. Thus began a personal and family relationship that has been rewarding to both families ever since. A finer worker and gentleman can seldom be found. K.K. Kawamoto, or just K.K. or Kay, was well educated as he had been preparing for the priesthood. He was married but left his wife in Japan to seek his fortune in the America. He was a quick learner, as we say today. His first job was the care and management of the skimming station and its subsequent forms as a collecting station. Quite often the smallest Munn child, George, would be left under the care of K.K, as some of the creamery operations involved waiting. There developed a special bond between Kaichi Kawamoto and George Munn that continued throughout their lives.

After Mr. Kawamoto became settled with his work and new community, he was able to return to Japan to see his wife and son. Sadly by then their first son had died. He was able to bring Mrs. Kawamoto back to the U.S. by way of Victoria, B.C. The couple lived in various homes about Leland. Their four children, Joseph, Jeanette, Pauline, and Alice, went to school in the Leland School and then at Leland Quilcene Union High School. Mr. Kawamoto worked hard and bought land just to the south of the Ryan place that was at the north end of Lake Leland. Son Joe Kawamoto turned the farm into a showplace dairy farm.

The immigration rules changed early in the 20th century and many other Japanese families found Leland Valley a good place to live and work. At first there were jobs in the railroad construction and then in the labor intensive logging operations of the time. A group of Japanese men formed a cooperative to cut cedar for the Quilcene shingle mills. There were as many as six Japanese families with homes near Lake Leland at one time. But as the logging operations closed, the families who had not purchased land moved elsewhere to find work.

INTERFARMERS TELEPHONE COMPANY, PART ONE: THE START UP

InterFarmers Telephone Company construction began in the summer of 1903. Matilda Edwards made three entries in her diary that referred to the phone company.

December 1, 1903, Tuesday: "Jim is putting up telephone wires. Rain most all morning. I sent letters to Jim and Meda, and Ana Ruggles and Henry Knight." (James Fitzgerald, Matilda's brother and wife Almeda, tried to homestead along the bank of Quilcene River. They became discouraged with the rain and flooding.) (Ana Ruggles was Dora's oldest daughter and Henry Knight was Elva's oldest son. Matilda followed the lives of all her grandchildren.)

December 10, 1903, Thursday: "Bill Hammond was here for dinner. They ran the telephone wire down." (Bill Hammond was hired as a telephone technician to get the construction started.)

December 11, 1903, Friday: "They put the phone in our house."

At the turn of the century, Port Townsend and Port Ludlow were the principle population centers of Jefferson County. They were served by Citizens Independent Telephone Company and Sunset Telephone Company. The railroads were served by telegraph lines and trunk telephone lines. Rural areas were slow to get telephones as the distance between customers made for expensive operations. Rural communities needed communications the most to encourage social contact and for emergency warnings.

State Senator William Bishop, for whom Jim Munn worked at Glendale Dairy in Chimacum, a banker/accountant named Mr. Albert W. Buddress and Jim and Ana Munn formed the telephone company. Jim Munn was the manager and majority stockholder. The license authorizing the company declared that it was to serve all of Jefferson County not then served by other companies. Incorporation documents were filed on February 1, 1907. The incorporation Preferred Stock was established at 100 shares. Jim and Ana owned 51 shares and William Bishop and Mr. Buddress owned 49 shares between them. Mr. Buddress continued to be a financial consultant as late as 1926.

Telephone lines using #14 (thick) copper wires were strung out along the existing roads that radiated from the Leland Bridge as the telephone switchboard was placed in Ana Munn's parlor. One line was along the Smith and Donnelly Road from the bridge over Strawberry Hill, past Matilda Edwards' and over Tarboo Hill to Dabob and Chimacum. One line went northward to Uncas and Gardner. One line went to Quilcene. Sunset Telephone Company had a long distance line from Port Townsend to Quilcene and along Quilcene Bay to Brinnon and Duckabush and on to Mason County. The company failed and InterFarmers bought the line to Duckabush. Finally there was a line up Leland Hill and a second line to Quilcene.

The original system was a "ground return" or single wire system. Where possible, the insulators holding the wire were nailed into trees. Telephone poles were added as necessary. The idea was to get the system up and running as soon as possible. Gradually improvements were made when a two wire system was installed and use of live tree as poles was eliminated. The ground return system used thick wire and booster batteries. The signal was very weak and could not be connected to a long-distance system. The system was powered by two dry-cell batteries in each customer phone box. No current was used until the receiver was lifted off its hook and the phone was cranked. The cranking movement turned a little generator to supply the call electricity.

The Munn compound needed a building to house the equipment and replacement parts. This shop was the first of a row of buildings across the creek and on the north side of Arcadia Road. The telephone shop was a marvelous place for pre-teens to play. The spare dry-cell batteries and extra phone boxes were all functional and could be rigged in interesting ways. The best was to make a shock circuit such that by turning a phone crank an electrical current would pass through a dozen bodies and shock only the hands that were grounded in some way. So the lads in rubber tennis shoes would surprise the fellow that had wet leather soles. Significant scientific knowledge was gathered in the phone shop.

Soon the girls in the family were trained in the operation of the switchboard. If customers wanted to call a neighbor on the same line, the ear piece was lifted off the hook and the crank was turned with "short" and "long" crank times similar to MorseCode used for telegraph communication. Customers did not have a number. They had a "ring". The switchboard was two shorts, for example. The longest ring was six shorts. Continuous "shorts" above six was the emergency ring. Everyone hearing that would immediately listen in to see what the emergency was and to decide if they could go to the aid of the emergency. Occasionally the "emergency" was that a new baby had been born or that Johnny was home from the Service.

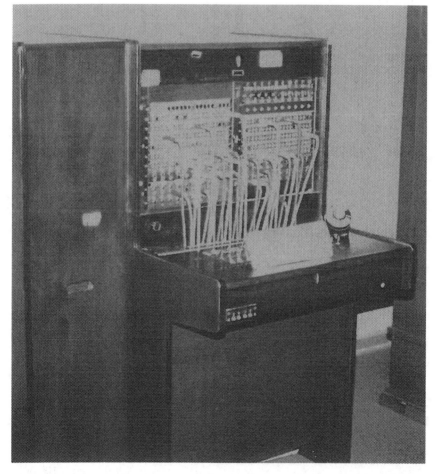

A Switchboard. The InterFarmers Telephone Company had only one switchboard. The "jacks" on the lower part were plugged into the vertical part. (Source unknown).

To call someone on a different line, the switchboard "central" had to be called. Then the connector "jack" that went from the incoming line to the outgoing line was plugged in. The operator would first ring the outgoing phone and if someone answered, she would say, "I have a call for you", and make the connection. The operator could stay on the line if needed, but that was not done unless asked. When the customers had finished the call, they could give the line a single ring. That is the origin of the expression of "ring off". However, it wasn't really necessary as a little light would go off on the switchboard when the caller returned the ear piece to its hook. The operator could break into a line if there was a perceived urgency and ask the parties to hang up. If there was no emergency to bump a customer, the operator just said, "That line is busy. Do you wish to wait on the line or call back?" A keen knowledge of social etiquette is necessary to be a switchboard operator.

Most of the initial equipment was purchased though a supplier in Sequim who serviced the systems all over the Peninsula. Mr. Kawamoto was called back into work to help install the telephone lines. He was trained by the original consulting engineers. He caught on quickly. Setting up poles in those days was a team effort. Digging the holes for the poles and raising the poles was only the start. Each pole had to be climbed in order to set out the cross-arms, attach the insulators and attach the wires. The climber had a rope and pulley arrangement with a bucket in which an assistant on the ground would feed up needed items. Pole climbing was the top skill of a lineman and smaller, quick fellows were better at climbing. The task fit K. Kawamoto's build and abilities. He excelled as a lineman. Line installation was completed after a time and Mr. Kawamoto always had other tasks he could do. He took his family away for a while, but came back to Leland to establish his farm. It is important to note that he was always a co-worker and friend to Jim Munn. He was always a welcome guest at Munn family activities and is often in family group pictures. Mrs. Kawamoto never learned much English and stayed at home. But she was always much loved by all.

Another aspect of the phone business was collection of bills. This was done in person going to customer's homes and businesses. Jim Munn took pride in his horses which were used to take the collecting agent around to the customers. Collecting was necessary to keep the business going. Collecting in person had both a positive and a negative aspect. Some customers enjoyed the collecting visit and would invite the visitor in and have a lovely social visit. People did not have many visitors. There were times that the economy dropped and customers would not have money or would expect to pay later. The truth is that the Munn collectors had a hard time keeping up with the collections and, if the bill was delinquent, to remove the phones. More is to be said on that topic later. Many young men and young women got their start in the work world through jobs with the phone company.

THE LELAND LUMBER COMPANY AND SAWMILL

Once the phone company was fully in place, the daily operation was mostly in Ana's hands. The maintenance was contracted to various workers. Jim Munn began to envision other projects. It was a concern to him that trees were being skidded to trains and taken to dumps in the bays and floated in huge rafts to sawmills in the cities on the east side of Puget Sound. Dick Brown's logging operation on Lake Leland was an example of how high value logs were lost to the local economy. The logs were skidded into the lake and pulled out on the other side where they were loaded onto the railcars. They were taken to Port Townsend for sawing into lumber. Finished lumber had to be imported for any local construction. There was still significant log resource in the area. To have a local sawmill that hired local workers and sold to local buyers seemed a good idea.

Jim found a saw mill that was going out of business and had the equipment brought by rail to a site about three miles south of Leland. (The location would be about 2500 W. Leland Valley Road today. Careful observation shows the remains of the mill pond.) He had an agreement with a land owner to cut the trees cut from the land there. Once the land owner saw the mill in operation, he decided his trees were worth more and Jim, in turn, decided he could move the operation to Lake Leland.

The mill equipment was re-assembled at the edge of Lake Leland south of the orchard and garden plot on his own land. Jim had hired Mr. Sturrock, a sawyer and carpenter, to help prepare the mill and direct its operation. Mr. Sturrock built a two-storied house at the "foot" of Leland hill between the current Munn Road and the creek to the south. Several bunk houses were set on the north side of Arcadia Road at the foot of the hill. Also, since the creamery was empty, it was also used as a bunk house. As most of mill workers were single men, a small kitchen and dining room (i.e. mess hall) was built behind the creamery.

Trees were then skidded from the hill south of the homestead. To power the movement of the logs from the hill to the lake and then from the lake into the mill, Jim purchased a steam donkey. A wood fired steam engine was mounted on wooden skids which were good sized logs that were beveled at each end. Cables were pulled by drums turned by the steam engine. The cables could be run out to anchoring trees and the donkey would pull itself across the land on the skids. Once in place, the cable would be taken out to the logs and they would be pulled in sets down to the lake water. The logs were floated to the edge of a ramp from the mill down to the water. The donkey then pulled the logs into place for the saws in the saw mill.

From a bill of sale:

"Purchased from R.C. O'Brien of Seattle, Washington for the sum of $1300.00 by J. H. Munn of Leland, Jefferson County, Washington the following personal property: One donkey engine 9" X10", Vulcan make, with the cables and equipment and everything in connection therewith, 15th day of April, 1913. The Bill of Sale was recorded at Jefferson County Courthouse on April 17, 1913. Vol.5 of Misc page 114."

The equipment of the mill had a separate steam engine and boiler to operate the saws and a planner. The product of the mill was quality lumber.

The added specialty was that the lumber was cut to specific dimensions and planed ready to be placed into a job without further wasteful trimming.

J.H. Munn sawmill at the edge of Lake Leland. 1914.
Log ramp from the lake is at right. The steam donkey is at the left. The men are making a new sled for it. Looking north east. Current location of Mrs. Robert Munn's house. (Munn family collection).

The mill was operational in April 1913. Its first contracted product was to replace the beams, braces and decking of Leland Bridge. The original bridge lumber had been split cedar and was rough and already rotting. The 1915 rebuilt bridge would last to 1931 when the decking was replaced again.

The lumber from the Leland Saw Mill was readily sold and since the trees were taken from the Munn property, the income was significant. Then, a major use of the product from the saw mill was for the construction of Jim Munn's barn. The barn was completed by the fall of 1915 and before it could be used as a shelter for cows and horses, Jim held a grand party. The story of the Jim's barn will follow later.

It didn't take long to fell, transport and mill the logs from the limited supply of trees on Munn property. Just as the trees were running out, the boiler for the saw mill became over heated and blew up from excess pressure. Leland Lumber Company came to a sudden end; at least as far as fir lumber was concerned.

Leland Sawmill. Circa 1916. A view from S.E. end of the Lake.
(Munn family collection).

THE SHINGLE MILL FIRE

There was still a good stand of cedar trees around the lake. Quilcene was home for three shingle mills. The Greene Mill was located in the "Linger Longer" area of south Quilcene. The product was loaded on boats and shipped out to the cities around the Sound. The Seaton Mill was north of the Greene Mill at the side of the Port Townsend Southern RR. Its product was loaded on flat cars and sent into Port Townsend. There was a third, smaller mill that was located on the north side of Quilcene River between the railroad right of way and the main road coming from the bridge over the river. (The structure was somewhere in the triangle where the Jefferson County road garages are today.)

The third shingle mill, the Butterfield Mill, had closed down as it was not able to compete with the two larger mills. Jim Munn decided to buy the small mill and move the equipment to his Lake Leland location. He had purchased the equipment and had it all ready to put on a railroad flatcar on the next Monday morning. A serious problem with shingle mills is that they create much powder saw dust. They used the saw dust and any extra cedar trimmings to fire their steam engine boilers. So a fire watch on the roof was necessary around the clock to douse embers from the boiler furnace. Perhaps the fire watch was off duty in the transition, but somehow on the Sunday night before the transfer of the equipment, the mill building caught fire and the equipment was a total loss.

The shingle mill plan ended about the same time that the lumber mill had closed because its boiler had blown up. No one ever knew for sure whether the cedar mill fire was an accident or if there had been someone who wanted to eliminate competition. It was a great financial loss the Jim Munn. His career began to wane from that time on.

There were business men who thought they could revive the Leland Lumber Mill, but none of them were successful. The equipment other than the boiler engine was gradually sold. The steam donkey with its supply of cable was still very useful and was readily sold. All the lumber and even rough trimmings gradually found use for building a set of garages near the telephone shop and for building a pair of poultry houses, one for chickens and one for turkeys and geese as well as a calf barn and a separator house.

Jim's oldest son Hector and Nate Stewart, a cousin who visited from Seattle, found the family home was too crowded and built a one-roomed cabin across the creek from the main house. It had framing from the "lumber pile" and they cut shakes for the siding and roof. They were soon too grown up even to use the cabin. It was left as an extra bedroom for the next generation of children. It was eventually moved in 1935 to be part of the "Alden" complex at the end of the orchard.

JIM MUNN'S BARN: DESIGN AND CONSTRUCTION

There could not have been a much better legacy than "The Barn" for Jim Munn to leave to his grand children. It seemed majestic to little eyes and limbs. It had nooks and crannies, mangers and mows, gables and gang planks, rope swings and rope ladders, tunnels in the hay, rafters hung with spider webs and cupolas and crows' nests. There were hiding places and danger ledges and places to sit by the hour to look out windows or to listen to rain falling on the roof.

The basic design of the barn is the "double crib". The framework consisted of two sets of braced post and beams with an alley between. The post and beams were 12" by 12" center cut fir. The upright posts were 12' apart, with three posts to a side with beams across each12'span. The angled braces were 12" X 3" planks. The main structure of posts and beams and braces were held together with wooden pins pounded into drilled holes. There were two "floors" of beams so that the lower 12' posts had an upper 12' post set on top. The basic crib would thus be about 26' high.

The foundation consisted of twenty-four (+/-) inch cedar rounds set under each main posts with the floor beams set across the spans. The rafters were of 3" X 6" planks set about a foot apart along the top beam. They were braced about four feet from the top with a horizontal brace and along the inner side there were braces that angled across the rafters.

Between the 12 X 12 beams for the outer walls on the three sides were 8" X 4" horizontal planks set midway between the beams. These beams were braced as well and served to support the outer wall planks. The outer walls were 1"X 12" planks placed vertically. The planks were closely set, but along the crack was a three inch covering strip. The edges and corners and soffits were covered with strips as well. These were eventually painted white while the outer wall was painted bright red, not the lighter "barn red". The roof was covered with cedar shingles nailed over a solid sheeting of planks.

The cow barn was about 40 feet wide and set to the center of the two cribs and with an alley that extended from the alley of the main barn. It extended back 50 or 60 feet. The posts and beams were probably 6" X 6". The alley extended back between stanchions on both sides. On the north side there was a large box room that was used as a calf pen. There were no windows and it was a poor place for calves. The outer wall of the cow barn did have windows. Calves were kept in the calf stall until they were weaned, after which they were taken to the calf shed or to an outside pen. On the south side of the cow barn were two horse stalls with a manger and a little walk-way in front of the manger. The horse stalls had a door to the outside. There was a window at the head of the stalls. Jim had a better idea of a horse's needs than calves' needs.

At the very end of the cow barn were the doors. Each side had a door set on a track so that they slid along the wall. Then the center had a double door that was also on tracks to slide each way, rather than swing in or out. At the front of the main barn there was a set of sliding doors as well. There was a long ramp that led up to the main doors. Horses could pull a wagon load of hay up the ramp into the center alley. Most of the hay was pitched off with hand forks into the right or north hay mow. The left or south mow had a floor at the second level. Below the floor was storage space or an area where extra horses or calves could be tethered. The upper level was a mow used in the early days for oat hay that was for the horses. In very good years, some grass hay or special hay was put there. Usually it was a grand play area.

To put the hay into the left mow or to put hay up higher than could be pitched off the wagon, Jim had a hay fork system. Along the tip of the barn peak ran a metal track that carried a carriage into which the top of the hay fork would set. The hay fork had a pulley at the top and ropes would lower it down to the hay on the wagon. The fork was jammed into the hay and "set". Metal points would extend to the sides of the hay fork and grip into the dry grass. The rope ran up to the top of the barn and with the pulley system could go either direction. The hay fork with a load would be pulled up to the top and then slide along the track over the mow. There was a quarter inch rope hooked to a trip catch so that when pulled, the prongs on the hay fork would pull in and release the load. Hay could be brought to the top of the rising hay mow. The hay had to be pitched back against the walls and stamped down to keep the mow evenly filled.

There were three special features of Jim Munn's barn. Centered at the top of each "barn" he placed a cupola. For the main barn the cupola was very high and not easily reached by children. The cupola on the cow barn was reached by climbing through the rafters and braces. This was called the Crow's Nest and was a favorite place to peek out to the outside. There was a weather vane "chicken" perched on top, which was crafted by George Nurnberg, Jim's son-in-law.

On the east side of the barn and centered above the big doors was a gable with windows. By very special effort, one could swing from rafter to rafter and pull into the windowed gable and look out over the lake and to George Thomas's farm on the hill above the lake. It is thought that a barn or house on the Belle River farm on Prince Edward Island had such a gable and was the model for Jim Munn's special feature. The cupolas were special as they are not often seen on barns.

Prince Edward Island barn. (Helen Bury collection).

LELAND FRUIT AND PACKING COMPANY, LELAND, WASHINGTON

Jim Munn painted his new barn bright red, not barn red. The trim was painted white. He was quite proud of his barn and staged and inaugural community dance. The new floor was smoothly laid down and danceable.

The breams and walls were festooned with lanterns. Musicians were hired. Ana and her teen-aged daughters put out a plentiful spread of refreshment. A grand time was had by all. The first use of the barn was to house the workers who rebuilt the Leland Bridge.

There would eventually be an adjacent bull barn and bull pen as well as a creamery/separator building. When there was no bull in the pen it would be used as a pig pen. However, Jim decided he did not want to mess up his fine, clean handiwork by keeping animals just then. He decided he could keep the "Nichols barns" for a few more years. He would use his new "barn" as a fruit cannery. Hence came about "**Leland Fruit and Packing Co. Leland Washington**", as the packing boxes read.

The Port Townsend Leader, Issue #73 for September 25, 1915 has this entry:

> **"Fruit Cannery: Articles of Incorporation: J. H. Munn, President and Manager; H. J. Munn, Vice-President; R. E. Ryan, Jr. Secretary. Capitalized at $3,000. Divided into 300 shares of $10 each."**

The Port Townsend Leader, October 21, 1915.
> **"Start-up of the Fruit Cannery at Leland."**

A company in Quilcene had tried to start up a cannery to can oysters. Unknown at the time was that oysters cannot be canned. There is no way, even in modern time to successfully can oysters, except as smoked oysters. So there was an immediate source of cannery equipment. What would eventually become the cow barn was set up with the equipment. There was a large steam pressure cooker. There were iron racks that slid into the cooker. A supply of #6 steel cans was purchased. Then amazingly for the time, Jim set up a gravity water system. He went up into the creek canyon that would have been just below the "Mudgett cabin", the first home of Jim and Ana. There he placed a source box which trapped water to fill the half-inch pipe that he ran down to the barn, now a cannery, to supply the water needs for washing fruit and cleaning the tables and equipment.

By this time the orchards of the homesteaders with apples, pears and plums were twenty or more years old and in peak production. The hotels, restaurants and logging camps could use all the canned fruit they could find. Also, Jim had four young daughters to clean, cut and pack the fruit.

The product was good. The first year canned fruit was all sold. Yet the company lost money. Jim Munn reasoned that any new business lost money at first. Then the second year was a greater financial loss. The supply of fruit was not large enough and the market was too far away for economical transport of the product. As is well known since then, Jefferson County had many fruit trees for fresh use by families, but nowhere near the number of trees to make a cannery profitable. Shipping to markets via the ferry system or via truck "around" through Olympia is simply too expensive. A cannery operated in Port Townsend for a few years during the depression and Second World War. Fruits and vegetables were home grown and taken home by the farm families. Not much was sold. The building is a bay-side condo today. So by the summer of 1917, the barn was finished off inside with stanchions and stalls to house the animals.

The "Nichols barns" were finally torn down to give Arcadia Road adequate room and the Munn household more open yard space. The steam cooker was sold. For years the rafter space above the cow barn had a pile of the racks used to hold the cans in the cooker. There were two large cartons of the #6 tin cans. The neighborhood children had an abundant supply of cans to play "Kick the Can". It was found that if one stepped down just right on the cans, the metal would crimp into the shoe just above the sole. This made a little stilt to walk about on that would keep the shoe about two inches off the muddy ground. There is always lots of mud about a cow barn. There was a call for scrap metal at the start of Second World War. Jim Munn's grandsons took the steam trays, the half-inch pipe that had a long time before been taken up and stored under the barn, and the metal debris from Leland Lumber Company's saw mill to the scarp drive. The scrap contribution lay in the elementary school yard much too long. The big barrel-like remains of the steam boiler tank became an invitation to tragedy as jumping on it made the school children sound powerful.

James H. Munn barn when it housed the Leland Cannery. Note the cartons in front. These held the empty cans in which the fruit was canned, circa 1917. (G. Munn collection).

A GRAND INTERRUPTION

In the fall of 1916 James H. Munn received a notice that he had been called to Grand Jury duty. This was not a trip into Port Townsend for a few days. It was a Federal Grand Jury that met in Seattle. For several months he lived with his sister Dorothy Stewart and her husband Alex in north Seattle on Aurora Avenue. There seemed to be no way that he could escape the obligation. It became a much greater problem than it seemed at the outset. He had to cut back on all his farm and business efforts. Fortunately the barn had been built. The sawmill operation had closed down anyway. He sold off his prize horses and all the farm equipment he could spare. The phone company always needed work done, so that had to be delayed or hired out. However, the telephone operation was not going smoothly. Patrons were not paying their bills and income was lagging.

The following is a letter he wrote to Ana from Seattle, dated November 24, 1916. It is being quoted in full as he wrote it in pencil on lined note paper of the day. Jim did not have a high school education. The quotation is not edited.

Seattle, Nov 24, 1916
4026 Area (Aurora) Av

Dear Ana it is a long time since I wrote you a love letter So I gesso I better start one now but if I call you all the honey bunchers and sugar plumbs I suppose you wood say that Jim has yor crasey but I will put all that stuff down without writing it well we got excused till Tuesday at 10 o'clock the cort goes aful slow one case a day is all that they dispose of as yet there is 3 women on the Jurey one of them looks like Mrs. Ryan and one looks like Mrs. McGuir and the other one looks like Mrs Fred Kerry wife So watch out for slivers the Judg told them that he wood excuse them if they wished but they said thay can go to it there is a lot of criminal cases and god help the man thay get down on thay look like if they cood chew . the. The.the. horns of a ____brass monkey _____Well I was down to se Budress yesterday and had a long friendly talk with him and ha said for you to take all the bad bills (off) the book before the first of the year or in his own wards to charge them (off). And for you to print off on the tipe writer the raits (rates) that we charge for the Phones and Post one up in the office and send one to him and one to Bishop and to be sure that one is up in the office he says the law is getting very stricked and he wants to know when Bishop is coming up to Seattle he wants us to get together here and have a meating so you call him up and find out when he is coming and call up Dorothy and let her know so I can meat him and arange to get to gather I leave dorothy's about 9 oclock in the morning but don't know what time I will get back in the eving.

Viola is out getting her teath fixed today. She is talking of going to Silverdale but I don't know when she is going. So I gess that is about all for this time I hope you are getting along all wright is the --------making aney trouble for you Let Georgie keep the Box stall locked.

So good by for now

From your oald Manan with lots of ---------------(post script) you will hafto correct this for your self."

THE ENVELOPE IS ADDRESSED: **Mrs. JH Munn, Leland, Wash. Jefferson Co.** Post marked "Seattle, Wash Nov 25 10 PM 1916". It was mailed with a magenta two cent stamp with head of G. Washington in left side pose.

James H. Munn and his sister, Dorothy Munn Stewart. In Leland, 1917. (Munn Family collection).

155

X: LIFE AND DEATH AT THE MUNN HOMESTEAD

⌒

ONE-ARMED TOM

The Munn family farm was a welcoming place. As an example was "One-Armed Tom". Little is known about him except that he had lost an arm in a saw mill accident and that his name was Llewellyn Thomas, a Welsh name. Some called him Lew. He showed up one day asking for work and a place to stay. There were lots of odd jobs around the farm. He could chop wood, carry wood, carry water, clean the barn, put out hay, and lots of things one wouldn't expect of a man with one arm. He wore long sleeved shirts and would use the empty sleeve to wrap around split wood or the handle of a wheel barrow or tool handles.

He found places in the barn to sleep and family members would see that he got food. He decided that there was plenty of lumber about and he built for himself a one room house between the orchard and the saw mill. It was quite well built so that Sarah Albright had it fixed up some by adding an "L" kitchen and a fireplace. It became a cozy little house with an extra sleeping room in the attic.

Tom (or Lew) would come and go without warning. He had family in the Tacoma area. He went everywhere on foot. Sometimes he was careless as to where he would walk in a road. He was finally struck down and killed by a car at night.

LELAND POST OFFICE: PART ONE

Jim Munn's grand business ventures came sputtering down. He tried other farming possibilities in the course of the next few years. He bought a flock of sheep. Sheep take too much care in the wet weather of the Olympic Peninsula. Ana was glad when he sold them. He planted the garden to loganberries. Again, there was no market for berries. The unattended vines eventually overtook the entire garden lake front. Ana was left with a few cows, her poultry, garden and InterFarmers Telephone Company. Then, however, there is the story of the Leland U.S. Post Office to tell.

Robert E. Ryan, Sr. was the first post master. He chose the name "Leland" for the post office. Actually, he had submitted the name "Lealand" to honor the regions first woman homesteader, Laura E. Andrews, "LEA" Land. But since the early script for a capitol S and a capitol L were so similar and because there was already a "Sealand" post office, the name was shortened to Leland.

Robert Ryan lived on a farm that occupied all four corners of what is today the intersection of Highway 101 and Leland Valley Road East/ West. His house was on the hill on the S.W. corner, which is a part of the Kawamoto farm today. Robert Ryan was a strong suporter of public education and gave a part of his farm to provide for Leland School. Today the site is a county park.

The mail was delivered by horseback from Port Townsend via Discovery Bay. When PTSRR was built, the construction actually ended at the Ryan property for a time and Robert Ryan wuld begin his work when the train came with the mail.

The Munn Homestead, circa 1922. (Munn family collection).

The barn has not been modified. There is the lane leading to the houses at the foot of the hill where the Hector Munn family lived in early 20s. There is a car (19??) parked in front of the post office. The structure behind the post office is the cook house that would be enlarged to be Ana's house. At the end of the orchard is "One-Armed Tom's" house, also not enlarged. There is a huge garden in early summer stage. There are no sawmill or old barns. But the telephone shop and cross arm on the bridge to carry the telephone wires. George Nurnberg was experimenting with Marconi radio and had erected tall posts for his antennae. The hill side still shows the extent of the 1901 fire.

James H. Munn and Ana M. Munn, circa 1917. (Munn family collection)

ANA'S NEW JOB

Ryan died 25 March 1922. The postal duties were turned over to his son, R.E. Ryan, Jr. The younger Ryan did not have the skills needed to handle the responsibility and soon, in frustration, his wife gathered the materials and mail paraphernalia together and took them to Ana Munn's house and dumped them in the center of her parlor where the telephone switchboard was kept. "You do it, Mrs. Munn," she said. She turned and left.

That was as official as it was for a time. To be a postmaster was a natural for Ana Mae Munn. She had long standing experience with mail service as her mother Matilda had the Ackley, Kansas post office in her parlor. Also, the telephone office was already a semi-public room with people coming and going a good bit. Now they had a second reason to visit at the Munn home. Jim built a wall cabinet of "pigeon holes" for customer boxes and set it just inside the door.

Ana made formal application for Postmaster. The application was accepted as of 3 May 1922. Her relationship with the U.S. postal service lasted until 1 October 1941.The job was not in her plans and dreams. Without question, she enjoyed the position and since it came with a retirement plan, she had basic financial support the rest of her life.

ANA M. MUNN, THE NEWS WRITER

Ever since Ana's mother had written a weekly article in the Minneapolis *Messenger*, Ana had thought that one day she also would be a news writer. The Port Townsend *Leader* became an official newspaper of record and switched to weekly publication. News from the far corners of the county was solicited. Ana had her "ear" to the news, so to speak. She began writing the Leland Valley News for each Thursday's paper.

Her first article of "Leland Valley News" in the Port Townsend *Leader* was printed on 3 February 1921.Her own family was a source of much of her news. In fact, since Matilda Edwards' diary ended with her death, Ana's weekly reportage in the *Leader* becomes the data and time check for most of the events that turned about her and her family for the rest of her life. So when it seems significant, her articles will be quoted. In reading Ana's account of Leland Valley, there is a sense that the facts are told but not the "information".

An example is the following entry that refers to the previous story of the Post Office:

January 20, 1922: "Mrs. J. H. Munn has been appointed (Leland) postmaster to succeed Mr. R.E. Ryan."

March 31, 1922: "Robert Edger Ryan, County leader of Territorial Days, died in Sequim March 25, 1922-----In 1885 he received his appointment as Post Master at Leland and served 37 years at the post."

September 8, 1922: There was a reunion of the Edwards family. Surviving members were: Joel, and U. Grant Edwards of Port Townsend, Mrs. Ed Wegner (Dora) and Mrs. P.J. Hansen (Vila) of Seattle, Mrs. L.W. Hall (Louisa) of Union, Iowa and Mrs. J. H. Munn."

September 22, 1922: "George Munn left for Pullman, Washington to start school at Washington State College".

November 17, 1922: "George Nurnberg, champion Marconi of Leland, has installed a three step amplifying radio set in the office of InterFarmers Telephone Co. This set replaces the two step set in use during the summer."

SCHOOLS, WEDDINGS AND WORLD WAR I

By 1916 the children were "young people" entering their adult lives. Viola was 23, Hector was 21, Alice was 20, Sara was 19, Vangie was 17 and George was 15. All had gone to Leland School and then to Leland-Quilcene High School. That is, all except Viola.

Ana had determined that Viola was more musically inclined and decided to send her to Port Townsend to live with the Edwards families and attend Port Townsend High School. She was given piano lessons and other music classes at the high school. When she graduated, she went to live with Jim's sister, Dorothy (Munn) Stewart, in North Seattle. (Recall Jim's letter written while on Grand Jury duty.) There was supposed to be a piano there for her to use. The plan fell through. Instead she got a job as a sales clerk with Sears and Roebuck, downtown. The Stewart home near Woodland Park Zoo was served by a city trolley. It was a good experience for her. She did play the piano when she could. She would help with the Leland Sunday School and played the organ there. Like her mother, she was left handed. She played the piano with a strong bass clef emphasis.

Hector finished high school in 1913. He didn't go to college until 1915. In the 1916-17 school years at Washington State College he was joined by Alice, Sara, and Vangie. They rented a house near campus and batched together. Hector was taking ROTC when the Great War broke out. But he was able to stay in school until the year was completed. He signed up for the U.S. Army on 6 April 1917. Alice took classes to be a school teacher. Sarah and Vangie took the nursing program.

Hector entered the U.S. Army at Vancouver Barracks, Vancouver, Washington. He was sent with a detachment of recruits to Great Falls, Montana. There was a metal smelter at Great Falls that required a very tall smoke stack. At that time in the war there was fear there were German sympathizes in the country and that they might blow up the smoke stack. This would disrupt the production of the special metals produced by the mill. So Hector and the men with him were sent to guard the smelter and smoke stack. While at Great Falls, as is always common, there were social events sponsored by the citizens to entertain the troops. There he and Miss Pearl Marie Bond met. At the end of that assignment, he was sent to Camp Hancock, a part of Camp Gordon, Georgia, where he received basic training. Just as he was ready to go to Europe, the Armistice was signed, 11 November 1917. He was discharged without completing the full three year enlistment. He went back to WSU long enough to qualify as a mining engineer. He never finished a four year degree. He went back to Great Falls and married Pearl Bond. There was still homestead land available in Wyoming that was especially available to ex-soldiers. Hector and Pearl took out a claim in northeast Wyoming, south of Gillette and proved up the claim. Their first daughter was on the way and Pearl went back to Great Falls for the event. They never went back to live permanently on the homestead. The rest of that story is better told by the second daughter Mary Beth.

During World War I Fort Warden, a U.S. Army base, had been built at the edge of Port Townsend on the northeast edge facing Admiralty Inlet where shipping has to pass in and out of Puget Sound. The fort had guns poised to fire on enemy ships that might be passing by. Young ladies of the county were welcome guests at many social events in connection with the "Fort". Alice met George Nurnberg, a medical sergeant, at one of these events. Following the war, George Nurnberg decided to attend W.S.C. when Alice and her sisters were still attending. He took classes in electrical engineering. He and Alice were married and moved to Leland where they purchased the Macomber place (aka

Nicola place) at the northwest shore of Lake Leland. They then went together to Bellingham where Alice completed her elementary teacher's requirements at Western Washington Normal School. Returning to Leland, Alice became the teacher at Leland School. George Nurnberg took charge of the maintenance of InterFarmers Telephone Company and was able to make major improvements in the technical quality of the system. They had one son, Donald, (born 4 July 1918) who was Jim and Ana's first grandson. The marriage did not last and George left Alice to raise Donald alone. Donald had just finished high school when he was diagnosed with tuberculosis. He and Alice travelled about, even to Toronto, Canada, in search of a cure.

The treatment for tuberculosis in those days was isolation (to protect the spread), rest, good food and open air. In the summer of 1937 several of Donald's friends in the neighborhood built him a special log cabin at lake edge south of Ana's house. It was only one room about 15'X15' with a wide, covered porch that overlooked the lake. The porch had a special swinging couch where Donald could lay and view the south end of the lake. By the next January, Donald was sent to a sanitarium. Donald never recovered from the disease as a cure had not been developed yet. He died at a T.B. sanitarium in Elma, Washington. Alice died of a massive stroke soon after Donald died. She had given her life to his care and well-being.

There was a local Port Townsend young man who was employed at the Munn saw mill for a time. Leroy "Roy" Albright became a dental student at Oregon Dental College in Portland, Oregon. He and Sarah decided to get married. Jim treated Sarah special sometimes. He said that he had always wanted a daughter to have a real "Scottish" wedding and this would be his chance. He invited every Scotsman he knew. They with the local neighbors packed out the little community school/ church on the hill (near the county park today.) Following the exchange of vows, the wedding party was lead up the railroad track and across the bridge by bag pipers piping traditional Scottish marches. It must have been a grand procession. Jim had an outdoor platform set up between the log house and the lake. The pipes and drums played the highland jigs and flings for the folks who knew the dances.

Ana says in her memoirs: "We ordered gallons of ice cream. I killed and roasted 24 chickens, baked 24 cakes and any number of biscuits. I prepared all the food and a thousand other things."

Everyone had a great time. There has never been such a party in Leland before or since. Jim spared no expense. The wedding was on 5 June 1921. "Roy" Albright had more schooling to complete in Portland. Their daughter Lorraine was born there. Roy set up practice in Sequim upon earning his dentistry degree.

Jim was truly please with himself to have arranged the big wedding. In contrast, the event tried Ana's patience to the limit, even as she recalled the occasion forty years later. Ana mentions Viola's wedding to George Alden on 21 February 1921 briefly and Vangie's wedding to John Norvell is just noted in passing. Ana thought that her husband should have treated all his daughters with equal consideration.

Vangie met a red headed soldier, John A. Norvell, who was stationed at Fort Warden. After they married, they stayed in Leland until their son, "Jack" (John A. Norvell, Jr.) was born (3 December 1919). John Norvell had separated from the army by then and took his wife and child home to Chicago. Vangie was not accepted by her in-laws and the couple broke up. Vangie came back to live at Leland. She was pregnant with Mary Jane who was born 17 September 1922, also at Leland. After the divorce from John Norvell was final, Vangie married Lloyd Tooker on 25 September 1925. Lloyd Tooker was then a mechanic living at Discovery Bay/Maynard. Together they built the auto repair business into a trucking company, Tooker Auto Freight, with headquarters at Discovery Bay. Lloyd adopted Jack and Mary Jane. They also had a son, Lloyd Jr., born 3 March 1928, and daughter Dorothea, born 14 February 1930.

George Munn did not start college until 1922 when he was 21. He had stayed home to help with the telephone maintenance and operation.

He was often the only one home during the transitional years for the older brother and sisters. There is one story that he loved to tell about his relationship to his father.

Jim decided that he must modernize the telephone bill collection process by getting a car. One can only imagine the pain that Jim had because it meant giving up his horses and depending on others to get around. Yet it was time to modernize. Jim ordered the car from the Ford dealer in Port Townsend. When notified that the car had come to the shop, he sent George in on the train to pick it up and drive it home. Of course the car would be absolutely new to George as well. His father told him to stay in town until he had learned everything he could about the car, how to drive it, how to maintain it and as much as possible about how to repair it. There would not be a garage in Leland to do repairs. Then when he brought it home, he was to teach everyone else what he had learned.

George was certainly the one to whom to give the responsibility. He stayed several days learning all the mechanical parts, how they worked and what might go wrong with each one. The car had a crank-to-start engine. It had a magneto system that could get wet. He learned how to change a tire and patch an inner tube. He went out and drove all around town, learned how to back up, how to park, how to shift on hills, how to use the reverse to back up a hill as reverse had more power and how to keep the engine and body clean. These were skills he learned well. Ever after when George was through driving a vehicle for the day, he would lift the hood and wipe down the engine and check the water and oil and look for any possible damage that might have happen while he was driving. He had rags and a little whisk broom to dust out the insides. He always kept any vehicle in his charge, even the school buses, in tip-top shape in and out. Arguably, no one ever loved automobiles more. He taught all his siblings to drive. Jim and Ana never learned to drive, even though they kept a car about when the children were gone. It was good that they had the train to get to Quilcene or Port Townsend. There was usually a young person around who was willing and ready to drive, if need be.

James and Ana Munn with adult children. 1920. (Munn family collection).

THE CHICKENS COME HOME TO ROOST

The post WW I time at the Jim and Ana farm was a period of bonding among the grandchildren. Alice and George Nurnberg were living a half mile north on the lake while Alice taught school and her husband George was helping to up-grade the telephone technology.

Hector had tried his hand at mining operations in Montana following his proving-up his Wyoming homestead claim. While working at a silver mine in Neihart, Montana, he came down with the deadly "Spanish flu" that was the scourge of post war America. He was truly near death. He survived but was left very weak. He and Pearl decided to move back to Leland with their two little girls, Helen (born 9 February 1921) and MARY Elizabeth (BETH) (born 3 November 1922). He and Pearl set up house-keeping in two of the bunkhouses left from the saw mill days. When his health improved he learned of a new mining operation that was starting in the North Cascade Mountains near the town of Index, Washington. He hired on as a principle engineer. He left Pearl and the girls at Leland and made infrequent trips home for special occasions.

The Munn family of Leland. 1924. (Munn family collection) Alice and George Nurnberg (from left back), Jim Munn with Mary Beth, Hector, Vangie Norvell (Tooker) with Mary Jane, George. Front: Sarah Albright with Lorraine in front of Donald Nurnberg, Ana with Iris Alden, Viola Alden with Margie, Pearl Munn with Helen, Jack Norvell (Tooker).

Pearl and father-in-law Jim Munn made an immediate connection. Both loved horses. Pearl was nearly raised on horseback in Montana. She was an excellent "grip and squeeze" hand milker and shared milking chores. She did her share of the cooking. She was an avid gardener. She even was quick to learn the operation of the switchboard. Pearl fit in well with the Munn family businesses.

The summer of '24 Pearl took the girls to Sunset Mine and she and the girls became acquainted with Hector's work place. But she returned in the fall in time for the last months of "confinement" before their son James Hector was born 10 December 1924. By then Jim and Ana had six granddaughters and two grandsons. This grandson was the first "Munn" son and what's more was named for his grandfather in true Scottish tradition. Before long the two, Jim and Jimmy were nearly constant companions. Grandpa Jim was not feeling well. He was resting much of the time and played with his name sake grandson as a way of being useful.

THE FINAL YEARS OF JAMES MUNN

Jim began to fail as early as 1916 when he was on Grand Jury duty in Seattle. The period during and just after the cannery venture, he was even less strong. Ana reports that up until then he had excellent teeth. But then the gums of his left upper jaw became swollen and he lost a few teeth. Ana reports in the Port Townsend *Leader* that on 15 February 1924 that Jim spent a week in Seattle having eye treatment. Ana's public news report gives the facts but excludes the information. In her memoirs she adds that a "growth" was removed from his left sinuses and that the growth had extended into the tear-duct of his eye. Jim seemed to heal and get back some enthusiasm for life. Jim had the sense that there was to be more "growth" problem. He and Ana began to have differences of opinions about things.

So often the details that are most important are the ones that folk seem to ignore or forget. Ana was very busy with her new Post Office duties. There were a growing number of telephone customers. When Jim had written to Ana from Seattle during the jury duty, he writes to say that he had had a meeting with Mr. Buddress, the business agent for the phone company. There had been a serious problem with bill collection and the loss on the books was dragging the bottom line down. Buddress told Ana (via Jim) to write the loss off. The company could not keep up with needs of the community if sufficient resources were missing. Public service businesses are expected to stay in operation, regardless of the financial situation.

Whatever was going on with the Munn finances at the time is not certain. But Jim and Ana took out a $3500 loan in 1918 as a mortgage on their 200 acres. Why the mortgage at this time? They had four children in college. There may have been medical costs connected with Jim's first surgery. It could have been money to buy the shingle mill that strangely burnt down. Or it could have been money to buy the cannery equipment. They may have needed to put money into telephone equipment and salaries of linemen. By the time of the Albright wedding, Ana was well aware of the loan not being up-to-date. Throwing such a grand party may have been seemed to Ana as an unaffordable waste. Such pressures took their toll on their relationship.

ANOTHER TRIP TO PRINCE EDWARD ISLAND(?)

There is an event during this time that has recently come to light in a strange way. The current living cousins were told of this project to write the story of James and Ana and asked if there were tales or pictures they knew of that could be included in the story. Well, my cousin Judy Munn had a full box of documents and pictures that her father George had put together in his later life. This resource has been invaluable to this writing project. Hopefully the most important data has been included.

Then Margie Alden sent some pictures from her family's collection. Among the pictures was a faint little picture that her father George had taken with a little box camera. It is a picture of grandpa Jim seated in their home in Lewiston. Margie, born 22 February 1921, is about 3 years old and is on one knee. Iris, born 8 December 1922, is nearly 2 years old. She is standing in front between her grandpa's knees. Margie said that the picture was taken when her grandfather was returning from a trip to the eastern Canada! She actually says he was returning from "Newfoundland". Certainly, if Jim had been in eastern Canada, he would have gone to Prince Edward Island! Then on the return trip, he made a "last" visit to Viola and the two grand-daughters who were not at Leland. As added confirmation, Margie Alden remembers that her Grandpa Jim had brought a big box of Hershey candy bars that he had purchased in Pennsylvania at a train stop.

Ana's article in the Port Townsend *Leader* for October 3, 1924 reads: "J. H. Munn returned Monday from a two week trip to Oregon, Idaho and Eastern Washington." If he had gone to Prince Edwards Island as Margie Alden must have meant, why didn't Ana say so? As said before, Ana was good at reporting the facts but not the information. The picture of the Alden girls fits the time frame.

It has been assumed all along that following James H. Munn's departure from the family Belle River farm that he never returned. Then the research revealed that he had returned in 1891 and was recorded on Canadian census to reside at the Belle River Old Farm. It was logical that that did happen because he needed to deed his inheritance to his brother John Daniel. He probably set up the grave marker for Maggie at the same time.

Grandfather Jim Munn with Iris and Margie Alden, September 1924.
(Margie Alden collection).

Now it seems that he also may have gone to P.E.I. in late September 1924, just two years before his death. We know that Jim wrote a letter to his Aunt Ann Munn in P.E.I. on 18 November 1907. She was living with John Daniel Munn at the time. He must have learned that she was ill as she died 18 December 1907. The letter was in possession of Edgar Munn, whose father was John Daniel Munn. John Daniel lived until 1945. It would have been to visit his brother John Daniel that James Hector went to P.E.I. as a very sick man. Other than Margie Alden's Hershey bar memory, there is no other evidence that he made the trip that far.

The reality of Jim's poor health now became obvious. He became weaker and weaker. He developed a partial obstruction of his throat.

He had good teeth only on one side. He was eating the food Ana had been eating all her life: milk, bread, smashed vegetables, meat broths, and, of course, ice cream and cottage cheese.

Finally, he had a neighbor lad drive him to Port Townsend to see a doctor. He couldn't face the idea of going to the hospital for examination and tests and returned home without much treatment. He finally agreed to be taken to St. Luke's Hospital in Seattle. (St. Luke's Hospital was owned by the Lutheran Church. The name was later changed to Virginia Mason Hospital, as it is today.)

Son George was in his final months of college at WSU. He had delayed his schooling to help with the telephone business for 2-3 years after finishing high school. He had come home in April 1926 to take his father to the hospital. Then he really had to get back to school to finish off the work to graduate.

Jim Munn never came home again.

A feeding tube was placed through an incision into his esophagus through which broth and water was fed to keep him alive. The cancerous growth had completely closed off his upper esophagus. He begged for water just to keep his mouth moist. He wasted away to 75 pounds.

Jim was clear of mind to the very end. He understood that his family was extremely busy. Ana was busy with the telephone and post office. Ana would call daily from Leland using her company's long distance line. He had visited Viola and her family in Idaho. Alice was teaching at Leland School. Vangie and Lloyd also had a thriving business to run. Hector was at Sunset Mine and in charge of the engineering. It was his sister Dorothy Stewart and daughter Sarah that came daily to visit. Kaichi K. Kawamoto, perhaps Jim's best friend had come to visit him as well and was present when he died.

Ana went to Seattle a few days before the end. Jim begged to be taken home. The medical people said he would not survive the trip and were probably right. Ana consented to one more surgery before she left. She received a call in the middle of the night, 25 May 1926 that her husband Jim had passed away. James Hector Munn was 61, two months short of reaching 62.

Sarah was with him at the time of his death. She said that **"Father had audibly prayed for each member of his family by name. Then he left."**

Ana Mae went back to Seattle the next day only to find his body was at the undertakers. His son Hector came down from Index to arrange for the body to go to Leland. The autopsy showed cancerous growth that had started in his jaw had spread throughout his body cavity as well as blocking his esophagus. Even today, all medicine can do in such cases is delay death with drugs and to make a person pain free but mentally dull.

The Grange organization took charge of the memorial service and the Presbyterian minister, Rev. Link, gave the message. James Hector Munn is buried in Quilcene Forester Cemetery. All nine of his little grand children were at the ceremonies as well as his children, except George. George had already said his goodbyes and had returned to Pullman to finish senior examinations. His graduation ceremony was on the same day as his father's funeral. George had had quality time with his father when he took him to Seattle to St. Luke's Hospital.

A TRAGIC POSTSCRIPT

There is one more event that must be included at this point. The Munn farm, originally the Nichols homestead, was at the edge of Lake Leland. The Munn family has a great fondness for the lake and the joys it brought while growing up. But little feet need a lot of watching.

Here is an account of the tragedy as reported by grandmother Ana in the Port Townsend *Leader* for July 2, 1926.

"The eighteen month old son of Mr. and Mrs. Hector Munn was accidentally drowned in Lake Leland Friday Eve, June 25, at about 6 o'clock. The mother was preparing the evening meal and the baby passed the kitchen window, stopped and patted his hands on the window and then waved good-bye to his mother, started in the direction of the barn, but evidently retraced his steps at once and went in the direction of the lake. After a lapse of about 10 minutes, his mother went to call him, but not finding him at the barn nor in the yard, went to the lake where he found him face downward in the shallow water where he had evidently stumbled and fallen and was unable to get up. Medical aid was instantly summoned, but to no avail. The little life could not be returned. Funeral services were held at the residence of Mrs. J.H. Munn Sunday afternoon, conducted by Rev. Geo. Link, and internment was made in Foresters cemetery at Quilcene. Little Jimmie sleeps beside his grandfather, who passed away just one month before. The parents are prostrated with grief over the loss of this baby boy, and the entire Munn family mourns the loss of their beloved little one."

For the record it might be added that once again, Grandma Ana reported the facts necessary for public knowledge but not the information. The story will be left as reported.

Hector was on the job at Sunset Mine when he received the news of the event at Leland. He drove home as quickly as possible. Following the funeral he took his wife Pearl and two little daughters back to Sunset Mine camp where the girls were the only children in the mining camp. The little family needed to be far away from the double tragedy of the spring of 1926.

XI: ANA MAE EDWARDS MUNN: ALONE

WHAT TO DO NOW? REORGANIZE!

Jim was nearly sixty-two years old when he died. Ana was only fifty-four years old and healthy. Who knows what a businessman like Jim Munn could have accomplished had he lived? He was the main motivator to start the regional phone company. He had a successful saw mill as long as the timber and equipment held out. He built a marvelous barn. He built a number of houses and barns for other folk. He had built his own house on the hill only to have it burn down. He built the Skimming Station/Leland Post Office, the first building in the valley using sawed lumber. But he never got around to building a family home for his wife.

The "Nichols" squared-log house had served the family well. Ana knew that she needed to have the post office and the telephone switchboard in a more public setting. But how could she accomplish that? Her oldest son had taken his sorrowing family to the foot hills of the North Cascade Mountains. Her daughters were busy with their own families. George had just graduated with his forestry degree, ROTC commission and a teacher's credential from WSC. He was ready to start his career. His mother prevailed on George to give her one year in which to restructure her situation.

He started by remodeling the empty skimming station/creamery. He put on a new shingle roof and a coat of white paint. Then he moved the telephone lines and switchboard to the building. He also moved in the tables, a roll-top desk and pigeon-holed mail box cabinet. He redecorated the creamery testing room into a bedroom so that Ana could sleep within earshot of the switchboard in order to respond to night calls. The building adjustment was excellent in size and location for the "Office".

Now the post office had a real, public waiting room with a warm wood stove. The Post Office porch was still the exchange depot for farmers to bring their cream two days a week to be picked up by Glendale Dairy. The building became the center of business and social contacts for Leland. It was much more accommodating than the ancient Nichols homestead house. The log building was eventually removed after George had rebuilt the "cook house" into a residence.

The cook house was located behind or south of the former creamery. It was a simple two-room rectangular building. The dining room was on the front and a small kitchen was across the back with a porch with steps leading down to the lake front. George added a "lean-to" on both sides. On the side toward the post office was an unheated alley/hall way that was a wood shed to store wood for the post office and the new house. Through the wood shed there was a door into a pantry with cupboards and shelving. There was a door into the kitchen and a door into a plumbed bathroom with hot and cold water. The bathroom had a flush toilet and wash sink. There was a cast iron tub with claw feet. It was all very modern for Leland of that day.

The lean-to on the south side had a bedroom in the center that opened into a sitting room extension to the dining room. Part of the old dining room wall was removed making an L-shaped living/dining room. There was a big black dining room table with expansion leaves. It was usually set back against the corner walls. The bedroom door was around a half-wall divider. This was the front bedroom. It was small with room for a double bed in the left corner, a dressing table near the window and a single closet. There was only room for a chair at the dressing table.

Remodeled house and Post Office, circa 1930. (George Munn collection).

To get to the back bedroom it was necessary to go though the kitchen door out to the porch and turn right. The bed room had about the same space as the front bedroom. It had room for one double bed, a dresser, a closet and two chairs. There was no stove or connection to the heated kitchen. In the winter, or most of the year, the procedure was to take a hot water bottle or a heated "sad-iron" to bed. Unfortunately, the iron would get cold before too long and be icy cold by morning. The bathroom was unheated as well. By having a roaring fire in the kitchen cook stove and opening the door to the pantry and then into the bathroom, the chill could be removed. Fortunately, there was electricity in the new house and there was a radiant space heater to dry by after bathing.

At some point in time a gravity water system had been brought in. George may have installed it or Jim may have set it up to provide water to the creamery and cook house. The water source for the system was in the western creek canyon, the creek that came down past the Nichols' barns and the homestead house. The ¾" pipe came from a feed box set at the side of the creek up into the creek canyon. The water line followed the creek down to a junction box on the south side of Arcadia Road. From the junction box a line went north to the homestead house, west toward the saw mill site and east toward the lake and into the house. The plumbed bathroom had a septic box up on the bank of the lake. It drained directly into the lake south of the bridge. The swimming "hole" was on the north side of the bridge. It was forbidden to swim on the south side of the bridge. The facts of sanitation were known, but folk didn't take them too seriously. George lived in the house he made for his mother until he could build his own house across Arcadia Road from the post office. His mother gave him the triangle of land from a few yards beyond the creek to the lake. The transfer was for a wedding present. Actually, he had earned it by giving his mother a year or more of work to reorganize her business and living situation. The deed to George's property on what he liked to call his homestead is dated 17May 1930. George married Hulda Marie Knutsen on 12 July 1929.

Ana Mae Munn with grand children. Mary Beth, Hector Jr., Bob, Helen Munn. 1931. Post Office in background. (George Munn Collection).

LELAND POST OFFICE, PART II: ROAD TO CLOSURE

With the post office and the switchboard in their new home and Ana in her new quarters in the room behind, she was much more in charge of the situation. By then the mail was brought by car or truck from Port Townsend. The mail carrier contractor would bid for the route, then Route 2, Port Townsend. About every two years or so a fellow would think he could under bid the current mailman and there could be a change. The route went through Discovery Bay and serviced the individual rural route boxes along the way.

At about 45 minutes to an hour before the mailman would arrive, folks would begin to gather about the fire at the Post Office. The time waiting was well spent with stories of the day past and news of plans for the days ahead. Ana carried subscriptions to newspapers and monthly magazines and had a collection of bound books. The patrons would chat or sit and read while they waited or even stay after the mail came to finish reading a magazine article. Calls would come in on the switchboard as well. Sometimes there would be fresh gossip from the callers, yet private news would never be shared.

When the mailman arrived the folks gathered would be enthralled by the flurry of activity. The first sack or box contained letters and packages picked up along the route. Those went directly to the stamping desk where Ana would arrange the letters so that she could make the postal hand stamp with rapid efficiency. The hand stamp would fly back and forth from the ink pad to the envelope so that each letter had a freshly inked mark giving the date and the name of the office.

Meanwhile, the mailman would bring the sack of mail for the Leland customers and would arrange the letters destined for customers between Leland and Quilcene. He'd take those out to the seat of the truck beside him. By then Ana would have the outgoing mail ready in a mail sack. There was a quiet moment when money and stamps were carefully counted and exchanged. In a matter of 15 to 20 minutes, the mailman waved good bye and was off. It was like a daily visit from

Santa. There was seldom time to gossip as there was a strict schedule to keep. In those days the mailman would go from Quilcene on to Brinnon where the carrier from Shelton would be met to exchange mail. Neither carrier wanted to be the late one. The Route 2 carrier would return to Quilcene where the office had more time to prepare the outgoing mail. The route would go on to Dabob that had a local office similar to Leland's and then to Chimacum and points north.

Back at the Leland Post Office, those customers who had been patiently waiting would get their mail picked out. The rest of the people served would have their mail sorted into the pigeon holes and Ana would return to her chair by the switchboard. The rest of the day would only have occasional folk drop by and then there would be more time to chat. Ana loved the opportunity to hear the news first hand.

Ana's entire day was spent in the office. When someone was living in the house, which was most of the time, her food would be brought in to her. Her only escape was that she had a herd of milk cows that she took care of as well as the office duties. At 4:00 AM she would handle the dairy chores herself before the Office opened. But at 2:30 in the afternoon she would have someone spell her off at the switchboard and post office. The post office part closed at 5 PM. When the milking was done, she'd be back at her post. The telephone business was sold in 1934, more on that later, and she only needed help in the afternoon.

Ana Mae Munn with grandchildren, circa 1931. Lake side porch of the Leland Post Office and telephone exchange. (Note telephone cables. The switchboard was just inside the window.) (George Munn collection).

When Hector's sons were old enough, Robert (Bob), would help grandma Ana with the barn chores after school. "Young Heck" was given the job of "watching" the post office after school from whenever the school bus came to 5 PM. He would have been 9 to 12 at the time. The mail boxes were behind a wall with a pass through window. When patrons would come, he could hand the mail through the window to them.

There was a radio in the post office and it was just the time to listen to the kid programs: Jack Armstrong, Green Hornet, Little Orphan Annie, Jigs and Maggie and Ma Perkins were some. It was not wasted time. For a lad to have a job with pay at age 9 would be quite unusual. Most of the income was spent on buying stamps for his world stamp collection or he would detour by the local grocery store, the Limit, for a double scoop ice cream cone for the walk home.

Ana Mae Munn was 70 years old when she retired on 1 October 1941. She was granted an annuity of $506.16 a month "to continue during life, unless otherwise terminated as provided by law." She was able to transfer the job of postmaster to her daughter Viola Alden. Young Hector was cut from the post office job only to take the barn job from his brother who was busy with high school athletics and was glad to be free from the daily milking chore.

Viola Alden held the postal job until 31 May 1959 when the post office was closed. Actually the Postal Service had wanted to close the office earlier in the year, but since Viola was so near retirement age, she was allowed to continue until she fully qualified with a Social Security pension. The pensions were very significant for both Ana and Viola for their old age. Air mail postage was 7 cents the year the Leland Post Office closed.

The post office building did not have significant use following the closure of the service route. With the loss of the postmark, the community also lost its identity. The rural routes were reorganized soon after that and mail patrons south of State Route 104 from just north of Crocker Lake were served by mail carriers route out of Quilcene. The postal service must always improve.

Viola Alden on closing day of Leland Post Office, 30 September1959.
(George Munn Collection).

INTERFARMERS TELEPHONE COMPANY, PART II: ANOTHER WRAP-UP

Jim Munn was the inspiration for InterFarmers Telephone Company, with Bill Bishop of Chimacum and Mr. Buddress, the legal and financial consultant. The company was incorporated with 100 Preferred Stock. Jim and Ana were majority stock-holders. They owned no less than 51, but may have had more originally.

Jim had many helpers to set-up the poles, wires and phone equipment. K. K. Kawamoto, George Nurnberg, technicians for some major line extensions and many of the young men of Leland and Quilcene.

Roscoe Thomas lived on the east side of Lake Leland just across the bridge with his wife Martha and children Leroy and Doriene. Roscoe was the son of George Thomas, so had lived in Leland most of his life. The Thomas families were all great friends of Hector and Pearl and their children. Roscoe was a dependable worker and soon became indispensible. Ana took care of the daily operation of the switchboard, billing and accounting. Her daughters and daughter-in-law Pearl helped with the switchboard. Jim kept his horses and a buggy dedicated to bill collection. Then in 1913 he purchased a Model T Ford to use for the collecting. Neither he nor Ana ever drove it, but the young women of the household took on that task.

Sunset mine folded in 1932-3 and son Hector was out of work. It seemed logical that he should come home and take over the lineman operation. By then Roscoe Thomas had become very well trained in the lineman's work and yet he was displaced. This was unfortunate as his wife Martha and children Leroy and Doriene depended on the job. Jobs of this caliber were scarce in Jefferson County during the Depression. Not long after starting on the job, Hector found that he was not physically adept to the rigors of pole climbing as he was heavier than the ideal lineman. After falling twice from a considerable height and undergoing slow recoveries, he vowed not to put on the climbing spikes again. Roscoe Thomas got his job back as he was very skillful at all phases of the lineman's work and had the physic necessary to climb poles safely.

The depression was taking its toll in other ways. Patrons were not paying the meager phone bills. Phone company income was down and ability to service the lines suffered. Since the start-up of the system nearly thirty years before, there had been much growth of the trees along the lines and winter storm damage kept service difficult to maintain. Ana was having a tough time keeping financially solvent. To make matters worse, the other major owner, William (Bill) Bishop, died. His sons, William Jr. and Steven, thought they should be getting more income from their part ownership in the company. They were also receiving complaints about the service.

Ana's back was against the wall.

On January 3, 1934 Steven H. Bishop called for a shareholders meeting. He claimed mismanagement and took over the operation. Ana had to sign over (i.e. "sold") shares of stock to cover the accrued losses and Roscoe Thomas's back pay. Mr. and Mrs. Mack Johnson were hired by the Mr. Bishop's sons. The switchboard was moved to a house across the lake to a house owned by George Thomas and Mrs. Johnson took over the inside operation and Mr. Johnson took over the line work. This put Roscoe Thomas out of work again. The Johnsons soon found out that operating the telephone business was not easy and they backed out of the contract.

Steven Bishop rehired Roscoe and Martha to manage the company. The equipment was moved to the main street of Quilcene across from Quilcene School. Actually, Ana Mae Munn was very relieved. Most certainly the phone company had been her life and livelihood, but she was aware of changing times and the need to upgrade the technology. A new switchboard had been purchased when she had moved from the log cabin. But the system was still a hand crank system. Business patrons were requiring better long distance connections. The repair of the lines with the need for replacing many poles was getting beyond her ability to finance.

Roscoe and Martha made a rare team. There were just 60 patrons when they took over the business. Martha had a soft but clear, recognizable voice. The call to "Central" changed from Ana's "LEE-land" to Martha's "Quilcene", which she said with a lilt that emphasized "QUIL-cene". Occasionally Roscoe would call on the Bishop family members to help in emergency, but they soon grew tired of the work and just left it all to Roscoe to organize helpers. Again, many young men of Quilcene had a first job setting poles or cutting brush. Many a young high school girl felt privileged to take a shift on the switchboard.

Year's later Roscoe Thomas was interviewed for his oral life story by a Jefferson County historian. This is his comment about the change over:

> **"I didn't take over until July 10, 1934. ......I put in a phone the first day that I went to work. That made sixty (patrons). ......The (phone service cost) two and a half (dollars) a month. We got sixty dollars a month, our house and lights. That's all. And (we had) the use of the company car. There was no truck."** (Roscoe Thomas, Jefferson County Historical Society, page 182-3.)

Roscoe said a patron told him that the management had been stealing money from the company and that was why the service was so bad. He responded, **"How much do you think 'they' could steal out of sixty telephones at two-and-a-half a month and a little out of long-distance calls, when they had to hire an operator, a lineman, run a truck, buy supplies, keep everything in repair? What was there left to steal?"** (Op. cit. page 184)

A young attorney from upstate New York moved to Quilcene in the early 40's. Arthur Garrett was looking for a business to buy and found that the Bishop family was ready to sell. Mr. Garrett became the majority stock-holder in August 1944. Roscoe and Martha had a new boss. Roscoe knew the technology and Arthur knew business. They made a good team. However, Martha eventually lost her job to the Garrett ladies. Mr. Garrett had three daughters, his wife, and his mother, all of whom took turns at the switchboard. Yet they still often hired high school girls to fill in on the switchboard.

Arthur Garrett made changes slowly and with planning. Before long he was able to bring in dial phones to the system and made the up-grades that made the system compatible with other systems so that long-distance service worked properly. Such changes cost money and he recapitalized by offering more stocks. The effect was to make the original preferred stock less and less valuable. For a time the heirs to the Munn stock received free phone service as stock dividend. Eventually the preferred stock was of such little value that all holders were bought out to close the books on that original company.

As the years went on Arthur Garrett expanded the company to include water systems, phone and electrical service in Southeast Alaska. The phone service to south Jefferson County was split off and sold. The utility has gone through a number of names. Most recently the community is served by Century Link.

JIM AND ANA AS COMMUNITY LEADERS

The Leland School was in place before Ana and Jim arrived on the scene. First Ana Mae Edwards was a teacher there. Then as the children became school aged and attended the school, Jim was a school director for most of his life. When Leland-Quilcene Union High School was organized, Jim Munn was a school director there as well. Then as Jim's health began to weigh in on him, Ana Mae ran for the director's position and served for many years. Perhaps when her son George became teacher and then superintendent of the high school, it was better that she not continue on the school board. She was a faithful in attending public school board sessions. Ana felt she was a good judge of quality teaching and was very out-spoken on school matters, too out spoken for some people.

The first modern school at Quilcene was a poured concrete building. It had three classrooms downstairs which housed most of the grade school. There were three classrooms upstairs that housed the upper grades and high school. One of Ana's major projects was the authorization of the construction of a school gymnasium and public meeting hall to the south of the main classroom building. That gymnasium had bleachers on one side, a regulation basketball court and a stage with curtains opposite the bleachers. At the end opposite the entrance was a kitchen. When the federal hot lunch program was started, the kitchen was expanded and the dining area was underneath the bleachers. This building served many functions on into 1944. It was all wooden and had become a fire hazard. The sports program needed modern showers for boys and girls, so was replaced by a modern, spacious gymnasium on the same spot. The new structure had a separate assembly hall with a stage, kitchen.

George Munn took a teaching position at Quilcene High School in about 1928. He drove the "Leland" bus and then became Superintendent as well. In 1933 he drew up plans for a new high school building. It was also a poured concrete structure and still stands. The high school classes started in the new building in 1934. Then the old school was just for the grade school. Since there were two grades to a room, only the first two grades were on the lower floor and six grades were on the top floor.

Leland School was closed following the 1936-37 school year. Whereas the high school students had been bused to Quilcene for several years, from 1937 on, all the children from Crocker Lake south were bused to Quilcene. Even then there were not many children in the school. Quilcene has never been a large program.

POLITICS AND RELIGION

The Edwards family grew up with strong Republican leanings. Thad Smith, G.W. Edwards' son-in-law was an active speaker for political events and was never shy to make his Republican ideas known. Matilda Edwards noted in her diary how each national election went. She was most pleased when women were given the vote while she could still cast a ballot. Her diary entry is:

November 5, 1912, Tuesday: "Cool and calm. I cast my first vote for a President." (Democratic President Wilson was elected. She doesn't actually say if he was her choice or not. Also, though Amendment 19 was made law 18 August 1920, the state of Washington gave women the vote in time for this 1912 election.)

If Jim and Ana had political leanings, they would have been Republican as well. At least Ana seemed to vote for Republicans. She respected President Roosevelt for his efforts during the Depression and WWII. She had little time for President Truman. She found his language not becoming for a president.

Jim was a Granger. Grange was a poor farmer's organization with a very open, public program. In contrast, George Thomas, his across the lake neighbor, was an active Democrat and a Mason. Jim was against secret societies. The two neighbors respected each other. George was more of a mechanic who had several interesting machines about his farm. When George Thomas died, the Masons conducted his funeral. The Grange handled Jim's funeral.

As recounted in the story of Ana's upbringing, G.W. and Matilda Edwards were active supporters of organized church and read the Bible to their children and gave table grace at meals. Ana had several religious experiences when she was troubled or sick and she credits prayer and faith to have brought good solutions to problems. So she had developed a firm moral basis for her life decisions. Her spoken language was clean and curse free as would be the case for most women of her day. Ana took responsibility for Sunday school at Leland when called on. As her parents had done, Ana hosted all ministers who were able to come to minister at the Leland church.

Jim Munn's family background in Prince Edward Island had been Scottish Presbyterian. His grandfather is listed on the church organization roll for the grand Church of Scotland building that still stands at Pinette, PEI. But Jim's childhood was brief. Since his parents died while he was quite young, he likely had little formal education or religious instruction. When he reached Vancouver, B. C., he attached himself to the Salvation Army and purchased a S.A. uniform. He had

S.A. friends in Everett and in Port Townsend. Ana reports the event when Jim and his friends had prayed loudly for her recovery from the flu and they were successful. She survived.

(LELAND-QUILCENE FRIENDS CHURCH: A VIGNETTE)

The nearest neighbor on Leland Hill was Dan Stutler. He and his family came from Ohio and had a Quaker up-bringing. He and his family were regular supporters of the Leland church. If a minister did not arrive for a service, Dan Stutler would share his testimony and faith.

In researching the history of the Quilcene Friends Church that was active from 1908 to 1964, it was discovered that Ana was a charter member of the church. That there ever was an organized Friends Church in Quilcene is a bit of an odd chain of events. In Quilcene there was a family named Sewell who had Quaker background. Whenever Quaker pastors came to Quilcene, they would also speak at Leland. One of these Friends/Quakers was named George W. Adams. He decided that Leland/ Quilcene was an appropriate location to start a "meeting", as Friends call their church as well as their worship service. He brought a request from the "Leland-Quilcene" Friends Church to Portland (Oregon) Friends Meeting for them to sponsor a request to starting the church. Then the Portland Meeting carried the petition to Oregon Yearly Meeting of Friends that was meeting in Newberg, Oregon. The Leland-Quilcene Meeting was granted standing. The "Minute" was "approved", (the Quaker way of agreement to the petition). The following "Minute" is recorded in the Minutes of Newberg Quarterly Meeting:

"On the fifth day ninth month 1908 the first meeting of the Leland-Quilcene Monthly meeting was held at the Leland school house." "Ana M. Munn, Recording Clerk". This was reported by George W. Adams.

Not only was Ana M. Munn shown as a charter member, but she is actually the one who officially recorded the event.

On the ninth day first month 1909, Pastor Adams reported to the Leland-Quilcene Meeting that the services of Samuel and Effie Taylor from Boise Friends Church had been secured. Again the Minutes show "A. M. Munn, Recording Clerk." The record of membership as charter members of Leland-Quilcene Friends Church lists Ana M. Munn along with Viola, Alice, Sarah, Evangeline and George Munn. Notably, James H. Munn and Hector J. Munn, Sr. were not listed as members. The Meeting (church) made immediate progress. The plan was that a worship service would be held on alternate Sundays in Quilcene and Leland and that the monthly business meetings would also rotate location between Leland and Quilcene.

W.J. Worthington, the prominent business man of Quilcene, donated land for a church building and parsonage in Quilcene. The members wasted no time in constructing both buildings. Early pastors kept up the alternating worship pattern. Before long it became more convenient to have all the morning worships services in Quilcene and to have a "Christian Endeavor" every Sunday afternoon at Leland. In case one would wonder, the Leland school building was owned by the community and no one questioned its use as a house of worship. In actuality, the community very much wanted the building to be used in any way possible. It had always been that way.

All was not well with the Munn/Friends Church connection. Ana Munn (and family) withdrew membership as reported just three years later in the November 4, 1911 Minutes. It was reported that the family would be joining a church (Methodist?) in Port Townsend. Strangely, the minutes of 13 May 1916 show that both the Sewell and Munn families withdrew membership. This time it was final as there is no later mention of Ana M. Munn in the minutes.

Then in the Oregon Yearly Meeting statistics for 1916, there are 24 members of Christian Endeavor at Leland and 20 at Quilcene. So an informal connection of Leland "church" and the Friends Church continued at least to 1916.

It is purely speculation as to why Ana and family had made such a grand start and then stopped. The years between 1906 and 1910 was when the Munn family was most occupied with the new business start ups. This was also the time the larger Friends Church was receiving enormous pressure from the Temperance Committee of the church. There were quite strident Christian Temperance promoters crisscrossing Oregon, Washington and Idaho. Additionally, one of the tenants of the Quaker Church is that women are given equality in conducting services. There was a very "evangelistic" woman Friends pastor in Seattle that had a disagreement with the larger church connection and as a ploy had "transferred" the membership of her Seattle church to Quilcene Friends Church so they could be geographically in Oregon Yearly Meeting. Otherwise they would be Outposts of Indiana Yearly Meeting. It all makes little sense today. Somewhere in this turmoil of religious and political events Ana had found more peace away from the Quakers. She never did join the Methodist Church in Port Townsend as far as is known.

The Quilcene Presbyterian Church had also been started about that time as the Friends Church. It would have been more realistic for the Munns to have been Presbyterians. In fact Rev. George Link, who was pastor of the Quilcene Presbyterian Church in the early '20s, held meetings at the Leland school/church and organized a Sunday school. From that connection, no doubt, Jim Munn's memorial service was held at the Quilcene Presbyterian Church and Ana made regular contribution to the Presbyterian Church in her later years.

None of Jim and Ana's children or grand children ever joined the Presbyterian Church. However, starting in1949, Hector Jr. became a member of the Friends Church and has been a Friend ever since. Hence he has had access to church records for this little essay.

ANA'S DOCTRINAL VIEWS

Ana often discussed religion with grandson Hector while they were busy with milking chores. The following observations can be made. Ana Munn was neither hot nor cold on religious matters. She was not a regular Bible reader, but had good Bible knowledge, perhaps gained from her parents. She never claimed to have been "born again" in the traditional sense. She had an intellectual Christian belief and strong moral principles. She accepted the Old Testament and Jewish History "intellectually" as well. She described her doctrinal belief as "dispensational". This is an older religious term that places biblical accounts as true for the time and people for whom they were written. She accepted the "Dispensation of Christ" but not the "Dispensation of Paul". Thus she agreed with the New Testament Gospels but was not committed to Old Testament except as a historical document. She had not changed her attitude about the Catholic Church and the Pope after her year of indoctrination experience at the request of her catholic suitor in Minneapolis.

Here is an anecdote told by Bernice (Leavitt) Jackson. The Leavitt family came to the area in the early '30's and lived on the Palm's Place, a farm in what is now part of the Ripley Creek Additions on the hill west of Lake Leland. Like everyone else in the mid thirties, they were poor. They seemed even worse off as members of the family are of small stature. Bernice and her siblings seemed undernourished as little children. One time, about 1937, as the children were walking home past the Munn ranch to go on up Leland Hill, Ana Munn met them and simply said, "You may have one of my heifers if you can lead her home." Of course the children immediately agreed to the offer. They were successful in getting the young cow home. Soon, the cow had its first calf. There was enough milk for the calf and for the children to have a daily glass or two of milk. They certainly had a supply of calcium and Vitamin D for their little bones. All grew to be fine people and raise fine families of their own. Bernice tells this story whenever she hears about Ana Munn. "Mrs. Munn was a Christian by anybody's definition," is how Bernice ends the story.

THE GOOD YEARS LEADING UP TO THE 1929 CRASH

As mentioned, George had moved Ana Mae out of the homestead house into the Post Office along with the post office furniture and the telephone switchboard. She had a nice bedroom in back of the post office so as to be close to the switchboard at night. George had then fixed up the former cookhouse that had served the saw mill workers. He lived there while he removed the homestead house. That log house had served the family well for about twenty-six years.

George was then well employed at Leland-Quilcene High School. Miss Hulda Marie Knutsen was a young teacher at the Uncas School and their common profession brought them together. They were married in 1929. As a wedding present, Ana gave them the triangle of property where the homestead house had stood. There George built a fine house with a brick fireplace and windowed dining room that looked out over the lake. In Ana's mind, however, she gave him the property as payment for the work he had done for her to get the house and post office set up.

Roy Albright had set up dental practice in Sequim. The time came for a new child for Hector and Pearl. Pearl and her two girls came from Sunset Mine camp where they were living and stayed with Roy and Sarah until a son, Robert Neil, was born in the Sequim hospital on 26 May 1927. The visit was brief as that fall big sister Helen needed to start school. A house was rented in the town of Index so they could move from the mining camp and be near Index elementary school. In recalling this event, Mary Beth bemoans the fact that Helen was an old 6 year old and she was still 5 years old and they started the first grade together. Helen blossomed and Mary Beth wilted.

Vangie and Lloyd Tooker were married on 25 September 1925 with Rev. Link officiating. Lloyd had an auto repair business in Maynard/Discovery Bay. They soon had additions to their family. Lloyd Jr. was born 3 March 1928 and Dorothea was born 14 February 1930. Lloyd Tooker officially adopted Jack and Mary Jane. He built a nice house at the edge of U.S. Highway 101 where Highway 20 begins. He and Vangie started a trucking business centered at that location. It was a very successful business during WW II when there was military construction on the Pacific Coast of the Olympic Peninsula.

George and Viola Alden were living in Lewiston, Idaho. Their family had grown from the two girls, Margie and Iris with the addition of a son, James Henry Alden, born 30 June 1926.

THEN THE CRASH

The 1929 Economic Crash did not immediately effect Ana's growing family. There began a difficult turn of event for Hector and Pearl who were doing very well the Sunset Mine and Index, Washington. Another pregnancy was coming to a natural end and Hector John Jr. was born on 7 February 1930 at their Index home. By July, Pearl became quite sick. Today there is a name for the malady, post-partum depression. It became increasingly difficult for her to cope with life as irrational fears gripped her. Her husband could not take time off to care for their children. Sarah and Roy Albright were able to come and help out. It was then decided that the family should move to Leland where there were more adults around. Sarah's daughter Lorraine came down with a bad case of measles. Lorraine's old baby bed was put in Ana's office bedroom for Lorraine, even though she was eight. Then on July 10, 1930,Sarah and Roy returned with Robert (Bob) and Hector Jr., who was five months old. Sarah took care of Bob. Hector Jr. was given to the care of grandma Ana. His bed was the recent "measles" bed in her bedroom in the post office. It was disinfected and fit him much better than it fit his big cousin Lorraine.

The baby was fed whatever his grandmother ate. Fortunately, her food continued to be crushed and mashed and was excellent baby food. Of course there was cow's milk. Hector Jr. continued to be "grandma's little boy" well beyond toddler stage. His earliest memories were of the switchboard and the activity of the postal operation. Relative to the other grandchildren, the bonding between him and his grandmother was unique.

Pearl was put into a hospital for a time. Typically recovery from this type of depression is quite rapid once daily stresses are eliminated. Then in November she was well enough to go to Great Falls, Montana to recuperate with her parents through the Christmas holidays. Helen and Mary Beth had remained in Index through the summer. Their father hired teenage girls to be with them while he worked. Uncle Roy Albright went back to Index with a truck and brought the girls and the family furniture to Leland. The move was reported by Ana in the 8 September1930 issue of the Port Townsend *Leader*. The timing was dictated by the need to have Helen and Mary Beth start at Leland School for the new school year. The move was good for Mary Beth as she was put back a grade from where she had been in Index. Pearl returned to Leland after New Years 1931 and quickly returned to duties as the mother of four children.

Quite soon there were problems that caused the close of Sunset Mine. Hector Munn and the entire mine crew were out of work. There were two factors causing the closure. Economically, the "crash" had hit and the price of copper had plummeted to 2 cents a pound. So there was no money for paychecks.

The second cause was structural. The procedure of the mine operation was for the workers to come to the work site at the end of the tunnel and load out the loose rock/ore. Then the crew would drill holes in the rock face into which dynamite charges were placed. The crew would then set the blasting caps, connect electrical wires and roll the electrical lines out of the tunnel as they left the site for the day. At a safe distance out, the dynamite charge would be electrically struck and the blast would shatter the rock of the working mine face. By the next morning the dust would have settled and rock would be ready to load out. The cycle was repeated daily.

One day the crew was following a vein downward below the main shaft. The work had progressed to "tens" of feet down. The blast had gone off as planned at the close of a shift, but when the men came back in the morning, the downward trending shaft had filled with water. No amount of pumping could drain the work shaft. They had hit an underground river. The mining operation was abruptly ended.

The mine operation ended in the summer of 1931. Hector continued to be involved with the shut-down activities while he looked for mining work. In October of 1932, it was decided that Hector could take over the lineman job from Roscoe Thomas. Roscoe reported that this was a near disaster for him. The rest of that story has been told. Roscoe got his job back. Hector went travelling again. He found a position in a cinnabar mine in Southern Oregon that lasted six months. He was home from that job by November 1934. By then the telephone company had changed ownership. The national economic depression was at its deepest.

XII: FARM IMPROVEMENTS

THE EXPANDED FARMSTEAD

When Jim and Ana bought the Nichols homestead, there was the log house and major barns on the opposite side of Arcadia Road. Arcadia Road started at the Leland Bridge and went straight west to the base of Leland Hill. Then it angled steeply up the hill and on to Ripley Creek and Howe Creek in Arcadia Valley. The county had the philosophy that getting access to a public road was what the settlers needed, which was correct. The roads were put through so as to give the best trajectory relative to creeks and hills. They did.not survey or purchase the land. This was indeed what the people wanted. If a homestead was missed by a public road, it was not long before the land was abandoned and sold as timber reserve.

Ed Nichols had removed stumps back from the lake only for six or ten acres. Rail or picket fences kept the farm into two main fields for hay. The areas back toward the hill were left as stump pasture for the livestock. Cows could range back up the hills without fences. Sometimes the cows would wonder through the logged off and burnt off land all the way to Ripley Creek. The Munn children would start out at 2 in the afternoon to find them and herd them back to the barn for milking time.

In March 1933 a road was built along the base of the hill to the Macomber/Nicola farm then owned by George and Alice Nurnberg. A deed was filed for this road granting the road to the county. The deed included a provision that the county could take gravel from a location to the south of Arcadia Road. The road in that direction was thereafter called the Gravel Pit Road and the north extension was the Nurnberg Road. These new country roads were well built, graded, graveled and set with proper culverts and ditches. They became the west edge of the farmstead and were fenced to keep the cows from wondering up the hill. When the County built Snow Creek Road in order to by-pass the Leland Bridge, the Nurnberg Road was abandoned in favor of private access roads to each lakeside home down from the new road.

Arcadia Road was fenced on both sides through the Munn farmstead with a lovely picket fence. The south side of the road had a wooden side-walk that extended from the Munn barns to the base of the hill. To keep the cows off the public road, a fenced lane extended from the new Jim Munn barn up to the "foot of the hill" where the cows could be turned into the various pastures. For a time there was a side-walk in the lane as well.

The men folk of the Munn family always had a job whenever everything else was done. That job was to remove the stumps in the stump pasture. Jim Munn cleared the stumps for his new barn. Hector Munn used blasting powder on the stumps in the north pasture. Finally, when Bob Munn took over the farm in the late 1940s, he brought in a caterpillar and cleared the south "creek pasture" to make one large hay field.

THE CHICAGO WORLD'S FAIR OF 1933

The Chicago World's Fair of 1933 was being advertised across America if not around the world. Ana decided she deserved a true vacation. Family members had no trouble taking care of the switchboard, post office and farm while she went. Everyone had a job to do so she could relax while on the trip. Ana made her way to Seattle and took the train to Chicago for a thorough visit to the World's Fair.

She returned with great stories about all the huge buildings of Chicago and the marvelous changes that were coming in the future.

She had a great time and returned rested and rewarded. She brought gifts and trinkets for her children and grand children. It was special for everyone that she had made such a fabulous trip.

THE ALDENS COME

As note already, Viola Munn had married George Otto Alden, whom she met at Fort Warden. Since July 1924, they lived on a fruit farm in Lewiston, Idaho. The family had grown with the addition of three children: Margaret (Margie), Iris and James Henry (Jim). The depression had not been kind to them either. So following the transfer of the Telephone Company, Ana was left with the Post Office and the dairy farm. It was decided that G.O. Alden could come and take responsibility for the dairy business. (There were so many "Georges" around at that time that it was decided that Mr. Alden would be called "Otto" or "Uncle Otto".)

Ana's house had become quite crowded when Hector and Pearl's children came. Sarah became ill with what was suspected to be tuberculosis. A tent deck and tent was set up for Sarah next to George and Hulda's house and daughter Lorraine stayed with them. Hulda took care of Sarah for a while. It was then that it was decided to improve "One-armed Tom's" cabin as a place for her and Lorraine to live. They were there for a time. Then when it was decided that the Alden family should leave Idaho and come to Leland, Sarah and Lorraine moved out of One-armed Tom's cabin to make room for them. Sarah took a job at the Limit Resort. She and Lorraine lived in one of the Resort cabins. The shake "cabin" that Hector and Nate Stewart had built as teenagers was put on skids and pulled over by One-armed Tom's house. The tent house was also moved to the edge of the orchard as a place to store the Alden's furniture. Thus there was a place for the Alden family.

The Alden's arrived on 4 February 1936. In anticipation of their arrival, it was learned that the children had the mumps. So Pearl insisted that her children not be present when the Alden's came. Bob and six year old Hector were sent over to "Auntie Al" Nurnberg's house and Helen and Mary Beth stayed with "Auntie Sara" at the Limit Resort. Donald Nurnberg was in a rest home at the time and Alice Nurnberg was the County School Superintendent. It was not long before the coast was clear and everyone was back in their normal beds. The Alden family had found room in the several spaces. Pearl and children lived in Ana's house.

THE CUMMING'S PLACE

An older couple had purchased the homestead that had once been the Edwards Place. The house that George Edwards had built had burned down a few years after they retired to live in Port Townsend. The well that had served the Edwards' was still there as was the cow barn, chicken house, equipment house and outhouse. So Mr. Cummings built a modern new house on the site of the burned house in August of 1923. Mr. Cummings died in October 1929. Mrs. Cummings lived there alone for a while, but moved to Port Townsend were she was employed. The house was vacant.

Pearl Munn had felt she needed to take charge of her family and with the arrival of the Alden family it seemed a good time to make changes. She rented the Cummings Place and moved her family there in February 1936, a few days after the Alden family came. Hector was not able to find local employment and travelled about the west looking for mining jobs. But he came home to make sure that his family was moved to the new house. Since moving from Index in 1930, Pearl's household goods, including her piano, had been stored in the buggy garage and had suffered damages.

From the Cummings place Bob and Hector Jr. were able to walk to Leland School. Bob was in the fifth grade and Hector was in the first grade. Though they were three years separated in ages, Bob had skipped the fourth grade. Skipping grades was easy in one room schools as children could do the lessons of the next class as well as their own. Big sisters Helen and Mary Beth went by bus to Quilcene

High School. Since first graders were dismissed from school at two in the afternoon, Hector would often walk down the county road toward the bridge with his classmates and visit his grandmother on the way home. He'd walk over the Strawberry Hill pathway. If he got home after dark, he was scolded. That didn't happen much as the trail went through thick young fir trees that made the trail spooky as darkness fell. Six or seven year old children would not be trusted to be alone like that these days.

Ana Munn's house from the south, circa 1938. Donald Nurnberg's log cabin is to the left. (Munn family collection).

Probably the main factor for the move from Ana's house was that Donald Nurnberg had returned from a stay in a rest home. One of the treatments for tuberculosis at that time was isolation, clean air and good food. It was decided that Donald should have his own living quarters. Some men of the community and some of Donald's buddies quickly built a log house just south of Ana's house. It set on the lake edge so that a corner perched out over the water. A fish line could be cast out from the porch. The building was only a 15'X15' structure. It had a south facing porch where the men rigged up a swinging bed where Donald could rest in the sun during the day. Ironically, Donald got even worse that summer and on 6 January 1936 he was returned to a sanitarium. He would leave confinement for short trips, but never did get better. He entered a sanitarium in Elma, Washington in October 1938 and died there. Donald's log house was never used as sleeping quarters. It was a "get away" place as the porch with the swing was quiet and secluded. Donald's log house was used as a changing room for summer swimmers and to change to milking clothes after school. It was never electrified.

Pearl was not happy to have a person with active T.B. close to her little boys. Her concern was not misplaced. The County Health Department had all the school age children tested for tuberculosis. All of her children tested positive to the disease. It was thought that Donald had contracted the disease from a tubercular cow, as indeed the Alice Nurnberg had a cow with a crooked horn, a sign of the disease. Pearl soon found where she could buy a nanny goat. She kept a herd of milking goats for several years. She served goat milk to the family during that time. As a plus, the goats cleaned up all the wild black berries. It was difficult to keep a garden, however.

Family reunion with Kawamotos present, circa1937. On Ana Munn's back porch. From left on railing: Sarah Albright, George Munn, Viola Alden, George Alden, and Ana Munn on right railing. Second from back: Viola Edwards Hansen (Ana's sister from Seattle), Vangie Tooker, Hulda Marie Munn, Mary Jane Tooker, Iris Alden (?) (crouching), Alice Nurnberg. Third row: Joe Kawamoto, Lorraine Albright, Margie Alden, Kaichi Kawamoto. Front row: Donald Nurnberg (in corner), Dorothea Tooker, Lloyd Tooker, Jr., Jim Alden. (George Munn collection)

UNCLE OTTO'S REMODEL OF JIM MUNN'S BARN

When Jim Munn set up his barn for keeping cows, his plan was taken from his memories of the Belle River buildings on Prince Edward Island. Winters were icy there and cows were kept inside much of the winter. They were kept in box stalls. Each box was about three feet wide and five feet deep. There was a stanchion for the cow to reach her head through to the hay and also could be locked about her neck. She could be left free as well as there was a door at back to hold her in. The doors swung open across the entry alley. The cows had to line-up and go into the barn in order, the fartherest one in came first. As the cow would come in, her door would be opened and then closed behind her. Cows are good at doing such routines. The stalls took up a lot of space and limited the number of cows that a barn/farm could have. The stalls were quite dirty places and hard to clean.

The first thing that Otto did was to rip out the stalls and replace them with new stanchions that put the cows next to each other and more cows could be handled. Something like 10 box stalls was replaced by 18 stanchions. There were stanchions on both sides, so the theoretical capacity of the barn went from 16 to 28 or so cows. Some of the second side was devoted to feed storage. It was also difficult to carry full milk buckets around to the separator room from the south stanchions. It was used mostly for non-milking cows.

Uncle Otto also remodeled the hay barn. Farm equipment had shifted from horse drawn wagons to tractor drawn wagons or to trucks. The floor of the barn was not strong enough to have a fully loaded truck drive up the ramp into the center alley. The barn had to be remodeled so that hay trucks could drive up outside on the ground and the hay brought in through a hay door cut into the north wall of the barn. This meant the hay fork and carriage could ride out from the barn on an extension, or "peak", of the roof. The operation of the hay harvesting and mowing remained the same.

Uncle Otto cut a large opening into the north wall above the upper 12 X 12 beam for the hay door. The door was on massive hinges and would befolded down to open it for the harvest season and pulled up tight as soon as the hay was all in. A new track for the hay carriage was set in below the old one. In fact, it was necessary to use the old track to install the new one. The track that Jim Munn put in was left in place. New ropes were purchased as well as the configuration was then different. Hay could be brought through to the south or upper mow that Jim used for oat hay, but there was seldom enough hay to need it.

The new peak had new shingles and thus is easily recognized in pictures. The barn never was repainted. "Uncle Otto's" barn was then the last time the barn was repaired. When grandson Bob Munn took over the barn and dairy, he and his father built a milking parlor on the south side. They used the boards taken from that outside wall, so they still had the red paint.

Cows could be brought in 4 at a time into the parlor and milked by machine. The milk could then immediately cooled and stored in cans set in cold water. Unfortunately, by then, the regulations for temperature and bacterial count were very stringent and Bob never received the permit to sell whole milk. He kept selling cream. The value of cream kept going down and it became impossible to do more than break even economically. It was impossible to raise a family with the dairy income. He shifted to just keeping beef cows while he became a full-time logger.

When the estate was settled following Ana's death, the barn was part of George's inheritance. By then there was no longer an economic value for the barn as a part of a business function. Two structural issues were brought into effect. The shingle roof began to rot out and leak. Even worse, Jim Munn had placed the building on large cedar blocks. These were rotting out as well. To replace the foundation would cost more than an entirely new building. So before the inner beams and wood began to rot or before someone was hurt in an uninsured structure, George sold the barn for its "barn wood", a very desirable resource. Somewhere there are nice houses with marvelous open beam construction using Jim Munn's barn beams. There is no evidence that Jim Munn's barn ever existed except in the photographs and in the memories of the children that grew up in its shadow.

George Munn continued to remove the other buildings of the once active farm. He left only the Post Office building. Finally that too was removed. Nothing remains of the J. H. Munn farm but memories.

J. H. Munn barn as remodeled by G.O. Alden, circa 1938. Looking eastward from Leland Hill road.1938. The roof extension and calf barn to the left. The school bus barn is at center right. (Munn family collection)

ANA AND HER DAIRY FARM

George Alden guided the remodel of Jim Munn's barn. He also upgraded the herd of milk cows by selling most of the older animals and buying several new ones. But misfortune soon overtook him. On 1 October 1936 he was working with a neighbor farmer when a team of horses went into a gallop and ran him down. He was hurt badly and was hospitalized. He was weakened severely and did not return to farming. Ana was back in the dairy business.

The Red Barn following remodel by George O. Alden, 1937/8.
Lane to west is present with fence to north extending faintly from the calf barn.
(Munn family collection).

Ana Mae Edwards started milking cows when she was nine years old. In her memoirs she said that was when she began helping her mother with their two cows, "straining" the milk, skimming the milk and washing up. So for Ana, dairy farming was a life-long skill.

There are two methods of hand milking, stripping or squeezing. Ana used the strip method. To do this one grips the cow's teat between the thumb and two fingers and slide downward. This catches the milk in the teat and strips it out. Two hands work one after the other on the same teat. To make the fingers slide down better, milk is used as a lubricant. The method gets milk all over but mostly in the bucket. The "squeeze" method takes a bit more skill and hand muscle. With the thumb and forefinger, the teat is squeezed at the top trapping the squirt of milk. The other three fingers are squeeze in sequence from top to bottom to squirt the milk out. Two hands are used at once but on different teats in an alternating squeeze. The hand never needs to touch the milk. Hand milkers develop strong forearm muscles and hand grips. A cow's udder can be quite dirty and needs to be thoroughly washed, no matter which method is used and with machine milking. The cow's udder is covered with hair and either system, even machine milking, will pull hair out. So milk directly from the cow is filtered to remove the hair. A little hair in milk never hurts the drinker, but it is a bit disconcerting if there is hair in ones food and drink.

When the dairy markets only the cream, as was the case in the early days, the cream separator removes "heavy" particles of hair and dirt as well as divides the milk into cream and non-fat milk. Fresh, whole milk enters the spinning separator bowl by a center opening in the center top from the source container above the bowl. Milk flows down to the bottom and is spun out and up through a set of closely spaced conical disks. The centrifugal force of the turning bowl moves the lighter cream to the inside, through openings and out the top spout and the heavier non-fat milk is moved to the outside and out separate holes to a lower or bottom spout. Heavier particles, dirt and hair stay in the bottom of the separator bowl and are cleaned out at the end of each session of milk processing.

Obviously, producing fresh milk is not an absolutely clean process. At best, milk carries bacteria of the cow regardless of the effort taken to keep it clean. Milk buckets, utensils, tubes of the milking machines and whatever milk touches has residual milk that dries on and is subject to bacterial growth. Actually, most types of milk bacteria are harmless and lead to sour milk, clabbered milk and cheeses. Never-the-less, every precaution is taken to have clean milk and hence to remove doubt, marketed milk is expected to be pasteurized. Raw milk was what the Munn children drank. The fresher the milk is, the better it was. No one wanted to drink sour milk. Amazingly, if one visits the third world cultures where cow's milk is a major food, the milk that is available is only sour milk as there is no refrigeration or pasteurization.

Meals in the Munn house in the early thirties were taken at the kitchen table. There was little room for everyone so each one had a special place. The smaller children were crowded into the back sides of the table. Everyone was served from the stove, which was near the side where the adults sat. Everyone was served a full glass of whole, fresh milk. Each plate and each milk glass had to be empty before one could leave the table. Somehow we would know if the milk served was from grandma Ana's milking or from mother Pearl's milking, as she was a squeeze milker. It was O.K. to leave a bit of milk at the bottom, in either case.

Ana Munn continued to have her dairy until her grandson took over the farm in 1946. She kept around 24 cows of which at least 14 were milking at any time. It takes 7 to 10 minutes to milk one cow. Therefore milking chores would take two or three hours twice a day. When she had help, it was only in the evening chores. She was often out calling the cows in at three in the morning. Cows soon learn any program and would wake up and come. There was always grain when they got to the barn and in the winter, there was hay ready. In really bad weather, the cows were left in over-night. That made for lots more cleaning! The grain was fed only just before the cow was milked. Cows "hold their milk up" until they receive the right signals and the grain was the main signal. But if a cow is spooked in anyway, they turn off. Dairy farmers do not change their routines or like to have guests or dogs about the front of the cows in the barn. Radios are often on with music. Some dairymen claim that cows prefer classical music.

Great grandmother Ana with great grandsons, 1950. Robert Bury (left), Leroy Woodman (Margie's son), James Bury in front of Bob Munn's remodeled barn/milking parlor. This is the barn that James P. Bury remembers and used to sketch the barn depicted on the cover. (Helen Bury collection).

ANA M. MUNN, THE NEWS CORRESPONDENT, WRITER, INTELLECTUAL

Matilda Edwards was also the model for Ana's literary efforts. The Edwards children loved schooling and words. Matilda became a regular correspondent for the Minneapolis Kansas *Messenger*, an Ottawa County weekly newspaper, when they lived at Ackley. This was somewhat amazing as Matilda was largely self taught. Her diary showed a distinct improvement from the first entries to the entries when her children began school and the classes were in her house.

As mentioned before, Ana began as correspondent from "Leland" to the Port Townsend *Leader* on February 3, 1921. The operation of the telephone switchboard and being postmaster put her in the flow of social information. She happily shared what she could glean from the neighborhood society. Births, marriages, parties, move in dates and move out dates, sicknesses, weather and openings of fishing season were all reported. She was as proper as she knew to be. Married women were mentioned with their husband's name. For example if she referred to herself in the news, she was "Mrs. J. H. Munn", even though her by-line was "Ana Munn, reporter". As her contacts narrowed, she could only report what she heard from children or visitors. Some neighbors began to resent being the only ones reported. She began to report people as "seen on the streets of Leland" or "transacted business" in Port Townsend, when the real news was a visit to a doctor or an attorney. Yet many Lelanders looked forward to having news reported of their wedding, school graduation, home from the army, or even new car purchase. For some it was fun to get their name in the paper once in a while. Entries such as "Mr. Hurd or Mr. Wills were seen on the streets of Leland" or "visited Mrs. Munn", really meant that a local grocery man had brought her groceries that she had ordered by phone. There was finally a change of management at the *Leader* and local news was cut from the paper except if submitted by their cadre reporters.

The newspaper never paid Ana by the word, as some thought. They did supply her with paper and postage paid envelopes. The paper was published on Thursday and copy was to be in hand by Monday noon. If it was a slow news week and there was space, sometimes they would accept news on Tuesday. Ana was usually good at meeting deadlines. She would write on Sunday afternoon and the copy would be in Monday's mail. In those days county mail was processed at Port Townsend and Monday's mail would reach the *Leader* office in the afternoon mail.

Ana's Memoirs, "Pioneering in Four States and I'll Tell You All about It", was completed in 1951 when she was 80 years old. The book, "The Egg and I", by Betty McDonald had been recently published. Its setting was somewhere on the Olympic Peninsula. Locals knew that Betty McDonald had drawn her characters from real people who lived in south Chimacum. In fact the actual road where she lived is memorialized as "Egg and I Road". Some of the characters in the book actually sued Ms. McDonald for libel. After reading the book, Ana bragged to her grandson Hector that "I could write a book like that, except it would be all true and wouldn't have to be dirty." She thought some of Ms. McDonald's words and scenes were a bit risqué. Well, her grandson challenged her to write her memoirs and bought her a package of manuscript paper, 8 ½ X 14 inch, and a box of carbon paper. She began typing something every day. She would compose in her mind and type it out. She never copied over or edited a draft copy. Sometimes her memory was not truly accurate. She was writing the truth, but would often omit names. For example, she never gave the name of the fellow she thought may have shot her suitor, Fred Rose. She did not always give accurate dates. Her outline was simple historical order. She gave greater detail to the earlier days. When her life became complicated with children and grandchildren coming and going there was much repetition of events. It was easier to only address more significant events. When her book was finished and made available to her family, some took issue with parts and for some reason a few pages found their way into the fire.

Ana Munn with book, circa 1951.
(George Munn collection).

Ana had a manual return Remington typewriter. When the carriage return bell sounded, about one more word could be added. If she was in the middle of a hot idea, Ana would often forget to return the carriage. Letters would pile up at the end of the line. She didn't rewrite, so a reader was left with a puzzle at times. She would compose her "Leland news" or a chapter of her book in her mind as she went about her daily activities, milking, gardening, resting, etc. then sit down at the typewriter and dash the copy off fairly rapidly.

Ana was left-handed, and she wrote with a fountain pen that was used for formal writing. She wrote by pushing the pen up from the bottom so that her hand would not drag into the wet ink. As a teacher writing with chalk on a black-board, she pushed the chalk from the bottom. In any case, she wrote with a distinct right slant. Her signature was a set of up and down lines that narrowed in height down to the last 'n' stroke.

About 1960, Hector Jr. made contact with Joel Edwards, who was a grandson of Ana's brother, Joel Edwards. When "Joel-the younger" learned of Ana's book he demanded to see it and was quite excited about it. This Joel Edwards had also been a local reporter for his home town newspaper in Camas, Washington. He would report high school sports news. He decided that Ana's original copy could use some editing and dates added. With a little imagination, he figured out missing words whose letters were piled at the ends of the line. He set up some chapter headings and improved paragraphing. He would say that "Ana's story is our family's story too". He was suffering with the aftermath of colon cancer surgery when he started to rewrite Ana's book. Like Ana, he would type something every day. His wife said it kept him alive. In fact, not long after he had finished the rewrite, he was taken by his disease. He kept a copy for his family and who knows who has that or photo copies made from it. A copy was given to Hector Jr. and several photocopies exist. Thanks to Joel Edwards, there is a more readable copy of Ana's memoires.

Ana read when she wasn't busy with something else. She read a few books or novels, but mostly read current magazines and newspapers. When at the telephone switchboard or waiting in the post office, she read the magazines from cover to cover and would leave the materials in the waiting area for patrons to read. She was always a soft touch for the neighborhood children who would come to sell Blue Birds to raise school money. She would buy one from every child every year. Her window was covered with Blue Birds. Sometimes the school children would sell magazine subscriptions. She would look through a list offered her and find one she wasn't already taking or renew an old one. She never renewed a subscription directly with the publisher, but would wait for the school child to come by so she could encourage their sense of accomplishment. She must have had a subscription to every national weekly and monthly news magazine published. This was in the 1940s and 50s, before television, when magazines were popular and abundant. Her parlor was the reading library for her grandchildren. She took special pleasure in having them come and visit and read.

ANA, THE GARDENER

The first thing pioneers did on a new place, along with getting a tent, cabin or sod house to live in, was to break sod and plant a garden. Potatoes always do well on new ground and were always a staple food that would keep in the root cellar through the winter. Gardens had "greens", i.e. lettuce, chard, cabbage, kale. The root crops of carrots, beets and parsnips would keep in the root cellar as would the winter squash and pumpkins. The latter spoiled sooner as they had more water in their flesh. Corn, beans and peas were a must to plant as well. They would be raised to maturity and dried. But as canning in glass jars became possible, they would get canned as well.

The Edwards had a big garden at their Kansas homes. Ana learned to plant and care for the crops. When G.W. and Matilda came to Leland, Ana helped them break ground and plant their first garden there. Each homestead in Leland had its garden plot. Actually, the garden plot between the orchard and the lake became quite tired. The soil was weathered shale rock brought down by the stream. Without lots of barn and chicken house cleanings, the garden became unproductive.

After grandson Bob took over the farm and cow responsibility, Ana was left with her chickens and her garden. The chicken yard was divided into two parts with a chicken wire fence around and down the center. One side was for chickens and other side was for turkeys or geese. She stopped raising turkeys and that yard, all nicely fenced off, became her garden. It was a rich soil for a few years. Then she stopped raising chickens and moved her garden to the chicken pen.

During her last four or five years, her garden was her life. Since the area had held chickens for many years, there were no weeds or grass. So she never turned the soil over. She would just scratch a ditch with a hoe and plant the seeds. Then as the plants grew, she would hill the plants on each side.

She liked to keep track of what she did in the garden. She had a diary or log of what she did each day that she kept on brown filing folders. The folders are dated from 1952-1954. The garden area had no water supply, so she would take a bucket or two of water out each day and carefully water plants where it would do the most good. The plants didn't get any more than needed to survive. In the late summer to late fall months, she records daily harvest of vegetables and greens far more than is possible to have grown.

She used the manila folders to record cash expenditures. She categorizes the items as "food", "medicines", "postage", "sales tax", "presents", and "fuel". She was not subscribing to as many magazines then. She kept a record of payments and when the subscription would expire. Her last entry is for "Farm Journal" for which a one year subscription was paid until 1956. Ana didn't use many medicines. She recorded the purchase of aspirin and something she called "kortozone", perhaps cortisone. She gave to "welfare", i.e. Red Cross, WildLife, and Tuberculosis League. She gave to "church and missionary" mostly to her granddaughters Helen Bury, whose husband was a minister with a radio broadcast at the time, and Mary Beth Munn, who was a missionary in Africa at the time. She made regular contributions to the Quilcene Presbyterian Church. These notations, though simple and repetitive, indicate that she continued to maintain her sense of involvement in life.

GOOD BYE TO MILKING DUTIES

After transferring the Post Office duties to her daughter, Viola Alden, Ana still kept milking the cows. These were war years and everyone needed to do something to help win the war. Grandson Bob had been helping her with the chores in the evening, but he wanted to do more afterschool sports in high school, so grandson Hector Jr. took over the chores. Then in 1944, Bob finished high school. He had just had his 17th birthday. He wanted to do his part in the war but was not eligible for military service. He was eligible for the Merchant Marines and began training for service with them. After basic training in San Diego, he was placed on a munitions ship that went into some dangerous areas of the South Pacific. He received triple pay when his ship entered war zones. Soon the war ended and he was discharged without incident.

Bob needed a peace time profession and it was decided that he should take over the dairy operation. He had done well with his military pay and decided to try to qualify the dairy for selling milk rather that cream. With the help of his father, a modern milking parlor was built on the south side of the barn. He put in a water system that pumped water from a spring in the meadow on the north side of the barn. He installed milking machines. He took over the cows that Ana had been milking and the cows that his parents owned and together he had enough cows to start the improved operation.

He also bought a new International Harvester tractor with some haymaking attachments, namely a "buck rake", mowing machine and a hay wagon. Ana was able to assist him in the purchase of the equipment, as we will soon learn.

A NAMESAKE FOR ANA MAE MUNN

Grandson Bob was also starting his family. In 1946 he married Dorothy Cook. They moved into "Red Woolard's cabin". Red Woolard was a retired army master sergeant who had fallen for the charms of Lake Leland. Ana Munn rented him a spot at the edge of the lake at "The Point" (in Lot 1). Here he had built a three room cabin "with a path" and lake water. He had moved out a few years earlier and it took little cleaning up to become a honeymoon house for Bob and Dorothy. They lived there for about three years. Their first two children were born while they were there.

First born daughter was named Ana Marie Munn. She was named for her great grandmother Ana Mae Munn and her grandmother Pearl MARIE Munn. Although the name "Ana" had been used by her sisters Viola and Dora to name nieces, none of her grand children had been given that name. Great grandma Ana was so pleased with the naming choice that she decided that Bob and Dorothy should be given the entire farm! They refused the offer but asked if they could have the lake shore land that had been the site of the Munn saw mill. This did happen. Bob eventually built his family home there and his wife Dorothy still lives there.

Ana Marie Munn about November of 1947. She is proudly modeling the brand new International Harvester tractor. (Dorothy Munn collection).

SOME NECESSARY BUSINESS

Unfortunately, Ana had another pressure on her mind that she wished to change. She was still paying on a loan on the farm that had been taken out in 1918! The timber on the "homestead" had not been harvested since 1915 and was again close to maturity. (Leland hills grow trees quickly). She consulted her family, which by then included Sarah's second husband, Bill Bryan. He was a professional forester with the National Forest Service. There was agreement that she should sell the timber. After considerable sorting out of possibilities, it was decided to offer the timber to Crown-Zellerbach Paper Mill. Crown Zellerbach managers looked at the timber and agreed to buy it but to let it be for several years more growth. The income was enough to pay off the longstanding loan, to help her grandson remodel the barn and to purchase the new International Harvester tractor and still have some money left for her "old age".

CLOSING DAYS

After finishing her book in 1951, Ana had very little to give her attention to except her garden. She had always kept cats about. While she was caring for the cows, she had too many barncats. There were a couple of cats that she fed at her house. They got bread and milk just as she did. She was always an early riser as her early morning chores started as early as three in the morning. Following chores, she would eat breakfast and then nap the rest of the morning. Afternoons were back to the chores. She kept this schedule after being released from the milking chores. She would garden in the morning and afternoon for a few hours each time. She rested and read between chores.

Ana's neighbors were son and daughter-in-law George and Hulda Munn, who lived across the "street" and her daughter Viola, who lived at the end of the orchard and was busy with the post office every day. Viola would check on her each morning and through the day. She would see that she got her groceries and medicines. She would check her before retiring for the night.

Her son Hector and family lived a half mile away at the south end of Lake Leland. Her grandson Bob had built a house on the old saw mill site and was nearby. Earlier he would bring her a quart of milk each night until he ceased operating the dairy. He and his wife Dorothy were close by if needed.

In the middle of the night of 29 August 1955, Ana got out of bed and fell. She may have struck her head on furniture. She was caught on the floor between the bed and a wall and couldn't get to her feet. Viola Alden discovered her in the morning on her usual call in. She got some help and managed to get her back in bed. Granddaughter Mary Beth was home at the time and grandson Hector and his wife Verna were also in Leland. Hector had just been separated from the U.S. Army and was on his way to school in Southern California. Mary Beth and Verna were both nurses and were going to stay with Ana on shifts until she was better. But during the early morning, Ana stopped breathing. That morning the two nurses made her ready for the undertaker instead.

Ana Mae Edwards Munn died August 30, 1955.

Ana was just a month short of being 85 years old. The commitment she had made many years earlier as she sat on Strawberry Hill and looked out over Lake Hooker to the Nichols Homestead was that she would one day live there and die there.

AND SHE DID

XIII: JIM AND ANA:
END DATA AND EPILOGUE

―――

FOLLOWING THE MONEY

One way to tell the story of a family is to relate how the economics of their lives works out. For most people, and Jim and Ana Munn are not exceptions, financial details are not very public. Often a couple does not want neighbors to know their business and often they do not want their children to know about any financial difficulties or successes. Children need to be shielded from worry, if there are difficulties. Nor do they need to know if there is excess money around. Who knows what children might expect? Most people in those pioneer days operated on a cash basis.

No one in the early days had much cash as wages were low and costs of goods were in small amounts by today's standards. Folks did not need banks for their savings or to write checks. They could use postal money orders to pay big bills or to transfer cash.

The records that are available for Jim and Ana's finances relate to the various times that their land was mortgaged and the payment plans that were generated. It turns out that the core 200 acres of land, i.e. the 159 acres purchased from the Nichols and the 40 acre "Orchard" homestead, were always under mortgage. Not until the Crown Zellerbach timber sale provided new money to pay off the loan was the land free and clear.

There was the 120 acres of timber land from Jim Munn's original homestead in Arcadia Valley. A 20 acre piece was sold to Ana's nephew Bob Henderson in 1895, which he sold later to a timber company. The story behind these transactions is lost. Bob was a young man looking for his future. It wasn't in Leland. Then there are several timber sale contracts on the property. Then finally, the land was sold to a timber company with any accrued trees. That acreage provided cash at some significant time in Jim and Ana's lives.

In Ana's memoirs she says that she kept her accounts separate from Jim's. At least up to the purchase of the Nichols homestead this was so. Ana says that to buy the homestead, Glendale Dairy Company loaned Jim the money, which "was paid off quickly." That may have been so, but there must have been more to the story.

The story told by the public deeds as recorded on the land does tell a significant story. Here is how that goes:

Jim and Ana took out a mortgage for $1,300 to buy the Nichols homestead. This was in addition to $300 paid immediately to Adelia Nichols in 1899 to confirm the deal. Mrs. Nichols assigned (sold) this mortgage to Lucy Ballou in 1906, as recorded in Erie County, N.Y. That mortgage was "satisfied" in August 1909 as recorded in Denver, Colorado where Lucy Ballou had moved. But a mortgage of $1,200 to Glendale Creamery was made in 1909. This money must have been used to satisfy the Nichols/Ballou mortgage less $100. The Glendale Dairy mortgage was finally satisfied on December 3, 1915. This was the year that the barn was finished.

It can be concluded that the saw mill was financially successful. The equipment was paid for in cash, employees were paid in cash, the barn construction and any final payments were made on the original mortgage were paid. Yet a new loan was taken out on the property on 15 December 1915. This loan was for $3000 from Merchants Bank of Port Townsend. This new mortgage had an 8% a year interest rate and was to be paid at $25 a month.

The 1915 mortgage was refinanced or renewed on 8 April 1918. This contract was for $3,500 at an interest rate of 5 ½ %. The 1915 contract was satisfied in the process. Little progress had been made on the mortgage. What is more, the new mortgage was for 34 ½ years from 8 April 1918. That is, it would not be paid until October 1952! This mortgage was still standing when on 1 September 1937 when Ana took out a second (junior) mortgage for $800. This one was at 5% and payable semiannually at $40 each 6 months until 1 March 1947.

Payment records exist for the last two mortgages. On April 1926, about the time Jim Munn died, the balance was $3154.13. Then in 1934, with a $2620.29 balance, it became delinquent. The second mortgage was paid on until September 1939 when it became delinquent with a balance of $600. At that time there is a gap in the information.

On 1 June 1949, with agreement from her children, Ana sold standing timber (not land) to Crown Zellerbach Corporation for $2,800. When the accounts were finalized by First American National Bank of Port Townsend, loans totaling $1,600 were paid off and the mortgage satisfied. When other costs were deducted, there was $1,670.30 balance left to pay. So somewhere between 1939 and 1949 a significant amount of the mortgage was paid off. Ana had been making mortgage payments with the income from the cream sales and her post office pension. She had no money in a bank account or significant cash on hand when she died. She was living on the postal pension, which by then was hardly adequate.

The mortgages seem quite small by today's standards. In actuality, they were significant when placed in relationship to the income levels of salaries or sales of a cow or a five gallon can of cream. In the thirties few people had cash. Living on a farm where there was meat, milk, eggs and garden vegetables made a lot of difference in supplying daily food needs for families. For most of Ana's life, she had no refrigerator, washing machine, car, or insurance costs. There were few medical costs except for the birthing of babies and hospital costs prior to dying. Ana never incurred significant medical expenses herself. It is said that Dr. Plut would come to visit her from time to time from Port Townsend. She died without hospitalization or consultation of a medical doctor. She did have two granddaughters available to help, but didn't need them either.

SETTLING ESTATES

Jim Munn's estate was not settled immediately after his death. On 26 February 1934 a Quit-Claim deed was filed by which the children and their spouses released their property rights to the land that was owned by James H. Munn, deceased, in favor of his wife and their mother, Ana M. Munn. The deed states that the net worth of the community interest of the deceased was $2900. This reflects James Munn's property when he died, 25 May 1926. In case there is any question, the property listed included the 157.34 acres of the "Nichols" homestead, the 40 acres of the "Orchard" homestead, and 40 acres remaining of the Arcadia homestead. Each family was awarded $100 in the settlement.

In the interim, Ana had sold the 80 acres of the Arcadia property and had deeded to George and Hulda Munn on 13 May 1930 a ½ acre parcel "lying between Lake Hooker and an unnamed creek and being north of the Arcadia Valley Road", i.e. their home site. She had also had this parcel excluded from the mortgage. The Arcadia Valley property had never been a part of the mortgages.

Following Ana's death the 197 acres was divided between the five living children approximately as follows: The northern "Lot 1", called the "Point", plus a north part of "the Orchard 40" was Sarah's inheritance. Most of "Lot 2", called the "Alders", as well as a south portion of the "Orchard 40" was Evangeline's inheritance. George was deeded the barn, the land around it and the balance of "Lot 2" as well as the north half of the "hillside 40". Viola received the Nichols orchard and lake front with Ana's house as well as the pasture/hay field of "Lot 2", with the exception of the "saw mill" property, and the south half, 20 acres, of the "hillside 40". Finally, Hector's family received the rest. Earlier his son Robert, Bob Munn, had been given the "saw mill" property for a home site when he took over the management of the dairy farm. "Lot 3", which is 45 acres, Hector divided into a western 20 acres which he deeded to his oldest granddaughter, Lyla Bury Hadley. The eastern remainder he deeded to son Robert. Then the southernmost "Lot 4", which is nearly 40 acres, he divided into a western 20 acres that he deeded the son Robert and an eastern 20 acres which he deeded to son Hector Jr. Hector Sr. never "kept" any of his inheritance but deeded it directly to his future heirs.

LAST WORDS: BLESSINGS

Ana Mae Edwards Munn includes a number of poems at the end of her memoirs. Perhaps these two can be used to illustrate her life of hope for all:

Give us, Lord, a bit o'sun
A bit o'work and a bit o' fun;
Give us in all the struggle and sputter
And daily bread and a bit o' butter;
Give us health, our keep to make,
An' a bit to spare for others' sake;
Give us, too, a bit of song
And a tale, and a book to help us along.
Give us, Lord, a chance to be
Our goodly best, brave, wise and free,
Our goodly best for our self, and others,
Till all men learn to live as brothers.
(An old English prayer)

And also this:

An Old Irish Blessing
May the road rise to meet you.
May the wind be always at your back.
May the sun shine warm your face,
The rains fall soft upon your fields and,
Until we meet again,
May God hold you in the palm of His hand.

THE EPILOGUE

James Hector Munn, the grandfather in this story, had major challenges in his life. The early death of his parents cut short his education. His first wife Maggie was ill when they married and he took care of her until she died. He survived his sorrow and found ways to gain skills as a carpenter that were effective. With hard work and the help of his second wife Ana, he was able to achieve major successes with businesses. As for most people in business, the economics of the times either helped or hindered his visions.

Though I never knew my grandfather Jim, in writing about him one lives out aspects of the imagined personality. Grandpa Jim is seen as a wise, right minded person who loved his God and who had great love for his family. He tried his best to make a good world for his wife and children. He loved to sing. He loved to play Santa Claus and stage Punch and Judy shows for his grandchildren.

He was highly respected by his neighbors and the men who earned wages from him as an employer. He was involved with public service as a school board member. He chose business ventures that would help the broader community of South Jefferson County.

Circumstances of economics, health and misfortune worked against him at times. But he did his best to rise above it all. We never get the impression that he showed anger or remorse. In fact he seemed happy and hopeful even as he accepted reversals and sorrow.

His barn was a great achievement for him. People would come from all around to see what he had built. Surely that pleased him greatly.

He was able to see his days numbered and made a special effort to bring closure to the memories of his life. Though his trip back to Prince Edward Island just two years before his death cannot be exactly confirmed, it is in his character to have made such a trip. One can imagine that he knelt before Maggie's grave marker and wept while he read those special words he had chosen to be carved in the stone, **"Where I am, you soon shall be."**

Prince Edward Island and his Scottish ancestry were important to him. It would also be important to him to have his progeny turn out well. He may have played favorites to some children, but one can be sure that he would encourage the best from each one and from his grandchildren. In his final moments he prayed for each one with his dying breath. Surely those prayers were meant to include even those heirs yet to come into the family either by birth or marriage.

Both Jim and Ana had significant love relationships before meeting each other. Jim's Maggie was never far from his mind. Ana's Fred Rose was an unfortunate learning experience in a young lady's coming of age experiences. She was forced by circumstances to set the memories aside and make the adult decision to care for family members.

Jim and Ana had a strong supporting relationship. Jim had imagination and entrepreneurship and wisdom gained in the school of hard knocks. While Ana had the educational and disciplined habits to keep the businesses operating as well as the family fed. There is no doubt that they played off each other's strengths and steadfast love. They shared a sense of responsibility for neighbors and the community.

Ana Mae was obviously fashioned by her up-bringing. Her unfortunate accident at such an early age gave her a determination to achieve regardless of difficulties. Though she and her twin brother were the youngest of the clan, she held strongly to her own goals and visions. Her mother Matilda was a confirming model in many ways. Ana's love of living things, animals and plants, was learned from her mother. She fancied herself as a postmistress and writer just like her mother had been. She could even be a midwife if needed. She had the firm notion that with the proper attention to education, progress could always be achieved.

Though she was certainly a dominant personality in her family and with the men in her life as well as her daughters, she could not be faulted for not caring for each one. She was careful not to find fault in others and always to promote learning and helpful community projects. She tried to encourage the best from her children and grandchildren and applauded their achievements and didn't fault their difficulties.

Once she settled in Leland, she seemed to pull life's edges around her. Business and school interests were fulfilled by the Leland-Quilcene circle. Except for the excursion to Chicago World Fair, she rarely left Lake Leland. Her occasional trips to Port Townsend to visit her family and her trips to Seattle to share final moments with her dying husband were the widest she pushed out from her comfort zone. The telephone switchboard, the dairy animals and gardening duties seemed increasingly to hedge her in as well as give her a sense of accomplishment. In the end, her garden was all she had left to do. She was a place as much as a person as a result of her vow to live and die at the edge of a lake that she named, that she loved, admired, respected and perhaps feared.

A REPRISE: THE GABLE WINDOW

Jim Munn's barn had a gable on the east side that was centered above the main ramp entrance and the double doors that could be rolled to the each side. The gable was set with a window that provided the only light inside when the doors were closed. There was no room behind the window. There was a space between the gable peak and the barn rafters. Without the gable, the roof would extend without a break.

The space behind the window could only be reached by a nimble lad who could swing hand over hand from rafter to rafter and get a leg over the middle rafter to pull up into the space. Once into the gable space, there was only room to sit on a thin rafter and look out. To get back down from the gable space required even more strength and agility. There was nothing to catch a leg on. After easing the body back between adjacent rafters, one had to lower through and hold tight until starting the hand over hand back to the high main beam of the barn. The whole operation of getting in and out of the gable space made the visit there special. One wanted to stay awhile and build memories.

Looking to the left out the window was a view nearly to the north end of the lake. The Limit Resort blocked the view of the very end. The lake-side wall of the Limit Resort had a greeting in big block letters that could be read by boaters on the lake. From the gable window it could only be seen in the mind's eye.

COME IN THE EVENING OR COME IN THE MORNING.
COME WHEN YOU'RE LOOKED FOR OR COME WITHOUT WARNING.
A THOUSAND WELCOMES YOU'LL FIND HERE BEFORE YOU.
THE OFTENER YOU COME HERE, THE MORE WE'LL ADORE YOU.
(Also quoted in Yntema, "The Story of Old Leland", page 185.)

Seen straight eastward from the gable window was George Thomas's farm. His two story house was styled from houses back in Maine. His unpainted barn was supported by cedar post set into the ground. It had a covered alley to the left into which hay wagons could be pulled by his horses for unloading. George Thomas had a pump house set at lake edge. It had a gas engine that ran the pump that pushed water up to a reservoir on the hill. When the pump was operating, it made an irregular sound that always seemed to be the last "kerchung-chung", but it somehow kept going.

To the right of the pump house was the east end of Leland Bridge. The bridge was hidden behind the trees of Uncle George Munn's house. On to the right was the set of garages with the orchard beyond that masked the south end of the lake.

Actually, the gable window was more of a place to imagine the world as it may have been when Grandpa Jim built the barn or to imagine the world that would one day happen. Yes, it was a quiet, secure place to be alone and still to be the observer of all that the world was past, present and future.

Grandpa Jim probably didn't imagine the gable window from the inside. He saw it as a special design feature that added character to

227

his prize. His vision was expressed most by his barn. Grandma Ana did not see the gable window as special, but as a source of light on an otherwise dark space. Her final words as she left the barn while I was doing the final chores of the day were, "Be sure all the doors are closed and fastened when you leave." She feared that a wind storm would blow out the roof or that a canny cow would slide a door open. When it came to the barn or to life, Jim was a visionary builder. It was Ana's role to follow through with life and maintain Jim's vision. In so doing she fulfilled her own vision.

The red barn turns out to be a parable for lives of Jim and Ana and our memories of them.

GOOD-BYE GRAMPA JIM AND GRANDMA ANA.

ABOUT THE AUTHOR

A study of one's genealogy can develop to more than a list of names and dates. As the author discovered more and more detail of his grandparents' lives, it became important to him to share his discoveries with his relatives and to leave a record to the progeny of Jim and Ana Munn. Today when families become spread to the far corners of the world, knowing family origins is important to a healthy self-concept.

Hector is the conservator of the family name. He has had access to many of the documents that Jim and Ana generated during their lives. Additional information has been gathered by visiting the places of their origins in Canada and Kansas.

Though this story is meant mainly for the family of Jim and Ana, it carries many records and stories that may be of interest to others, especially current and future residents of South Jefferson County.

The author is a retired college chemistry teacher and college registrar. He now lives in a retirement community with his wife Verna in sight of the campus of George Fox University in Newberg, Oregon where he worked for 34 years. They still own twenty acres of the land by Lake Leland once owned by Jim and Ana Munn. The community is now a part of Quilcene, Washington. Since their two sons live in that community, they make frequent visits to the location of the book, "Jim and Ana".

APPENDIX I: MUNN GENEALOGY

PART I: BEGINNING WITH DUNCAN MUNN AND FLORA BROWN

L. Ann Coles and Linda C. Harding have authored a complete Munn genealogy beginning with Neil Munn (b.1797). It is called *"From Island to Island: The Family of Neil Munn and Elizabeth MacLeod,"* published about 1996/7 and printed in limited edition by private printing. It has 377 pages. (ISBN # 0-9699-9430-3)

Since copies of *"From Island to Island"* are no longer available, the genealogy for the branch of the family related to this publication, *"Jim and Ana"*, is hereby reproduced in part.

Coles and Harding begin their genealogy with Neil Munn and Elizabeth MacLeod who lived at Mermaid, Lot 48, Queens County, Prince Edward Island. Neil Munn is reported to have arrived at P.E.I. in 1818 from Colonsay Island, Argyllshire, Scotland.

Coles and Harding also point out that Neil Munn's parents are unknown to them. They list two possibilities as reported by family members: 1. Neil and Elizabeth's first son, Donald, holds that Neil came to P.E.I. with a twin brother named "Archibald". It was held that Archibald went on from P.E.I. to Ontario and no one has found a record of his existence. He may have been accompanied by a "Mrs. Walker" who may have been an aunt. Both parents of the twins were either dead before Neil left Colonsay or died en route. 2. Neil's second son,

Roderick, simply reported that his father emigrated to P.E.I. as a single man and took up a job as a school teacher in 1818 in Mermaid.

Thus, no names are available for Neil's parents by way of his descendents, even though Neil and Elizabeth name their first two sons Donald and Roderick. Roderick is known to be Elizabeth's father's name. It would be most reasonable to suggest that "Donald" was named for Neil's father.

Parochial records of Colonsay have come to light since Coles and Harding did their search for a record of Neil's parents. This records that Donald 'Mun' and Sarah McLean were parents of twins, born 11 January 1797 on Colonsay. The twin's names were Neil and Alexander. It is now assumed that Neil Munn's parents were Donald Munn and Sarah McLean. Additional rational for this assumption is that Neil and Elizabeth name their first daughter Sarah, perhaps for her grandmother Sarah McLean. The naming custom would dictate that the first daughter would be named for Elizabeth's mother, the wife of Roderick McLeod. This woman is only shown with the name "Mrs. Mackenzie" in the records with no given name provided. It is as if "Sarah" would be the next best name for Elizabeth McLeod's first daughter.

Another line of information is that Sarah Munn, this first daughter of Neil and Elizabeth, becomes married to Hector Munn, the third son of James Munn and Elizabeth McMillan of Belle River/Wood Islands, P.E.I. Hector Munn's family holds that Hector Munn and Sarah Munn were cousins at some level, a reasonable conclusion to explain why they had the same surname. James had three brothers who emigrated with him and their father Duncan. They came on the ship Spencer *from* Colonsay Island, Argyll, Scotland to P.E.I. in 1806. None of these brothers had a son they named "Neil". Then it becomes a possibility that Donald Munn, (aka Mun) was a son of Duncan Munn who remained on Colonsay when the rest of the family left for Canada.

That Donald was an additional or "fifth" son of Duncan Munn and Flora Brown is a reasonable deduction. Donald's probable birth year is 1780.This is an appropriate date between birthdates of his "brothers", Neil, born 1778, and Malcolm, born 1783. This makes Donald the third son, Malcolm the fourth son and James the fifth son of Duncan Munn and Flora Brown.

Why did Donald choose to stay on Colonsay and not go to Prince Edward Island in 1806? He and Sarah McLean had twin sons that were then about 8 or 9 years old and well into their schooling years. It is known that Neil obtained a quality education as he was qualified to teach school upon arrival at P.E.I. in 1818 as a young man of about 20/21 years of age. It is also possible that the mother of twin boys was not healthy enough to make the trip in 1806. At least she never was recorded as getting to P.E.I. and was thought to have died early.

Not only is Sarah Munn, the first daughter of Neil Munn and Elizabeth McLeod probably named for her grandmother Sarah McLean, but Neil and Elizabeth name their first son Donald, probably for his grandfather Donald Munn. Then after their second son is named Roderick for Elizabeth McLeod's father, there is never any use of the name Archibald, if Neil's twin were so named. But Neil and Elizabeth name their fourth son Alexander. This would be in favor of Neil's **real** twin brother.

With all this rational in mind, it is possible to proceed with a Munn genealogy beginning with Duncan Munn and Flora Brown and placing Neil Munn in a proper sequence. The eventual result is that Hector Munn of Belle River marries Sarah Munn of Mermaid and they would be "first cousins once removed". That is, **Hector** Munn would be Sarah's father Neil Munn's first cousin.

Cousin marriages were quite common in the early days. Actually as eugenics is studied today, it is realized that there is adequate gene distance with cousin marriages that the problems of inheritance of bad recessive gene pairs is greatly diminished at this genetic distance. There is of course even greater genetic distance as first cousins once removed.

MUNN GENEALOGY PART II:
COLES AND HARDING GENEALOGY OF THE MUNN FAMILY BEGINNING WITH "THE WOOD ISLANDS MUNN'S":
(Page 281)

1. **DUNCAN** (John?) **MUNN** b. abt 1746[1] Scotland. (Possibly Kilfinnan, Cowal Peninsula, Argyllshire.) m. FLORA BROWN, b. abt 1748[1]. DUNCAN died abt 1821 P.E.I[2].
   (It is thought that Duncan Munn was a fisherman/boat builder and moved his family to Lower Kilhatten on Colonsay where the family cottage was at the edge of Port Mor, a major bay on the west side of the Island. The home site would have been at the pleasure of McNeill, the Laird of the Island.)

   CHILDREN:
+2. *i*ANGUS b. abt 1774/5[1].
  3. *ii*NEIL MUNN b. abt 1778. Argyllshire, Scotland.[1] m. 6 June 1803, Argyll, Jura.[3] **CATHERINE CURRIE** b. abt 1784.[1]Very little is known about Neil. He appears to be the same as the man variously appointed a fence viewer and a constable for Belle Creek/Wood Islands between 1812 and 1827. In 1841 Neil Munn and a wife lived alone in lot 62. Both were natives of Scotland and both were between 45 and 60 years of age. Both had paid own passage. And a 21 years of a 999 year lease had expired. He was a farmer.
+0. *iii*DONALD MUNN b. abt 1780/81.
+4. *iv*MALCOLM b. abt 1783.
+5. *v* JAMES b. abt 1784/1786.

+6. *vi*ANN b. abt 1787/1789.

+7. *vii* EFFY b. abt 1791.

Second Generation

2. **ANGUS MUNN** (1.DUNCAN[1]) b. abt 1774/1775, Argyll, Scotland.[4] m. 10 Dec 1803 in Colonsay and Oransay Parish, Argyll,[5] **MARGARET MCNEIL,** b. abt 1784, Argyll, Scotland, d. 21 Feb 1871, Little Sands, P.E.I.[6] ANGUS died 27 July 1837,[7] buried: Wood Islands Pioneer Cemetery. Angus' grave marker reads: 'Native of Isle of Colonsay, N.B. (North Britain). He is listed on the *Spencer* passenger list as Angus McMunn age 31. Margaret McNeil appears on *Spencer* list as age 21 in the Munn family group, though she is likely the daughter of DOUGLAS MCNEIL and FLORA MCMILLAN, who were *Spencer* passengers. ANGUS owned 100 acres in lot 62 between plots of NEIL and JAMES at Belle River. They had 10 children. (See Coles and Harding page 282 as further referenced there.)

0. ***DONALD MUNN*** (1. DUNCAN) b. abt 1780/1781, Argyll, Scotland. m. **SARAH MCLEAN** abt 1796. SARAH MCLEAN b. abt 1780 as inferred from baptismal records of their children[8]. No records of deaths. See Coles and Harding, page 19 for clues.

CHILDREN:

+1 (*i*)**NEIL MUNN** b. 11 Jan 1797[2], Colonsay, Argyll, Scotland.
AND TWIN:

> 00 *(ii)* **ALEXANDER MUNN** b. 11 Jan 1797[9], Colonsay, Argyll, Scotland. Because of a confusion of names, ARCHIBALD for ALEXANDER, research into the existence of an Archibald Munn have been unsuccessful and have lead to a denial of the family other than NEIL MUNN, who is the progenitor of the genealogy published by Coles and Harding. Thus no information concerning Alexander Munn (1797) is forthcoming.

4. **MALCOLM MUNN** (1.DUNCAN) b. abt 1783, Argyll, Scotland[1], m. **MARGARET (Peggy) SHAW,** b 1786,[10] d. 1873. MALCOLM died before 29 Aug 1837 as Peggy was a widow when the youngest two children were baptized at Belfast on 29 August 1837. These two children were Angus and Malcolm. They had seven children. (See Coles and Harding page 282 and following as further referenced there.)

5. **JAMES MUNN** (1.DUNCAN[1]) b. abt 1784/1786, Argyll, Scotland,[11] occupation shipbuilder, m.29 Dec 1805 in Jura, Argyll, Scotland,[1]**ELIZABETH (BETTY) MCMILLAN**, b. abt 1786/1788, Argyll, Scotland, d. 22 Nov 1873,[7] buried Wood Islands Pioneer Cemetery. JAMES died 5 June 1868, buried Wood Islands Pioneer Cemetery. The marriage is recorded in Parochial Records for Jura. (It speculated that the marriage took place in Kilfinan on the Cowal Peninsula where the ancestral home of the Munn family may have been. The Parochial Record[8] is listed as James Mun and Bety McMillan.) James is recorded as owning 100 acres freehold in lot 62 at Belle River between lands recorded for his brothers Angus and Malcolm. In 1831 James was appointed a fence viewer for Wood Islands and in 1833 he was appointed a constable. In 1861 there were 2 females aged 5-16 and one female aged 21-45 living with James and his wife at their lot 62 location.

Children:

+25.   *i* **FLORA** b. 1806

+26.   *ii* **DUNCAN Howard** b. abt 1807.

+27.   *iii* **GRACE** b.1810.

+28.   *iv* **MARY** b. 1820.

+29.   v **MARGARET** b. 1823.

30.   *vi* **JOHN MUNN** b. abt 1824, Wood Islands, d. 31 Aug 1855. Buried: Wood Islands Pioneer Cemetery. John was not known to have married.

+31. *vii* **HECTOR** b. abt 1826.

32. *viii* **ANN MUNN** b. abt 1827. Wood Islands. d. 18 Dec 1907, Wood Islands. Buried: Wood Islands Presbyterian Cemetery. Ann was unmarried. In 1891 she was living with the Crawford's, probably as housekeeper to her widowed brother-in-law. She died at the home of her nephew John Daniel Munn. The last to die of this generation.

+33. *ix* **NEIL.**

+34. *x* **JAMES MUNN** b. 2 Aug 1832, Wood Islands. bapt 29 Aug 1837, Belfast Presbyterian Church. d. June 1859, Woodville, buried: Wood Islands Pioneer Cemetery. A death notice in *The Islander*, 24 June 1839 reported that he died at Woodville, Lot 62 of consumption at age of 24. James Munn. Jr. was youngest.

Third Generation

(**Note:** Coles and Harding bases their presentation on the assumption that Neil Munn, born 1797, holds the beginning position as progenitor of the Munn genealogy. This presentation is based on the assumption that Neil Munn would actually be the grandson of Duncan Munn and Flora Brown. **However,** to maintain the integrity of the exceptional research and design of the genealogical presentation of Coles and Harding, their notational method and numbering system will be continued as much as possible.)

NEIL MUNN and FAMILY of MERMAID, Lot 48
From Coles and Harding, page 19

1. **NEIL MUNN** b.11 Jan 1897, Colonsay, Argyll, Scotland. m. 22 Feb 1831, **ELIZABETH (Betsy) MACLEOD,** b. abt 1804, Orwell Cove, Prince Edward Island. (daughter of **Roderick**

MacLeod and **Mrs. MacKenzie**) d. 9 Dec 1865, Mermaid, P.E.I., buried: Calvin Presbyterian Cemetery, Mermaid, 61 years. NEIL died 29 Oct 1869, Mermaid, P.E.I., buried Calvin Presbyterian Cemetery, Mermaid, 71 years. His family claims that he became a school teacher at Mermaid in 1818 when he came to P.E.I. On 8 March 1830, a year before his marriage, Neil leased 100 acres in Lot 48. In 1840 he added a further 62 acres to his holdings. On 22 Feb 1831 Neil married Elizabeth MacLeod. She was generally known as Betsy. She was the daughter of Roderick MacLeod and his wife, a MacKenzie, who had emigrated from Kendrone, Isle of Skye in 1803 on board the brig *"Polly"* and had settled in Orwell Cove. Though Betsy should, according to her age at death as recorded on her gravestone, have been born about 1804, she claimed to be Scottish born in both the census of 1841 and 1861. Her sons all indicated that their mother was born on the Island. Some even claim that she was the first child born in Canada of the Sellkirk Settlers that came on the *Polly* in 1803. (There is additional information and commentary available in Coles and Harding.)

Children :

+2. *i***SARAH MUNN** b. abt 1832.

+3. *ii* **DONALD MUNN** b.17 July 1833.

+4. *iii* **RODERICK MUNN** b. 17 April 1835.

+5. iv **MARY MUNN,** b. 26 April 1837.

6. *v* **DOROTHEA (DORA) MUNN** b. abt 1840, Mermaid, d. 24 April 1903, Duxbury, Mass., buried: Mayflower Cemetery, Roxbury, never married. (There is additional commentary of page 21 of Coles and Harding.)

+7. *vi***ANN (ANNIE) MUNN** b. abt 1841.

+8. *vii* **CHARLES MUNN** b. abt 1843.

+9. *viii* **ALEXANDER MUNN** b. 10 Dec 1844.

10. *ix* **WILLIAM MUNN** b. 1848 Mermaid. d. 21 May 1937, East Royalty, buried: Calvin Presbyterian Cemetery, Mermaid,

89th year. (Additional information, pages 23-24, Coles and Harding.)

11. *x* **JAMES MUNN** b. 1851, Mermaid. d. 25 Jan 1824, Tewksbury, Mass., buried: Calvin Presbyterian Cemetery, Mermaid. (Additional information, pages 24-25, Coles and Harding.) (Except for +2 SARAH MUNN, see Coles and Harding for further information.)

SARAH MUNN, lot 48 MERMAID and HECTOR MUNN, lot 62 WOOD ISLANDS/BELLE RIVER

("Wood Islands Munn's" begins with page 281 of Coles and Harding. The reader is referred to pages 281-290 for the second and third generations of the Duncan Munn family up to his grandson Hector. Then, the genealogy including Hector's siblings will also be identified as available in Coles and Harding on 292 and on.)

(It is also worth noting that the four Munn brothers settled on four adjacent 100 acre lots that are along Belle River or Creek. The adjacent village to the east is Wood Islands. Often the names are used interchangeably in the Coles and Harding genealogy.)

31. **HECTOR MUNN** (5.JAMES, 1.DUNCAN) b. abt 1825, Wood Islands. Occupation farmer. Married: 23 Oct 1851.

  1. **SARAH MUNN** (daughter of **NEIL MUNN** and **ELIZABETH MACLEOD**) b. abt 1832, Mermaid. D. 15 Dec 1882, Wood Islands, buried: Wood Islands Pioneer Cemetery. HECTOR died 21 April 1876, Wood Islands, buried: Wood Islands Pioneer Cemetery.

Children: (The first number is sequenced from NEIL MUNN of Mermaid. The second (number) is sequenced from DUNCAN MUNN and the Wood Islands Munn's).

2. (124). *i* **DUNCAN HOWARD MUNN** b. 25 June 1853, Wood Islands, occupation farmer, d. 23 Oct 1876, buried, Wood Islands Pioneer Cemetery. Unmarried. Probably died of consumption. Edgar Munn claimed that the middle name was "Hector".

3. (125). *ii* **ELIZABETH ANN MUNN** b. 26 Nov 1854, Wood Islands. m. 69. **DANIEL MUNN** (19. DUNCAN, 4. MALCOLM, 1.DUNCAN) b. 15 Nov 1855, occupation carpenter/farmer, d. 5 Oct 1911, Hopefield, buried: Wood Islands Presbyterian Cemetery. Elizabeth died 16 May 1927, buried: Wood Islands Cemetery. Eight children. (See page 298, Coles and Harding).

4. (126). *iii* **MARY SARA MUNN** b. 9 Feb 1857, Wood Islands, m. 9 Feb 1878, **WILLIAM NEEDHAM,** b. 25 Dec 1851m (son of **William Needham** and **Charlotte Douglas**) d. 18 Nov 1935, Danvers, Mass., buried: Brookdale Cemetery, Dedham. MARY died 8 Nov 1935, Danvers, Mass. Buried: Brookdale Cemetery, Dedham. Eight children. (See Coles and Harding, page 30.)

5. (127). *iv* **FLORA GRACE MUNN** b. 25 Dec 1858, Little Sands, m. 20 Feb 1879, **JOHN HENRY COMPTON,** b. 27 Jan 1854, Belle River, (son of **John Compton** and **Mary Grant**) occupation cabinet maker, d. 30 Dec 1928, Belle River, buried: Belle River Church of Scotland Cemetery. FLORA died 25 Sept 1945, Belle River, buried: Belle River Church of Scotland Cemetery. Eleven children. (See page 31, Coles and Harding). John Henry's great-grandfather William Henry Compton lived in New Jersey. "They were Loyalists who, following the American Revolution brought their family including a son John to Belle River." There John married Mary Grant. Data from this

family's history was a major source for the Coles and Harding book.

6. (128). *v* **DOROTHEA (DOROTHY) JANE MUNN** b. 26 Nov 1861, Wood Islands, m. 22 Jan 1884, **ALEXANDER (ALEX) STEWART,** b. 12 Aug 1859, Charlottetown, (son of **Angus Stewart** and **Mary McLeod**) occupation carpenter/ engineer, d. 6 Sept 1943, Seattle, Wash., buried: Evergreen Memorial Park. Dorothy died 24 Feb 1949, Seattle, Wash., buried: Evergreen Memorial Park. Dorothy and Alex were second cousins as both were great grandchildren of Donald MacLeod of Kendron, Isle of Skye and Orwell Cove. (Coles and Harding, page 33). They moved to Seattle, Wash., where Alex was chief engineer for Seattle Public Schools.

Children:

38. *i* **MARY (MAMIE) STEWART** m. **THOMAS HAMMER,** They lived a Gig Harbor, Wash.

39. *ii* **NATHANIEL (NATHAN** or **NATE) STEWART** b. 6 April 1895, Quincy, Mass. NATHAN was a concert singer of note, having appeared with the Philadelphia Grand Opera. He may have been married, but no children.

40. *iii* **ARTHUR (ART) STEWART** m. **Catherine** ---. They had no children. Art was a programmer for KING radio and TV in Seattle.

7. (129). *vi* **JAMES HECTOR MUNN** b. 26 July 1864, Wood Islands, occupation: businessman, farmer/carpenter, m. (1) 1 Feb 1884, **MARGARET (MAGGIE) MACLEOD,** b. abt 1862, d. 3 March 1886, buried: Wood Islands Presbyterian Cemetery. No children. Possibly they were second cousins. Married (2) 2 Dec 1892, **ANA MAE EDWARDS,** b. 24 Sept 1871, near New Providence, Hardin County, Iowa. Occupation: school teacher/postmaster, d. 30 Aug 1955, age 84, buried: Quilcene Community Cemetery. James was naturalized 1898,

died 25 May 1926, age 61, buried Quilcene Community Cemetery, Quilcene, Washington. They homesteaded at Lake Leland in Jefferson County.

Children: (6)

+41.　*i* **VIOLA Dorothy MUNN** b. 31 Aug1893, occupation: postmaster. m. **GEORGE Otto ALDEN,** b. 7 Nov 1889. Viola died 22 March 1975. Three children: Margaret (Margie), Iris, James.

+42.　*ii* **HECTOR John MUNN,** b. 19 Jan 1895 Leland, Washington, occupation: mining engineer, m. 3 Apr 1920, Great Falls, Montana, **PEARL Marie BOND,** b.19 Aug 1896, Winterset, Iowa, (daughter of **Alpheus Bond** and **Julia Elizabeth Maxwell)** d. 10 Dec 1967, age 71, Port Townsend, Wash., buried: Quilcene Community Cemetery. Hector died 31 Dec 1965, age 69, Leland, Wash., buried: Quilcene Community Cemetery. Five children: Helen, Mary Beth, James, Robert, Hector Jr.

43.　*iii* **Margaret ALICE MUNN** b. 29 March 1896,Leland, Wash., occupation: teacher, m. Jan 1918, Leland, Wash., **GEORGE NURNBERG,** b. 7 April 1952, Nurenburg, Germany, occupation: electrical engineer, d. 7 April 1952, Los Angeles, Cal. ALICE died 19 Oct 1951, Elma, Wash., buried: Quilcene Community Cemetery. One son, **DONALD HECTOR NURNBURG,** b. 4 July 1918, Raymond, Wash., d. 8 Feb 1951, Elma, Wash., buried: Quilcene, Washington.

44.　*iv* **SARAH MATILDA MUNN,** b.29 Aug 1897, Leland, Wash., occupation: nurse, secretary, m. (1) 5 June 1921, Leland, Wash., **LEROY (ROY) ALBRIGHT,** b. 30 June 1892, Humburd, Wisc. One daughter: Ellen LORRAINE, b. 24 Jan **1922**, Portland, Ore.

Married (2) 21 Sept 1937 Everett, Wash., **Wilbur (BILL) BRYAN,** b. 18 June 1899, Rochester, Wash., d. 17 Jan 1980, buried: Quilcene Cemetery. SARAH died 2 Dec 1993, Port Townsend, Wash., buried: Quilcene, Washington.

+45.   *v* **Evangeline (VANGIE, VAN) MUNN,** b.16 Feb 1899, Leland, Wash., occupation: school teacher/accountant, m. (1) Mar 1919, Leland, Wash., **John ALEXIS (ALEX) NORVALL, JR.,** b. Chicago, Ill. Two children. John (**JACK**), Mary Jane.

Married (2) 25 Sept 1945, Quilcene, Wash., **LLOYD Ackley TOOKER,** b. 6 Mar 1897, occupation: trucking business, EVANGELINE died 2 June 1974, buried: Quilcene Cemetery. Two children: Lloyd, Jr., Dorothea.

+46.   *vi* **GEORGE Edwards MUNN**, b. 16 June 1901, Leland, Wash., occupation: teacher, U.S. Air Force officer, m. 12 July 1929,at Everett, Wash., **HULDA MARIE KNUTSEN,** b. 4 Dec 1902, Irene, S.D., d. 10 July 1983, Port Angeles, Wash., buried: Laurel Grove Cemetery, Port Townsend, Wash. GEORGE died 26 Feb 1993. Buried: Laurel Grove Cemetery. Two children: Gerald, Judith.

(For the extended information re: +, see the continuation in the Genealogy of James Hector Munn and Ana Mae Edwards Munn which may be in another publication.)

8.   (130) *vii* **JESSIE Euphemia MUNN,** b. 24 May 1865, Wood Islands, m. **EDWARD ROBERTS.** JESSIE died 15 June 1890, Wood Islands, buried: Wood Islands Presbyterian Cemetery. 25 years old. No information on her husband and a possible child that died early.

9.   (131) *viii* **NEIL Alexander MUNN,** b. 6 April 1867, Wood Islands. d. 22 March 1889, Wood Islands, buried: Wood

Islands Presbyterian Cemetery. 23 years. Unmarried. His father willed one-third of the Belle River estate to him. He willed his portion to James Hector and John Daniel, his brothers.

+10.   (132) *ix* **JOHN Daniel MUNN,** b. 26 Nov 1868, occupation farmer/ miller, m. **SARAH Ann STEPHENS,** b. 12 July 1869, England, d. 31 Oct 1945, Belle River, buried: Wood Islands Presbyterian Cemetery. JOHN died 17 April 1939, Belle River, buried: Wood Islands Presbyterian Cemetery. Eleven children: eight sons and three daughters. (See Coles and Harding, page 35 for more information.)

REFERENCES:

1. Computed from ages as recorded in the *Spencer* passenger list.
2. Personal records of Gordon T. Munn (b. 1913). Gordon's last address was 92 First St. N., Stoney Creek, Ontario, Canada L8G 1Y3
3. International Genealogical Index, 1984 version. PAROPEI. Also Parochial Records, Colonsay/Jura Parish.
4. Computed from age as recorded on the *Spencer* passenger list.
5. IGI, 1984 version.
6. Death notice. *The Island Argas*, 28 Feb 1871.
7. Wood Islands Pioneer Cemetery, grave marker.
8. Parochial Record Colonsay/Jura Parish.
9. Op. cit.
10. Munn family record via Gordon T. Munn, Ontario. (see #2).
11. Computed from *the Spencer* passenger list.

APPENDIX II: EDWARDS GENEALOGY

———

For the purposes of this genealogy as it relates to the text of "JIM and Ana", only a limited genealogy will be set out. This will begin with Joseph JESSE EDWARDS, born about 1896 in Adair County, Kentucky, it is thought. His father may have been William Edwards, but there is more than one "William Edwards" in the records and it hasn't been shown for a fact which one is Jesse's parent.

Yet there are extensive references to the Edwards name dating back to the colonial or pre-Revolutionary War. Much of this literature had been generated by the "Edwards Heir's Association" in an attempt to document relationships to William Bayard Edwards and Thomas Edwards. These men were granted land in the State of New York by the King of England prior to the War of Independence. The most notable land grant was on Manhattan Island where the financial district is today. Another tract of land was in Herkimer County, New York. Since the lands were given to loyalists who died or left their holdings, the land was confiscated by the Federal Government.

The Edwards Heir's Association made legal efforts to regain rights to the property. If the suit would have been successful, then anyone who could prove relationship to the Loyalists Edwards brothers might have some benefit from the properties. Considerable effort and expense was made by attorneys in the courts. No one gained a penny except the lawyers.

Ulysses Grant Edwards kept track of the case in his later life and as of his writings dated 1930; nothing was proven as to his grandfather's relationship to that Edwards lineage. Jesse Edwards' family seems to have had considerable property in Adair County, Kentucky. Yet exactly where that was or who Jesse's parents were, all seems to be unrecorded or the records lost. Undoubtedly the family originated in Virginia or North Carolina. Some of the Edwards families did originate in New York, but the name is common in the colonial era.

For the purposes of this story, we will begin with Joseph JESSE EDWARDS b. abt 1796 and his wife ELIZABETH BRIANT b. abt 1810.

The Family of Joseph JESSE EDWARDS and ELIZABETH BRIANT.

1. **Joseph JESSE EDWARDS**, b. abt 1796, Adair County, Kentucky. His father's name may have been "William Edwards" and his grandfather may also have been William. Men with these names may be found in the censuses of 1800 and 1810. Only numbers of people in the households were given.
   Married (1) abt 1827, **ELIZABETH BRIANT**, b. abt 1810. (Daughter of GEORGE BRIANT, b. abt 1782 and SARAH DeMOSS, b. abt 1784.)
   George Briant (or Bryant) was the son of John Briant of Ireland. George Briant was one of eight brothers lost in the War of 1812. The father of Sarah DeMoss is said to be David DeMoss from Alsace-Lorraine who had German citizenship.
Children:
+2. *i* **JOHN BRIANT EDWARDS**, b 14 June 1828/9.
+3. *ii* **SARAH EDWARDS**, b. abt 1831.
+4. *iii* **GEORGE WASHINGTON EDWARDS**, b. 5 April 1836.m.
   (2) Jesse left Elizabeth in Morgan County, Ind. He returned to Adair County, Kentucky and remarried. Data of second wife

and children are not known. George W. Edwards never knew his father though John did visit Kentucky.

NOTE:

ELIZABETH BRIANT EDWARDS, b. abt 1810, remarried after Jesse left her.

m. (2) 1838, ELI RITSMAN, b. abt 1804 d. 1847.

Children:

i NANCY L. RITSMAN, b. abt 1840.

ii CHARLES I. RITSMAN b. abt 1842.

iii PETER B. RITSMAN b. abt 1844. (Changed his name to Wrightsman, which may be true to the pronouncement of the name, i.e. "long I").

m. (3) 1848, JESSE OVERTON, b. 1806 Tenn. He had 6 children by a prior marriage to Eve?

Children:

i WILLIS OVERTON, b abt 1874

(See: Edwards-Cole pages E, 7-9 for data on Ritsman and Overton families.)

2. **JOHN BRIANT EDWARDS**, b.14 June 1828/9, probably Adair County, Kentucky.

m. (1) 26 Dec 1849, **PERMELIA FITZGERALD**, b. abt 1831. (Daughter of John Fitzgerald and Mary Martin. Permelia was a sister of MATILDA FITZGERALD, wife of George E. Edwards. Since Edwards brothers married Fitzgerald sisters, the children of the two families were double cousins.)

Children: (14) Sylvester and twin Sylvanus, Sarah E., James A., Calvin, Sylvania, George, John, Dora, Matilda and twin William, Laura, Vastella, Emma.

m. (2) 7 Nov 1896, Mrs. REBECCA NELSON, separated.

Children: none

(See: "John Briant Family as told by U. Grant Edwards and by Elva Salome Edwards-Cole.)

3. *ii* **SARAH EDWARDS**, b. abt 1830, Adair Co., Ky, m. (1) 1846 **James Fitzgerald, Sr.**, b. 1807, Tenn. (His second marriage. His first wife was Mary Martin, who was the mother of Permelia, Matilda, and John Fitzgerald, and others.) He died 1857. Sarah and James had five children:
m. (2) 1859 Joseph Hartley, b. 1831, d. in Civil War, no children.
m. (3) ?, William Grandstaff, b.?, d.? No children.
Sarah died 1890 in Indiana.

4. *iii* **GEORGE WASHINGTON EDWARDS**, b. 5 Apr 1836, Owen Co., Ind. or Jackson Co. m. 3 Sep 1854 Hardin Co, Iowa. **MATILDA FITZGERALD**, b. 1 Feb 1837, Morgan Co. Ind. d. 8 Feb 1919, Seattle, Wash...Buried: Laurel Grove Cemetery, Port Townsend, Wash.
George died 26 Sept 1914, Port Townsend, Wash., Buried: Laurel Grove Cemetery.
Occupation: Farmer, Carpenter, Justice of the Peace, Union Army, Co. B, 11th Iowa Reg. re-enlisted.
Children: (10): Louisa, Veroque, Joel, Elva, Ulysses GRANT, Eldora, Viola, Ana, James PORTER, John LEWIS.

+5 *i* **LOUISA EDWARDS**, b. 19 June 1855, New Providence, Iowa. m. (1) 25 Jan 1872, Hardin Co., Iowa, **LOUIS VINSON HALL**, b. 8 May 1847, East Bend, N.C., d. 14 June 1921. Occupation: business man, inn keeper. d. 14 June 1921.
Children: (8) Clayton, Daisy, Edwin, Hester, Jessie, Lester, Elva, Porter.
m.(2) 12 May 1823, Union, Iowa, Ed Mothersell, b. July 1853, d. 6 May 1933. His first wife was Louisa's sister-in-law.
Louisa died: 26 Oct 1938, Union, Iowa.

(See Elva Edwards-Cole, p 15 and following.)

+6 *ii* **VEROQUE EDWARDS**, b. 17 Nov 1856, Morgan Co., Ind., m. (1) 1875, Ellsworth?, Kan., **DAVID HENDERSON**, b. 17 Mar ??, divorced 23 Oct 1885. Ellsworth, Kan., He was a railroad engineer. He remarried, no children, d. Butte, Mont. Children: (3) Robert, Elva, John ALLEN .

m. (2) 3 Feb 1887, Minneapolis, Kan., **THADDEUS STEVENS SMITH**, b. 12 June 1843 Pennsylvania. He had a previous marriage and a son, George Smith, b. abt 1881. Thaddeus Smith was a Union soldier and earned the Congressional Medal of Honor for service in Battle of Gettisberg. Marriage (3) to Lottie Smith, Port Townsend. Son----. Thad d. May 1933, at Port Townsend. Buried: Laurel Grove Cemetery, Port Townsend.

Veroque died 19 April 1891 at Leland, Wash., Buried: Laurel Grove Cemetery, Port Townsend. On her death the three children were raised by G.W. and Matilda Edwards until they went to high school.

Veroque and Thad had one son: **PORTER EDWARDS SMITH**, b. 9 Jan 1889, Leland, Wash. d. 9 Nov 1904 by accidental gunshot by neighbor boy, Ralph "Hap" Currier. Buried: Laurel Grove Cemetery, Port Townsend. Porter was raised by G.W. and Matilda Edwards until Porter was shot. (See Elva Edwards-Cole, p. 22-23)

+7 *iii* **JOEL EDWARDS**, b. 8 Dec 1858, Martinville, Morgan Co., Ind., occupation: carpenter, farmer, motorman/conductor Port Townsend street car, Councilman, Baptist.

m. 13 April 1861, Minneapolis, Kan., **Clarissa ALICE Morse**. b. 8 Mar 1859, Lake Co., Ind., teacher. d. 9 Dec 1936 Seattle, Wash., Buried: Laurel Grove Cemetery, Port Townsend. Joel died 12 July 1929 in Swedish Hosp, Seattle. Buried: Laurel Grove Cemetery, Port Townsend.

Children: (6) Lulu, Lola, Ray, Elva, Guy, Schuyler.
(See Elva Edwards-Cole (granddaughter), pages 24-27.)

+8 *iv* **ELVA MAUDE EDWARDS**, b. 25 Mar 1861, Hardin Co., Iowa,

m. 26 June 1877 Ackley, Ottawa Co., Kan., **Edwin Richard Knight**, b. 6 Aug 1841, Sandusky, Ohio; d. July 1931, Olympia. Occupation: businessman, took U.S. Census for Jefferson County, 1890. Remarried: 13 Jan 1894, Mrs. Lewis who had two daughters. They had one son: Russell Knight, b.?, d. Aug 1954, Anacortes, Wash.

Elva died suddenly of "acute malaria" according to family tradition. She had been taken with intense headache. She died 4 June 1889 just a month after arriving at Port Townsend. Buried: Laurel Grove Cemetery, Port Townsend.

Children: Henry Granger, Chandler, Charles, Claude. After Elva's death, Henry lived independently. Chandler and Claude were raised by G.W. and Matilda Edwards, though Chandler did not live to be an adult. Charles died soon after birth. (See Elva Edwards-Cole, p.28)

+9 *iv* **ULYSSES GRANT EDWARDS**, b. 20 Dec 1864. Hardin Co, Iowa. Occupation: teacher, county school superintendent for Jeff. Co. Wash., U.S. Customs/Revenue Inspector of ships. m. 29 Aug 1897 **Elizabeth Forbes Dalgity,** b. 18 Apr 1868, Forfar, Scotland. Occupation: teacher. She died Jan 1930, Seattle, Wash. "Grant" died 13 Aug 1936.

Children: (4) George, Archibald, Jean, Matilda.
(See Elva Edwards-Cole, p 29.)

+10 *v* **ELDORA (DORA) Permelia Edwards,** b. 30 Sep 1867 (a twin born before midnight), Cainsville, Harrison, County, Mo.,

m. (1) 28 Sep 1884, Ackley, Ottawa, Kan., **Hiram C. Ruggles**, b 12 Mar,1859,

Penn., Divorced 1904, d. 1950 Phoenix, Ariz. Occupation: railroad engineer.

Children: (8) boy, stillborn, Agnes, Ana, George, Hiram, Viola, Franklin, John.

m. (2) 8 Jan 1910 Port Townsend, Wash., Baynard Fletcher (annulled 14 June 1910.

m. (3) Oct 1910 Seattle, Wash, Edward Wegner. B. abt 1887, d. 12 June 1964, Seattle, Wash. No children.

Eldora died 18 Sept 1930.

(See Elva Edwards-Cole, p. 30-33.)

+11 *vi* VIOLA ALMEDA EDWARDS, b. 1 Oct 1867 (a twin born after midnight), Cainsville, Harrison Co., MO.

m. (1) 14 Jan 1886, Minneapolis, Kan, JOHN RICHARD MERRILL, b abt 1865, divorced 1906. Farmer, musician, builder. Died Aug 1950, Tacoma, Wash.

Children: (4) Ana, LeRoy, Dora, Grant.

m. (2) 7 May 1914, at Port Townsend, Wash., Peter L. Hansen, b. 1872. D. Jan 1936, Walla Walla, Wash.

Children: none

Viola died 30 June 1958, Seattle, Wash. Cremated

(See Elva Edwards-Cole, p. 34-5)

+13 *vii* ANA MAE EDWARDS, b. 24 Sep 1871, (a twin), near New Providence, Hardin Co., Iowa. Occupation: business woman, postmaster, farmer.

m. 2 Dec 1892, Everett, Wash., JAMES HECTOR MUNN, b. 26 July 1864˚, Belle River, Queens County, Prince Edward Island. Carpenter, telephone business, sawmill owner. D. 25 May 1926, St. Luke's (Virginia Mason) Hospital, Seattle. Buried: Quilcene Cemetery, Washington.

*(The year on his grave marker, in the Elva Edwards-Cole record, and reported on page 27 of Coles and Harding, "From Island to Island". It is also calculated from the marriage date of 2 Dec 1892 when he was 28 years old. However, his nephew in P.E.I., Edgar Munn, reports the year as 1863. This is the year that appears in all of Mary Beth Munn Ynetma's writings. She submitted the year as 1863 to contributions to Coles and Harding, "From Island to Island" and it is included in that publication on page 291.

Ana died 30 Aug 1955, Leland, Wash., buried Quilcene Cemetery, Washington.

Children: (6) Viola, Hector, Alice, Sarah, Evangeline, George. (See Elva Edwards-Cole, page 36 and Coles and Harding, pages 34-5, 43-45).

14 *viii* JAMES PORTER EDWARDS, b. 24 Sept 1891 (a twin), near New Providence, Hardin Co., Iowa, d. 14 July 1890, Port Townsend, Wash. Buried: Laurel Grove Cemetery, Port Townsend, Wash. PORTER was a barber in Kansas and Port Townsend. He died of lung problems due to pneumonia or tuberculosis contracted from human hair. Never married.

15 *ix* JOHN LEWIS (LOUIE) EDWARDS, b. 26 Jan 1876, Ackley, Ottawa Co., KAN., d. 27 Oct 1877, Ackley, Ottawa Co. KAN. Buried: Ackley Edwards Cemetery. No certain cause of death. Possibly snake or insect bite, according to Ana Munn or childhood cholera, according to Elva Edwards-Cole.

REFERENCES

Berton, Pierre, "Klondike", McClelland & Stewart, LTD., Toronto, 1962.

Burris, Oliver (family), Columbia County (Ore) Historical Society, Page 39-41, Vol. VI, 1967.

Cole, Elva Salome Edwards, "Genealogy of Edwards-Fitzgerald Family, to December 1972", B.A. Copy Company, printers, 4222 University Way, Seattle, WN 98106. 1972.

Coles, CG(C), L. Ann (MacLeod) and Linda C. (Matheson) Harding, "From Island to Island: The Family of Neil Munn and Elizabeth MacLeod". Privately published, Linda C. Harding, 264 Mount Edward Road, Charlottetown, C1A 5T7, PEI. ISBN #0-9699-9430-3. @ 1996. (Copy purchased 29 Dec 1997, $48.00).

Columbia County Historical Society (no author), "The Coming of the Railroad to Columbia County, CCHS, page 47, Vol. IV, 1963-64.

Edwards, U. Grant, "Edwards Family History", unpublished compilation, 1930-31.

Faber, Jim, "Steamer's Wake", Enetai Press, Seattle, 1985.

McDonald, Betty, "The Egg and I". New York, Lippincott, 1945.

Munn, Ana Mae Edwards, "Pioneering in Four States and I'll Tell you All About It", Unpublished memoirs, Leland, Washington, 1951.

Thomas, Roscoe, "Railroad Line to Party Line: Leland Valley Early Times", Marjorie Last-Rogers, Interviewer. WITNESS TO THE FIRST CENTURY: 1889-1989, Volume 29. Jefferson County Historical Society, Oral History Project, Jefferson County Historical Society, Port Townsend, Washington, 1989.

Yntema, Mary Elizabeth (Beth) Munn, "The Story of Old Leland", privately published, 2000.

Yntema, Mary Elizabeth Munn, "Head Waters: Munn-Edwards, Maxwell-Bond & Tributaries". Book One. Unpublished research and family memoirs, written 1990.

Yntema, Mary Elizabeth Munn, Additional works are: "Merging Streams- Homestead and Honeymoon, 1920-1923"; "The Hector Munns Move to Leland, Washington, 1923-1926"; "Sunset Mines – 1926-1928"; "Index—1928-1930"; "Leland—1930 and Beyond". Mary Beth Munn Yntema, 2184 Beacon Place, Port Townsend, Washington 98368.

PICTURE INDEX, CREDITS AND NOTES

~~~~~~~~

Book cover: Drawing by great grandson James Peter Bury of Fresno, California.

Page 2   Forward photo: An aerial photo of the south end of Lake Leland.

Page 3   Mr. and Mrs. James H. Munn on the "main street" of Leland, Arcadia Road, circa 1917. (George Munn collection)

Page 9   James Hector Munn, circa 1893. (Munn family collection)

Page 13   Hector Munn family at Belle River "Old Farm", Prince Edward Island.1866. (Greg Munn collection). (Greg Munn's great grandmother is also in the picture. He is a great, great, grandson of Malcolm Munn, James Munn's brother.)

Page 28   Ana Mae Edwards Munn at age 33. The photo is extracted from an Edwards family portrait taken August 3, 1905. (George Munn collection)

Page 34   Cpl. George Washington Edwards and Matilda Fitzgerald Edwards, 1894 while on furlough. Notice the chevrons on G.W.'s uniform. (George Munn collection)

Page 47   Twins James PORTER Edwards and ANA MAE Edwards, 1878. The Edwards family was living at the Coal Creek/Ackley homestead at that time. (Munn family collection)

Page 54   Porter and Ana Mae as teenagers in Minneapolis, Kansas, circa 1887. (Munn family collection)

Page 58   Central School, Minneapolis, Kansas, circa 1885. The Edwards family moved to the county seat so that Grant, Ana and Porter could go to school. Ana completed her senior class studies before leaving for Port Townsend. She was granted her diploma in absentia. (Ottawa County Museum, Minneapolis, Kansas).

Page 65   The railroad ferry *The Tacoma*, circa 1908. (Columbia County Historical Society, St. Helens, Oregon).

Page 66   The passenger ferry *The Olympian*. Circa 1889. (Faber, *Steamer's Wake,*p.100).

Page 74   Fred E. Rose, of Minneapolis, Kansas, circa 1888. (Munn family collection).

Page 91   Edwards/Cummings place at Leland, circa 1920. The house is not the original house built by George Edwards. The other buildings are the original structures built by G.W. Edwards. The Olympic Highway was built in 1926 that would come just along the fence line in the foreground. (George E. Munn collection).

Page 95   Leland School Picnic, 1892. Ana Mae Edwards and U. Grant Edwards were teaching in neighboring schools for the 1891-2 year. It is thought that Grant had just organized the Tarboo school, but the source citation indicates that he brought students from the "Tookey" school. Tookey or "Tukey" was a family at Adelma Beach on the eastern shore of Discovery Bay. (Jefferson County Historical Society, Allen Beach collection).

Page 99   George Washington and Matilda Edwards at their Leland House, circa 1893. (Munn family collection).

Page 103   Leland hill west of the Munn barn. (George Munn collection).

MAPS

MAP 1: BLOCK 6 PORT TOWNSEND, WASHINGTON 1890.

Seaman's Bethelis the building at 881/2 Quincy Street "Reading Rooms".

The buildings east of Water Street were built on the wharf and did not survive into modern times.

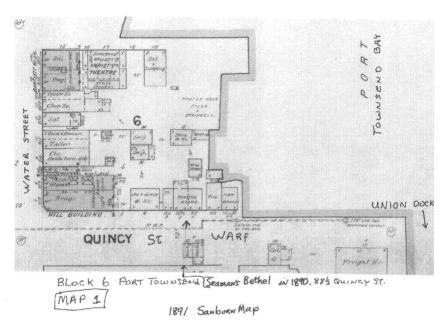

1891 Sanborn Map provided by Jefferson County Historical Society.

MAP 2: ARCADIA HOMESTEAD.

James H. Munn completed a120 acre homestead in Section 22 TWP 28 R 2 WWM. NE1/2 NE ¼ 80 acres and NE ¼ SE1/4, 40 acres. Thaddeus Smith's claim was in Section 25 north of the letters "BM220".

Map 3: Munn/Nichols Homestead in Section 26, TWP 28 R 2WWM, Jefferson County, Washington.

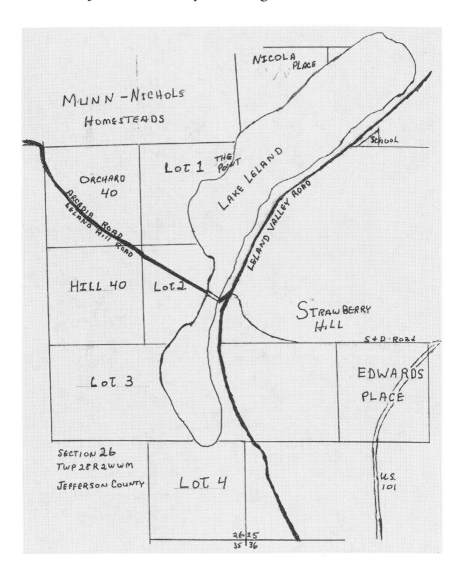

MAP 4: OTTAWA TOWNSHIP, OTTAWA COUNTY, KANSAS ,1884.

North east corner, not the entire TWP. Note the Quarter sections of Section 18. The NW ¼ of NW ¼ is the Timber Culture 160 acres given to Joel Edwards. The SW ¼ of NW ¼ is the Homestead 160 acres earned by G.W. Edwards. The Ackley P.O. is shown on the homestead. The SE ¼ is the Ackley Homestead.

(Source: Ottawa County records.)

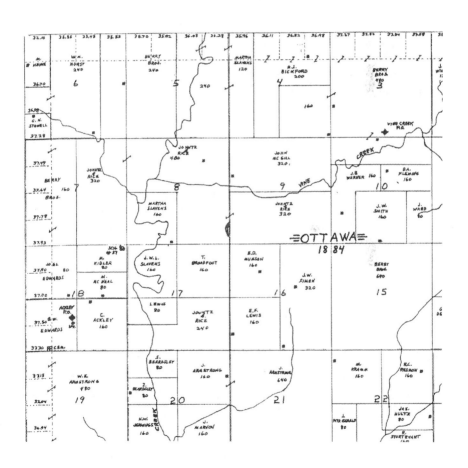

Map 5: MINNEAPOLIS, KANSAS, 1889

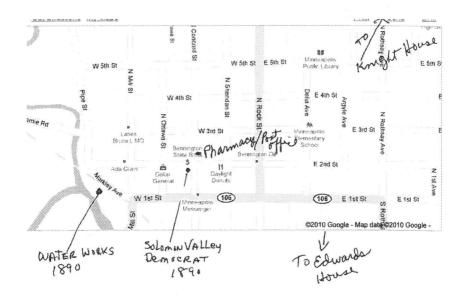

INDEX